Sparrows of the United States and Canada

The Photographic Guide

David Beadle dedicates this book to Katie and James.

Jim Rising dedicates this book to Justus David and Nigel James
– the next generation.

Sparrows of the United States and Canada

The Photographic Guide

David Beadle and J. D. Rising

Princeton University Press
Princeton and Oxford

Published in 2003 by Princeton University Press, 41 William Street,
Princeton, New Jersey 08540
In the United Kingdom: Princeton University Press, 3 Market Place,
Woodstock, Oxfordshire OX20 1SY

First published by Academic Press

ISBN-13 978-0-691-11747-8
ISBN-10 0-691-11747-0

Library of Congress Control Number 2003104200

British Library Cataloging-in-Publication Data is available

This book has been composed in Stone Serif

Printed on acid-free paper. ∞

www.nathist.princeton.edu

Printed and bound in Spain by
Grafos S.A. Arte Sobre Papel, Barcelona

3 5 7 9 10 8 6 4 2

Contents

List of Species Covered

Acknowledgments

Following the publication of our first book, *A Guide to the Identification and Natural History of The Sparrows of the United States and Canada*, many people – more than we can acknowledge here – contacted us with helpful comments and additional information for which we are profoundly appreciative. We do wish to mention a few of these, however, whose contributions were especially helpful: Alfred Adamo, Dick Banks, Jon Barlow, Bob Behrstock, Brad Bergstrom, Michel Bertrand, Rich Bradley, Bill Bremser, P. A. Buckley, Jim Burns, William Carter, Allen Chartier, Will Cook, Chris Corben, Jeff Cox, Don Crockett, Marty DeHart, Martha Desmond, Rich Ditch, Gary Felton, David Fix, Ted Floyd, Larry Gardella, Kurt Gaskill, Dan Gibson, Jon Greenlaw, Horst Grothman, Anthony Hertzel, Chris Hobbs, Tyler Hicks, Jean Iron, Pete Janzen, Al Jaramillo, Andrea Jones, Paul Lehman, Ron LeValley, Barry MacKay, Paul McKenzie, Jamie Meyers, Marty Michener, John Miles, Alex Mills, Joe Morlan, Todd Newberry, Pia Öberg, Noreen Palazzo, Michael Patten, Keith Peters, Ron Pittaway, Will Post, Paul Prior, Van Ramsen, David Rintoul, Barbara Ross, Steve Rottenborn, Larry Sansone, Fred Schaff, Scott Seltman, Tom Shane, Brian Small, Macklin Smith, Mark Szantyr, Noel Wamer, Phil Wedge, Clayton White, Tracy Wohl, Gene Young, and the many contributors to Birdchat. Jim Dick (now retired), Glen Murphy, and Mark Peck of the Royal Ontario Museum have always been helpful. Janet Mannone helped with the photos and Trudy Rising with the text.

As well, we are greatly indebted to Andrew Richford of Academic Press who asked us to write this book and has encouraged us at every step in its development. As in the past our families, especially Trudy Rising and Katie Thomas, have been both patient and fully supportive. Thanks to you all!

Introduction

Our objective in producing this photographic guide to the North American sparrows is to illustrate with clear photographs each of the 64 species that has been recorded in the United States and Canada (biogeographically, most of Mexico is in North America, but we are not covering Mexican sparrows other than those that also occur north of there). We will also illustrate as many different plumages of these as space and the availability of photos permits. Many species of sparrows show a great deal of geographic variation – that is, individuals from different parts of the range differ in appearance; biologists have often named different populations of geographically variable species as different *subspecies* (for more on subspecies, see Geographic Variation, below). Although space – and again, availability of good photographs – does not permit us to illustrate all of this variation, or all of the named subspecies, we have selected photographs that show much of the range of variation in each species.

We view this guide as a companion volume to our book *A Guide to the Identification and Natural History of the Sparrows of the United States and Canada* (Academic Press, 1996), not as a replacement for it. The text in that book is substantially more extensive and not so focused on identification as is the text in this volume, and it is illustrated with color plates and line drawings. There are manifest advantages to paintings: a good illustrator can pose the painting in a way that emphasizes selected features, and similar species can be conveniently juxtaposed on a single plate. But there are also advantages to photographs: a photograph more nearly captures the way the bird actually appears in the field. The authors (and probably you) often have found that a good photograph helps us to identify an individual that we have not been able to identify using illustrated field guides.

General Identification Problems

There are a number of general identification problems in birds that one often encounters, such as judging size, variation in lighting, and age and seasonal variation in appearance. As well, with many sparrows it is often difficult to get a good look at the bird. To help deal with these problems, there are a number of questions that an observer should ask in the field when confronted with an identification problem.

1 How large is the bird? Generally, it is not possible to measure the individual in the field, but often there will be some other object near the bird that can be used for comparison. If the bird is with other birds, is it relatively large or relatively small? With experience it often becomes possible to assess the size fairly accurately even if the environment gives few cues. Thus, with practice, you can tell that, say, a White-crowned Sparrow is simply too large to be a Clay-colored Sparrow.

2 What are its markings? With sparrows, you should always note breast color and patterning – does it have a streaked breast or a plain one? Is there a central breast spot? With sparrows, the head pattern often gives important clues for identification, so take special note of this. Note soft part colors – are the feet and legs pink, or dark? Does the bird show white in the wings or tail when it flies? What is its

general appearance – does it have a relatively long tail or a short one, a rounded tail or a 'sharp' one? And so forth.

3   How does it act? Is its flight direct like a Savannah Sparrow, or floppy like a Song Sparrow? Does it flush, fly a short distance, then drop into the vegetation, like a Le Conte's Sparrow, or does it fly up into a bush, like a Chipping Sparrow might? Does it walk or hop? Does it scratch on the ground for food, like a towhee, or feed from a seed head like a Field Sparrow?

4   How about its ecology? Is this the sort of place where you would expect to see the species you suspect you may be observing? For example, it is very unlikely that a Lapland Longspur would be visiting a feeder in the middle of a city, and it is also unlikely that you would find a White-throated Sparrow in the grassy margins of an airport runway.

These are things that you will learn to note, consciously or otherwise, when identifying sparrows. Often the list runs through your mind quickly, and you immediately can identify your bird. Largish sparrow, with streaked breast, rusty shoulders, narrow white eye-ring, white along edges of tail, along a roadside in open country: Vesper Sparrow. However, if you cannot quickly identify your bird, take notes about it, writing in your notebook the features we have listed above, then go to your books and try to figure it out. It is often far more effective to do this than to flip through your guides trying to find a picture similar to the bird you are observing. If you are with another person, quietly exchange observations. The other person may have noted something that escaped your attention. Lastly, be especially careful identifying something that appears to be out of range, in atypical habitat, or present at the wrong season according to field guides such as this one, especially if you do not have previous experience with the species. Also remember that some birds are simply aberrant. White wing-bars on a junco do not a 'white-winged' junco make.

What are sparrows?

The word sparrow is an English word, originally and still quite appropriately applied to birds in the genus *Passer*, and some of their close relatives. In North America, there are two species of *Passer*, both introduced, the House (or 'English') Sparrow and the European Tree Sparrow. The early English-speaking colonists in North America, however, applied the name sparrow to the small brown birds that they found that superficially resemble the *Passer* sparrows of the Old World, and that name has become well established as a part of the English names of many American species. (These are generally called buntings in the Old World.) It is the American sparrows, and some of their close relatives that are covered in this photographic guide. The *American Ornithologists' Union Check-list of North American Birds* (7th Edition, 1998) [AOU Check-list] places the New World Sparrows in the Family Emberizidae, and although the classification of sparrows is debated by ornithologists, the AOU classification is used in most lists and books about American birds, and we, with a few exceptions, noted below, shall use it here. The New World Wood-Warblers (Family Parulidae), Bananaquits (Coerebidae), Tanagers (Thraupidae), Cardinal Grosbeaks (Cardinalidae), sparrows (Emberizidae) and New World Blackbirds (Icteridae) (using the AOU Check-list classification) are all closely related to each other.

Overview of the Genera of Sparrows from the United States and Canada

The species in the Family Emberizidae are divided into a number of smaller groups, called genera. The following is a list of the genera and some of their features that are found in the United States and Canada. These are the ones that are discussed in this book. It is conventional to italicize generic names as well as the Latin ('scientific') names of species, e.g. the genus *Melospiza* and the species, the Song Sparrow, *Melospiza melodia*.

Genus *Sporophila* (Seedeaters). Seedeaters are small birds with stubby, but thick bills with convex culmens (upper bills). Unlike most sparrows, they are conspicuously sexually dimorphic in plumage (that is to say, the males and females have different plumages). Some biochemical evidence suggests that they are tanagers not sparrows. Only one species, the White-collared Seedeater, occurs north of Mexico.

Genus *Tiaris* (Grassquits). Grassquits are small sparrows with stubby bills with straight culmens. They are sexually dimorphic in color; the young are unstreaked. Like the *Sporophila*, these birds may be tanagers. Two species have been recorded north of Mexico, but both are extremely rare in the area covered by this book.

Genus *Arremonops*. These rather chunky sparrows are mostly found in Mexico and Central America, although one species, the Olive Sparrow, is common in southern Texas. Although called sparrows, they are probably more closely related to the towhees (*Pipilo*) than the other North American sparrows. Like towhees, they often use their rather large, stout feet to scratch in the leaf litter for food.

Genus *Pipilo* (Towhees). Towhees are large, long-tailed sparrows (the tail is usually longer than the wing), with stout feet. Adults are unstreaked, and some species are sexually dimorphic. They commonly feed on the ground, scratching for food, using a characteristic 'double scratch,' in which the bird remains stationary while scratching backward with both feet. *Pipilo* are apparently closely related to several Mexican and Central American genera, including *Arremonops*. Six of the eight species occur north of Mexico.

Genus *Aimophila*. The sparrows in this genus are variable, and careful work will probably show that they should be divided into three different genera or at least groups. The first group contains Bachman's, Botteri's and Cassin's sparrows; these are certainly closely related, and can be difficult to tell apart in the field. The second group is represented north of Mexico by the Rufous-crowned and perhaps the Five-striped Sparrow, and the third only by the Rufous-winged Sparrow. They are medium-sized sparrows with rather long, often rounded tails, and rather short rounded wings; the sexes are alike in plumage. The *Amphispiza* sparrows are probably closely related; some workers place the Five-striped Sparrow in this genus. Some, particularly some Mexican *Aimophila*, also are probably closely related to the towhees.

Genus *Spizella*. The *Spizellas* are small, slim sparrows with relatively long and usually slightly forked tails. Adults have unstreaked underparts. The sexes are alike in most species, but the female Black-chinned Sparrow is less brightly colored than the male. The separation of some of the species in their first autumn is one of the more difficult field identification challenges. Most *Spizellas* are sparrows of open, brushy habitats, but not grasslands without many bushes; the Chipping Sparrow, however, breeds in open woodlands, parks, and urban areas. All seven species occur north of Mexico, although one, Worthen's Sparrow has been recorded outside of Mexico only once. Their relationships to other sparrows are unclear.

Genus *Pooecetes*. The widespread Vesper Sparrow is the only member of this genus (such a genus is called 'monotypic'), and its relationship to other sparrows is not clear. They are fairly large sparrows, have a streaked breast, notched tail, and conspicuous white edges to their outer tail feathers.

Genus *Chondestes*. *Chondestes* is another monotypic genus of unclear affinities. The only species, the Lark Sparrow, is a fairly large sparrow with a brightly colored head, and conspicuous white in the tips of the outer tail feathers; the sexes are similar in coloration. Adults have an unstreaked breast although juveniles are lightly streaked below.

Genus *Amphispiza*. The two to four species (here we treat them as three species) of *Amphispiza* all breed north of Mexico. They are small to medium-sized sparrows with rather long tails, pointed wings, have relatively small bills and, as adults, are unstreaked below. The sexes are similar in coloration. The facial pattern in the genus is distinctive and strikingly similar to that of the Five-striped Sparrow, suggesting to us that they may be closely related to at least some of the *Aimophila*.

Genus *Calamospiza*. The Lark Bunting, the only species in this genus, is an unusual sparrow. It is a large, chunky, large-billed sparrow that is strikingly sexually dimorphic in plumage. The male in breeding plumage is a showy black and white bird, the female brown and streaked, and much more sparrow-like. As with several other of the sparrows the relationships of Lark Sparrows are unclear, but it has been suggested that they are allied with the Snow Buntings (*Plectrophenax*).

Genus *Passerculus*. The Savannah Sparrow, the only species in this genus, is a widespread and highly variable species – and indeed, closer study may show that they really are three or more distinct species. They vary considerably in size, but all are streaked both on the back and breast; the sexes are alike in coloration. *Passerculus* is closely related to *Ammodramus*, and is merged with that genus by many.

Genus *Ammodramus*. *Ammodramus* is a fairly large genus with nine species, seven of which breed north of Mexico, and the other two in South America. They are medium-sized sparrows with relatively short, thin tails and wings; the sexes are similar in coloration. They are found in grasslands. In the genus there are two groups, those that are found in wet grasslands (Le Conte's, Seaside, and the two sharp-tailed sparrows), and those that are found in the dry grasslands (Grasshopper, Henslow's, and Baird's sparrows; the Savannah Sparrow is probably in this group).

Genus *Passerella* (Fox Sparrows). Fox Sparrows are large, with strong conical bills, long legs, stout feet with strong claws, and rather long double-rounded tails; the sexes are alike in coloration. They vary a great deal geographically, but all are heavily streaked with rusty or brown. At present, only a single species is generally recognized, but pending research that is being done, we feel that soon they will be divided into at least two and maybe as many as four species; we treat these as four species. Fox Sparrows are put in the genus *Melospiza* by some, and these in turn are close to *Zonotrichia* and *Junco*, but a strong case can be made for keeping them in their own genus.

Genus *Melospiza*. The *Melospiza* are rather small to large sparrows with short rounded wings, rather long rounded or double-rounded tails, and most are conspicuously streaked; the sexes are alike in coloration. All three species are widespread in the United States and Canada; they are very similar in juvenal plumage. The Song Sparrow is one of the geographically most variable of all birds. They are closely related to *Passerella*, *Zonotrichia*, and *Junco*.

Genus *Zonotrichia* (Crowned Sparrows). The *Zonotrichia* are medium-sized to large sparrows with large conical bills. The tail is about the same length as the wing, and all have striking crown or at least head markings. In some species the sexes differ somewhat in coloration. There are several known hybrid crosses in the genus as well as records of White-throated Sparrows (*Zonotrichia albicollis*) crossing with Dark-eyed Juncos (*Junco hyemalis*), indicating a fairly close relationship between these two genera.

Genus *Junco* (Juncos). The juncos are a distinctive group of medium-sized sparrows. Adults are unstreaked, and (with the exception of the Central American Volcano Junco) they have white lateral tail feathers, are predominantly gray, or gray and pinkish, and white in coloration; the sexes are similar, although females commonly are not so brightly colored as males. Most have pinkish bills. Although juncos are highly variable, at the present time only three or four species are recognized, and only two of these occur north of Mexico. They are generally thought to be closely related to the *Zonotrichia* sparrows, and the existence of hybrids between juncos and White-throated Sparrows (see above) supports this. There are also close chromosomal similarities between them.

Genus *Calcarius* (Longspurs). All four species of longspurs breed in North America and one, the Lapland Longspur also breeds in northern Eurasia (where it is known as the Lapland Bunting). Longspurs are medium-sized terrestrial sparrows with long pointed wings, relatively short bills, and a long slender hind claw (hence the name 'longspur'). All are strongly sexually dimorphic in plumage, and they are gregarious in migration and winter. Their relationships are unclear. Because they are brightly colored in plumage and superficially resemble many Eurasian buntings (*Emberiza*) they are commonly placed close to them in lists. However, some molecular data suggest that they are neither close to these nor to any of the other American sparrows. It has been suggested that the Lark Bunting may be a close relative. The striking sexual dimorphism and spectacular flight displays characteristic of both Lark Buntings and longspurs could be taken as evidence supporting this.

Genus *Emberiza* (Old World Buntings). The 38 or so species of *Emberiza* all breed in the Old World, and although eight of these have been recorded in North America, none are known to breed in North America. The sparrows in this genus are quite variable in plumage; most of the species that have been recorded in North America have white in their tail.

Genus *Plectrophenax* (Snow Buntings). The Snow Bunting is a large, chunky bunting that breeds commonly not only in Arctic North America, but in Arctic Eurasia. The closely related McKay's Bunting, the only other member of the genus, however, breeds only on a few islands in the Bering Sea. The Snow Buntings are strikingly colored, largely black and white birds, and are sexually dimorphic in coloration; they have different summer and winter plumages as well. They may be closely related to either *Emberiza* or *Calcarius*, but this remains to be carefully studied.

Organization of the Guide

The main section of the guide consists of the species accounts. These are arranged in the sequence of the AOU Check-list (7th Edition, 1998). This sequence is slightly different from that in most of the guides currently available (including our earlier guide to sparrows), which were based on earlier editions of the Check-list. We have not followed the species-level taxonomy of the AOU Check-list completely, anticipating some taxonomic changes that we think are soon to come.

Each account begins with **measurements** (total body length and wing length both in metric and English units, and mass in grams). The measurements are from Ridgway (1901), Rising (1996), or the references cited at the end of the account. The data on mass are either from Dunning (1993a), Rising (1996), or other sources cited in the accounts.

Then there is a brief statement of the important features that aid in identification. Bold typeface is used to highlight identifying characteristics. This is followed by a summary of the species' **habitat** preferences, **behavioral characteristics**, and **song**. Following this we describe **similar species**, followed by a summary of the species' **geographic variation**. Named subspecies are mentioned, and general trends of variation are noted. For the most part, geographic variation is clinal, that is to say, there are gradual geographic trends in features such as color and size. In the past, ornithologists commonly 'chopped' up these clines, describing different parts of them as different subspecies. *A subspecies is a geographically and morphologically defined population (or group of populations) of a species.* Individuals from different subspecies of the same species are presumably interfertile; if they were known to be otherwise, they would be named as different species. Subspecies are given a three-part name; the first two parts are the same as the specific name. Thus, an individual called *Passerculus sandwichensis beldingi* is a Savannah Sparrow (*Passerculus sandwichensis*) in the subspecies *P. s. beldingi*. When portions of clines are named as different subspecies, geographically adjacent subspecies usually grade into one another, and therefore *it usually is not possible to identify each individual as to subspecies*. It is important to emphasize that each subspecies has a specific breeding range. A non-breeding bird that is migrating or on its wintering grounds, therefore, cannot be positively identified to the subspecies level, although if the subspecies is well marked, a bird can be identified outside of the breeding season with a high degree of probability. Also, it is important to note that essentially *all* of the individuals breeding in the range of a named subspecies, unless they are on the edge of that range, are members of that subspecies *by definition*. Thus, Savannah Sparrows breeding in a saltmarsh near San Diego, California, are members of the subspecies *Passerculus sandwichensis beldingi* because that is the name given to the birds that breed there. In the case of very well marked subspecies, we might judge otherwise. For example, *P. s. princeps* is a distinctive subspecies of Savannah Sparrow that breeds on Sable Island, Nova Scotia, but rarely on the adjacent mainland, and it would be reasonable to assume that such a bird really was a member of that subspecies; conversely individuals of the subspecies that breed on the mainland, *P. s. savanna*, rarely breed on Sable Island, but can safely be assumed to be out of range if on Sable Island. However, for the most part, the variability among individuals breeding in the range of a subspecies defines the variability in that subspecies.

Following the discussion of geographic variation, we give a brief summary of the species' **distribution**, then discuss its **conservation status**. This is followed by a description of the species' **molts**, and a rather detailed **description** of its appearance. Lastly, there is a summary of records of **hybrids** and a list of the principal **references** consulted for the account.

Age Terminology

We follow Humphrey and Parkes's (1959) terminology for plumages and molts, which, in sequence, is as follows: **Natal down, Prejuvenal molt, Juvenal plumage, Prebasic I** (or **First Prebasic molt**), **First basic** (or **Basic I plumage**), **Prealternate I molt, Alternate I plumage, Definitive Prebasic molt, Definitive Basic plumage,** etc. Molts may be complete (involving all of the feathers) or partial. For most North American sparrows, the Prejuvenal molt is complete, and takes place before the young leave the nest. The Prebasic I molt may be partial or complete, and takes place in the late summer or fall (commonly, but not always, before migration). Thus, the bird winters in Basic plumage (in the first year, this is the First Basic plumage). Commonly in sparrows there are no Prealternate molts, but if they occur they are generally partial. Sparrows breed either in Basic or Alternate plumage, depending on whether or not they have a Prealternate molt. Some sparrows have an additional molt, a **Presupplemental molt** that takes place before the Prebasic molt.

We use the term **nestling** to refer to a bird in the nest, **juvenile** to refer to a bird in Juvenal plumage, and, generally, **adult** to refer to a bird in Basic plumage. In some species, such as the White-crowned Sparrow, it is possible to differentiate birds of different ages in the field, in which case we refer to them as, for example, **first fall** or **first winter**.

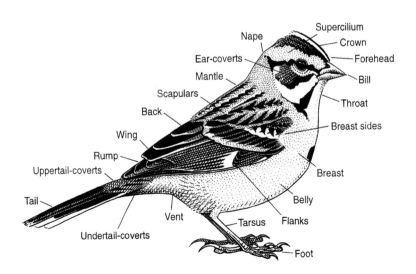

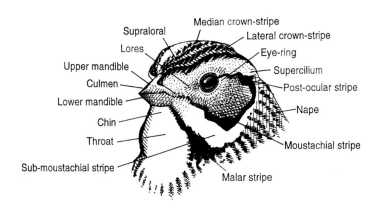

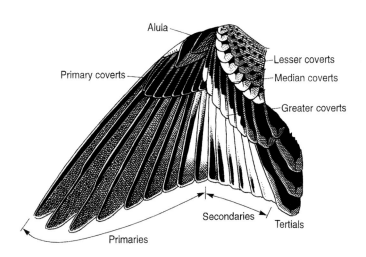

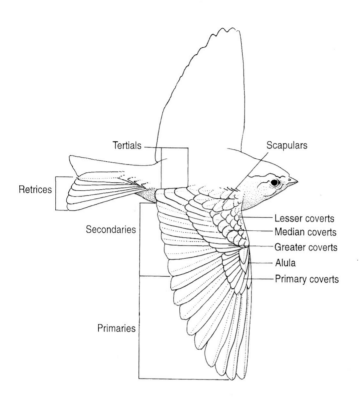

Tertials

Scapulars

Retrices

Lesser coverts
Median coverts
Greater coverts
Alula
Primary coverts

Secondaries

Primaries

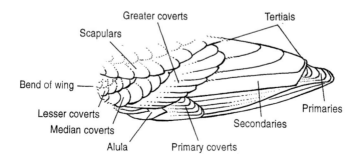

Greater coverts

Tertials

Scapulars

Bend of wing

Primaries

Lesser coverts

Median coverts

Secondaries

Alula

Primary coverts

Habitat Photographs

On this hillside covered with low brushy alders and willows and cow-parsnips, near Portage, Alaska, both Golden-crowned and Sooty Fox sparrows were common. June 1993 (J. D. Rising).

Snow Buntings were the commonest birds on this rocky, tundra site on St. Paul's Island, Pribilof Islands, Alaska, but Lapland Longspurs also occurred there. June 1993 (J. D. Rising).

Lapland Longspurs breed in fairly high density in this tundra habitat; Smith's Longspurs can also be found here. Central Alaska, June 1993 (J. D. Rising).

California Gulch, in extreme south-central Arizona, is one of the few places north of Mexico where Five-striped Sparrows can be found breeding. They were fairly common at this site. Early June 1993 (J. D. Rising).

This saltmarsh, where cordgrass, blackgrass, and marsh-elder are common, is prime habitat for Seaside and Saltmarsh Sharp-tailed sparrows. Coastal New Jersey, May 1993 (J. D. Rising).

Gambel's White-crowned Sparrows were breeding commonly in this dwarf birch and willow habitat. Danali Highway, Alaska, June 1993 (J. D. Rising).

This stunted black spruce, tamarack and sedge bog at the edge of the treeline is good breeding habitat for American Tree, Savannah, Harris's, and White-crowned sparrows. Churchill, Manitoba, June 1979 (J. D. Rising).

This area near Popham Beach, Maine, is one of the few areas where both Nelson's and Saltmarsh Sharp-tailed sparrows breed; as well, hybrids occur here. June 1989 (J. D. Rising).

On Umnak Island, in the Aleutian Islands, Alaska, Lapland Longspurs are the commonest sparrows. Savannah Sparrows, however, are also common. Also the very large Song Sparrows and rosy-finches (not sparrows) breed here, but not in this habitat. June 1974 (J. D. Rising).

This is prime habitat for breeding Bachman's Sparrows (formerly also known as Pine-woods Sparrow). Although most commonly found in the grassy understory of open mature southern pine woodland, Bachman's Sparrows may be found in other grassy habitats. Okefenokee National Wildlife Refuge, Georgia. May 1993 (J. D. Rising).

In this low, wet area of deciduous brush, Savannah, Song, and Lincoln's sparrows were all common. Near Portage, Alaska, June 1993 (J. D. Rising).

'Timberline' (Brewer's) Sparrows breed in this montane krummholz in western Montana. June (Milo Burcham).

Pawnee National Grassland in north-central Colorado is prime nesting habitat for McCown's and Chestnut-collared Longspurs, Lark Buntings, and Grasshopper and Cassin's sparrows, and a few Savannah Sparrows. (Kevin Karlson).

Range Maps

A range map is provided for each species of sparrow covered in this book that breeds in the Americas. (The different groups of subspecies of Dark-eyed Junco are treated separately in the text; however, like the other species, a single range map is provided for the entire species). A typical range map is shown below.

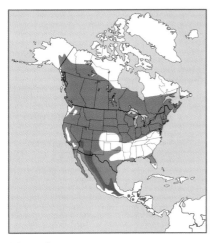

Map colors:
Red: Areas where the species may be found nesting in suitable habitat.
Blue: Areas where the species may be found more or less regularly in winter.
Purple: Areas where the species may be found throughout the year.

The colored areas show the usual distribution of the species (places where the species is usually reported each year). *The text (**Distribution** section) should be consulted for a more detailed account of each species' distribution, especially for information on where the species occurs only occasionally, or as a vagrant.* As well, for migratory species, there are comments on the usual **migratory routes** as well as the principal times of migratory movement. Although migrant individuals may turn up anywhere, during the breeding season and in winter each species is generally found only in a specific preferred habitat. For example, juncos generally breed in coniferous woods, so within their delimited range they should be expected to be found breeding only in such woods, and at all seasons, longspurs are found in open country.

‖ White-collared Seedeater

(Sporophila torqueola)

Measurements
Length: 9.5–11.2 cm; 3.7–4.4 in.
   (males slightly larger).
Wing: 47.8–54.6 mm; 1.9–2.1 in.
Mass: 6.3–12.0 g, av. 8.7 g.

White-collared Seedeaters are the small-est North American sparrows, and have **blunt bills** with a **convex culmen**. *Males* have a **blackish head, whitish throat**, and a variable amount of dusky on the breast, and **black wings and tail**. *Females* are **dull brownish green above** and **yellowish buffy below**. *Juveniles* resemble adult females, except that their wing-bars are darker and more richly colored.

Habitat
Seedeaters are found in open grassy areas, including pastures, weedy fields, roadsides, and in grassland along irrigation ditches. In Texas, they prefer areas with dense ground cover 2–3 m high, with scattered clumps of cattail, coarse grasses, trees, or low bushes (especially retama and huisache).

Behavior
Males sing from a perch near the top of a small bush, or a tall weed or grass. Territorial defense is not particularly vigorous, but males will chase other males from their terri-tory. Females are difficult to see as they feed in the grass most of the time. In winter they form loose flocks, formerly of 100 individuals or more. Seedeaters commonly cling to the thinnest of grass stems as they extract seeds.

Voice
The song is high-pitched and variable, a clear *sweet sweet sweet cheer cheer cheer*, or *sweet sweet sweet cheer cheer cheer chee swee swee r r r r r*. The flock note is a dou-ble *tick tick*. The call is a soft *che* or *chip*. Males sing frequently from Mar to Oct.

Similar species
They are variable, and males do not obtain their full plumage until early summer. They do not resemble any other sparrows, and their small size and blunt, distinctly curved bill separate them from female and first-winter **buntings (*Passerina*)**. Female **Yellow-faced Grassquits** are greenish in tone, and have a straight bill and a dull yel-lowish supercilium. **Lesser Goldfinches** have white in their tails.

Geographic variation

This is a highly variable species, but there is no geographic variation north of Mexico. The subspecies that breeds in southern Texas, *S. t. sharpei*, is found south to e San Luis Potosí and n Veracruz. There is an increase in the amount of black on males as one moves south, with the Texan birds having the least.

Distribution

Apparently resident from the lower Rio Grande Valley in s Texas south through eastern Mexico to nw Panama, and along the w coast of Mexico from Sinaloa south to w Oaxaca. Recently, most recent Texan records are from Zapata Co. (San Ygnacio and Zapata). Apparently wanders in winter.

Conservation status

The clearing of woods and brush along the lower Rio Grande river during the early 20th century created good habitat for seedeaters, and they were reasonably common there until the 1950s when cotton replaced citrus as the principal crop in that area, and the use of DDT and other insecticides, as well as weed killers was increased. Today, they are marginal and local in southern Texas.

Molt

The Basic I plumage is acquired by a partial Prebasic molt, June–Nov, that does not include the primary coverts, secondaries, and primaries; sometimes the rectrices are molted. There is no Alternate plumage. The Definitive Basic plumage is acquired by a complete Prebasic molt, June–Oct.

Description

Adult males—Small. *Head:* crown and side of face black, often flecked with brown; thin white crescent under eye; malar region and throat white, sometimes flecked with black; side of neck whitish buff; *back:* nape and mantle grayish-brown, variably flecked with black; *rump:* light buffy; *tail:* uppertail-coverts and rectrices blackish, edged with buff in unworn individuals; *underparts:* throat whitish, sometimes flecked with black; breast variable, but with some black, sometimes forming a thin black crescent breast-band; flanks, belly, and undertail-coverts rich buffy; *wing:* remiges very dark with the bases on the inner primaries white, forming a wing stripe in flight and a white rectangle on the closed wing; coverts black, tipped with white, forming two wing-bars; *bill:* black in breeding season, dusky otherwise; *legs* and *feet:* dusky brownish or gray; *iris:* dark.

Adult females—*Head:* crown and side of face pale olive-brown; *back:* pale olive-brown, not contrasting with rump; *rump:* somewhat paler than back; *tail:* the same color as the back and unpatterned; *underparts:* throat, breast, flanks, and belly pale, buffy olive-brown, somewhat paler on belly; *wing:* median coverts tipped with cinnamon-buff and greater-coverts tipped in cream-buff, forming two dull wing-bars; *bill:* yellowish olive-brown; *legs* and *feet:* dusky brownish or gray; *iris:* dark.

First-winter males (after Oct)—Resemble adult females, but often with some darker feathers, especially on crown, and blackish wings with white or buffy wing-bars.

First-winter females—Resemble adult females.

Juveniles (Apr–Sept)—Resemble adult females except that wing-bars are darker and more richly colored; males have darker wings and white at the base of the primaries.

Hybrids None reported.

References Eitniear (1997), Oberholser (1974).

1.1 Adult male White-collared Seedeater *S. t. sharpei*, Zapata, Texas, USA, May 1998. This is the only member of this neotropical genus to occur in the region. The small size, stubby bill with strongly curved culmen and shortish, rounded tail are distinctive. Note the mottled gray and black head and upperparts, blackish wings with two narrow white bars and largely pale buffy underparts. A whitish crescent under the eye is noticeable (Brian E. Small).

1.2 Adult male White-collared Seedeater *S. t. sharpei*, Zapata, Texas, USA, May 1998. The underparts are mostly pale buff, whiter on throat and grizzled with black on malar and lower ear-coverts. The tail is black with narrow whitish tips visible on underside (Brian E. Small).

1.3 Adult female White-collared Seedeater *S. t. sharpei*, San Ignacio, Texas, USA, Mar 1991. Plain brown upperparts contrast with buffy face and underparts. The dusky wings show two buffy bars. Note the short, stubby bill with strongly curved culmen (Kevin T. Karlson).

2 Yellow-faced Grassquit

(Tiaris olivacea)

Measurements
Length: 9.2–10.9 cm; 3.6–4.3 in.
   (males slightly larger).
Wing: 48–54 mm; 1.9–2.1 in.
Mass: 8.9–10.3 g (Panama).

The Yellow-faced Grassquit is a small, **olive-green** sparrow with a bright **yellow supercilium** and throat, and a **gray belly**. The **culmen is straight**. Adult males have a dark gray breast; females and young birds have less yellow in their supercilium than adult males, and sometimes none.

Habitat
Yellow-faced Grassquits are found in weedy fields, roadsides, edges of clearings in tropical deciduous forests, and second-growth and lowland scrub, from 0–2000 m.

Behavior
Courting males hover with rapidly vibrating wings near females while singing. In their range, they are often found in pairs or, when not breeding, in small flocks.

Voice
The song is a series of thin, high trills, varying in speed and pitch, **tsi-tsi-tsi-tsi**, described as an insect-like trill. In the West Indies the song resembles that of a Worm-eating Warbler. The call is a soft **tek**, **sik** or **tssip**.

Similar species
Adult males are unmistakable. Females and young may closely resemble female **Black-faced Grassquits**, but show the species' facial pattern.

Geographic variation
There are several subspecies of Yellow-faced Grassquits. The Mexican subspecies, *T. o. pusilla* which is resident in Mexico north to s Tamaulipas and central Nuevo León, is the one most likely to occur in s Texas, whereas the Caribbean *T. o. olivacea* appears to be the one that has been reported in Florida. *T. o. pusilla* has more black ventrally than *T. o. olivacea*, and in full adults the ear-coverts are black rather than green.

Distribution
Resident from s Tamaulipas and central Nuevo León south along the e coast of Mexico to Guatemala and Belize, and along both coasts of Honduras, the Caribbean slope of Nicaragua, and both coasts of Costa Rica and Panama. They also occur in the

Greater Antilles and in the Cayman Islands. Individuals seen in Florida (the Dry Tortugas [April and May], Homestead [July], and Flamingo [Jan]) were probably from the Great Antilles, whereas a bird reported from the Santa Ana Refuge, se Texas, 22–24 Jan 1990, was probably from Mexico.

Conservation status
Common in many places where they occur, but vagrant in the United States.

Molt
No information. Breeding is tied to the advent of the wet season, and thus could be quite variable. Molting probably occurs when the birds are not breeding.

Description
Adult males—Small. *Head:* crown olive-green; ear-coverts olive-green or black (Mexican); forehead, lores, and submoustachial stripe black; supraloral spot and super-cilium bright yellow, broad toward bill becoming narrow behind eye; yellow crescent under eye; ***back, rump,*** and ***tail:*** olive-green, not contrasting in color with crown; ***wing:*** greenish-olive and unpatterned, with slight yellow on the alula; ***underparts:*** chin and throat bright yellow; breast black; flanks gray or grayish-olive; belly and undertail-coverts grayish to olive-green, often (especially in birds from Mexico) with black on upper belly; ***bill:*** black; ***legs*** and ***feet:*** brownish; ***iris:*** dark.

    Adult females—Similar to males, but duller in color, and lacking black; the yellow on the face is variable, and may be absent (probably in young birds).

    Young males (any time of year)—Resemble adult males, but the yellow is reduced, and the black on the breast and throat is reduced or absent, and the chin is grayish-white or dull yellowish. Older young males have a dark malar stripe outlined by a thin yellow submoustachial stripe and yellow throat.

    Young females—Similar to adult females, but probably duller, without yellowish or whitish on throat.

    Juveniles—Like young females.

Hybrids None reported.

Reference Howell and Webb (1995).

2.1 Adult male Yellow-faced Grassquit *T. o. olivacea*, Flamingo, Everglades, Florida, Jan 2001. Grassquits are small and chunky, like seedeaters, but have straight culmen to the bill. The striking black and yellow head pattern of this male is distinctive. Otherwise quite olive above with grayish underparts. Note the restricted amount of black on the upper breast which is characteristic of this form. (Kevin T. Karlson).

2.2 Immature male Yellow-faced Grassquit *T. o. olivacea*, Dry Tortugas, Florida, USA, 1994. Very similar to female but note black border to pale yellow throat and some black above the supercilium (Kevin T. Karlson).

2.3 Female Yellow-faced Grassquit *T. o. olivacea*, Grand Cayman, Mar 1998. Differs from male in any plumage by complete lack of any black on head. The throat, supercilium and lower eye-crescent are paler lemon yellow. The ear-coverts and crown are concolorous with the olive upperparts (Kevin T. Karlson).

2.4 Adult male Yellow-faced Grassquit *Tiaris o. pusilla* or *T. o. intermedia*, Yucatán, Mexico, Mar 1998. These forms show more extensive black on head and, especially, on breast than *T. o. olivacea* (Rick and Nora Bowers).

3 Black-faced Grassquit

(Tiaris bicolor)

Measurements
Length: 9.8–11.8 cm; 3.9–4.6 in.
   (males slightly larger).
Wing: 50–56 mm; 2.0–2.2 in.
Mass: 7.8–11.2 g (av. = 9.7 g)
   (Puerto Rico).

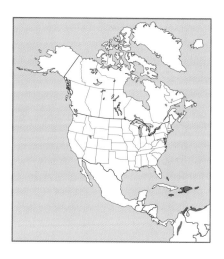

The Black-faced Grassquit is a small, drab sparrow with **no conspicuous markings**. Adult males are dark and have black heads, throat, and breast. The bill is small, conical, and black with a pink gape; the **culmen is straight**. Females are olive-green above and grayish-beige below. Young are pale bellied with a paler bill.

Habitat
Black-faced Grassquits are birds of roadsides, the edges of fields, and lowland second-growth scrub and forest edge, from 0–1300 m.

Behavior
Black-faced Grassquits often occur in small flocks or pairs. Displaying males fly a short distance slowly, with rapid wing-beats, while singing.

Voice
The song is a weak, but emphatic buzzy *tik-zeee, tik-tik-zeee, dik-zeezeezee*, or *tzee-teeeteeee*. The call note is a soft *tsip*.

Similar species
In all plumages **Yellow-faced Grassquits**, which are similar in size and shape, have patterning on their heads. The similar **Cuban** or **Melodious Grassquit** has been reported several times in southern Florida, and for several years a small population nested in Dade County. These are all thought to have been escaped cage birds. Males have a bright yellow post-ocular stripe that runs behind the ear-coverts and broadens into a broad puff of bright yellow feathers, nearly forming a band across the throat (there is a thin black line separating the puffs on either side of the throat, but this is difficult to see); females are chestnut on the head and throat, and the yellow is less bright than on the males. Female Black-faced Grassquits could be mistaken for wintering **Indigo Buntings**, which are larger.

Geographic variation
There are several named subspecies. Strays to Florida probably come from the Bahamas, where *T. b. bicolor* occurs.

Distribution

Resident throughout the West Indies (except Cuba), islands in the western Caribbean, Netherlands Antilles east to Trinidad and Tobago, and n Colombia and Venezuela. Very rare in winter (Oct–May) on the coast of se Florida and the Keys. The Florida birds are probably from the Bahamas.

Conservation status

Common where it normally occurs, but a very rare visitor to Florida.

Molt

No information. Breeds year round and inasmuch as it probably does not molt while breeding, molting times are doubtless quite variable.

Description

Adult males—Small. *Head, throat, breast*, and upper *belly:* flat black; *back, rump, wing, tail*, and lower *belly:* dark olive-green; *bill:* black; *legs* and *feet:* brownish; *iris:* dark.

Adult females—*Head, back, wings*, and *tail:* dull, grayish olive-green; *throat*, and *breast:* grayish; *flanks:* grayish, and sometimes washed with dull olive; *belly:* whitish-gray; *bill:* brownish, with lower bill paler than upper; *legs* and *feet:* brownish; *iris:* dark.

Young males (may occur at any time of year)—Like adult male, but paler, especially on the flanks and belly, and with a pale lower bill.

Young females—Like adults, but paler.

Juveniles—Like young.

Hybrids None reported.

Reference Raffaele *et al.* (1998).

3.1 Adult male Black-faced Grassquit *T. b. bicolor*, Bahamas, Jan 2000. Small and chunky with straight culmen. Olive upperparts contrast with mostly blackish face and breast. Lower underparts fading to gray with olive suffusion on lower flanks. Bill dull horn with blackish culmen (Kevin T. Karlson).

3.2 First-winter male Black-faced Grassquit *T. b. bicolor*, Bahamas, Jan 2000. As adult male but with patchy black on face and breast and slightly paler belly. Bill variably pinkish, especially on lower mandible (Kevin T. Karlson).

3.3 First-winter male Black-faced Grassquit *T. b. bicolor*, Bahamas, Jan 2000. Very similar to female but note some dusky-black on chin and malar area. Bill mostly pinkish with slightly darker tip (Kevin T. Karlson).

3.4 Female Black-faced Grassquit *T. b. bicolor*, Bahamas, Jan 2000. Upperparts dull olive grading into gray head. Throat and underparts pale off-white with grayish-olive suffusion on breast and lower flanks. Note narrow pale eye-ring. Bill pinkish with dusky culmen (Kevin T. Karlson).

4 Olive Sparrow

(*Arremonops rufivirgatus*)

Measurements
Length: 13.4–15.2 cm; 5.3–6.0 in.
  (males slightly larger).
Wing: 59–67 mm; 2.3–2.6 in.
Mass: 15–30 g (male av. = 23.2 g;
  female av. = 21.7 g).

Olive Sparrows are chunky sparrows with **dull olive backs, pale olive-gray head and underparts**, and a **yellow edge to the wing.** Sometimes the pale cinnamon-brown lateral crown-stripe can be seen. The sexes are alike. Juvenile birds have dusky streaks on the neck and breast, and have a broad, buffy supercilium; they are not greenish.

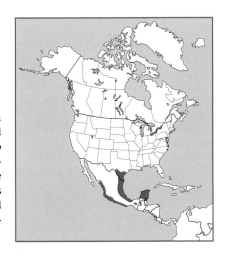

Habitat
In southern Texas, Olive Sparrows are found in thorny chaparral, brushy clearings, and weedy thickets, commonly in mesquite, Texas ebony, and huisache. They may occur in streamside thickets of ash, cane, and live oak.

Behavior
Males most commonly sing from a hidden perch close to the ground, but may sing from a fairly high, exposed place. Olive Sparrows run, and scratch for food on the ground. Their flight is low, and they usually fly only a short distance.

Voice
The song is a distinctive and accelerating *chip chip chip chip-chip-chip-chipchipchip* on a single pitch. Singing is most frequent Mar through July. The call note is an insect-like *tsip*, which is often rapidly repeated, or a sharp *tsik* or *wheee-k*.

Similar species
The **Green-tailed Towhee** is somewhat larger and in adult plumage is much more brightly colored with a rusty cap, grayish side of the face, and a whitish throat. **Botteri's Sparrows**, which occur in the same area as Olive Sparrows, are much browner and have streaked backs. Juvenile **Green-tailed Towhees** are similar to juvenile Olive Sparrows, but Olive Sparrows are smaller, have a somewhat paler throat, and less ventral streaking; their breeding ranges do not overlap.

Geographic variation
Nine subspecies have been named. *A. r. rufivirgatus* breeds in southern Texas, and is the form described here. *A. r. ridgwayi*, which occurs from s Tamaulipas to n Veracruz is little different.

Distribution

Resident from s Texas south through Coahuila, Nuevo León, e México, Yucatán, n Guatemala, and Belize, and along the Pacific Coast of Mexico from central Sinaloa south to central Oaxaca, n and central Costa Rica.

Conservation status

Olive Sparrows avoid areas where thorn-scrub has been removed, and extensive clearing reduces their numbers. South of the United States clearings resulting from slash-and-burn agriculture in some cases are suitable habitat for them.

Molt

The timing of the Prebasic I molt is uncertain, but probably occurs June–Sept; it involves body feathers and some tertials. The Definitive Prebasic molt is complete and occurs June–Sept.

Description

Adults—Medium–large sized. **Head:** lateral crown-stripes variable, but usually dull rusty or cinnamon-brown; median crown-stripe greenish-olive; supercilium grayish; eye-stripe and lores olive-brown; thin whitish eye-ring; ear-coverts greenish-olive; throat grayish, often with a thin, dull malar stripe; **back:** nape, mantle and **rump** dull brownish olive-green; **tail:** greenish-olive; **wing:** greenish-olive, with yellow in the bend; **underparts:** throat grayish-white, breast and flanks buffy-grayish; **bill:** upper mandible dusky brown; lower mandible paler; **legs** and **feet:** light brown to flesh-colored; **iris:** light brown.

First-winter (after Sept)—Like adults, but usually duller in coloration; coverts may be tipped in brownish-yellow, forming two indistinct wing-bars.

Juveniles (May–Sept)—Brownish, with brown streaking on the crown, nape, mantle, throat, breast, and flanks; supercilium broad, and buffy.

Hybrids None reported.

References Brush (1998), Howell and Webb (1995).

4.1 Olive Sparrow *Arremonops r. rufivirgatus.* Santa Ana National Wildlife Refuge, Texas, USA, Dec 2000. This species is distinctive within its US range, but could be confused with a wintering Green-tailed Towhee; note the difference in head patterns (Michael D. Stubblefield).

4.2 Adult Olive Sparrow, *A. r. rufivirgatus* Concan, Texas, USA, May 1995. Quite chunky and long-billed with generally dull olive upperparts (with brighter yellowish edges to wing and tail feathers) and pale underparts (Brian E. Small).

4.3 Adult Olive Sparrow, Concan, Texas, USA, May 1995. The head pattern is distinctive. The face and crown are mid-gray blending into a whitish throat. Note the thin sepia-brown eyeline and lateral crown-stripes. Also note the whitish split eye-ring and supraloral area. The longish, spike-like bill is pinkish with a dusky culmen (Brian E. Small).

5 **Green-tailed Towhee**

(Pipilo chlorurus)

Measurements
Length: 15.7–18.0 cm; 6.2–7.1 in.
  (males slightly larger).
Wing: 71–82 mm (male av. = 78.2 mm;
  female av. = 74.8 mm); 2.8–3.3 in.
Mass: 22.5–39.4 g. (male av. = 29.1 g;
  female av. = 27.6 g [California,
  July–Oct]).

The Green-tailed Towhee is a large sparrow with a **rusty cap, whitish throat,
black malar stripe,** and **greenish back**
and **tail.** The sexes are similar in
plumage, but the females are generally
duller. *Juveniles* are heavily streaked with
the primaries edged with green.

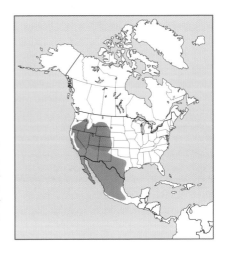

Habitat
Breeds on dry shrubby hillsides with low brush interspersed with trees and chaparral,
up to 2400 m. Often associated with burns. Commonly occurs in sagebrush or open
piñon-juniper; also found in mountain mahogany, chokecherry, snowberry, and antelope brush. In California, they are in montane thickets. In winter, they are found in
low weedy brush, and arroyos with mesquite.

Behavior
Male Green-tailed Towhees sing from the tops of shrubs; if alarmed, they dive into a
bush or to the ground. They either hop or run. Their flight is low; in flight, they often
pump their tail while flapping, then close their wings while raising their tail. They
glide just before landing on a branch.

Voice
The Green-tailed Towhee's song is a lively Lark Sparrow-like warbled **wheeet clur
cheeeweee-churr**, or a rapid wheezy **eet-ter-te-te-te-te-te-ti-si-si-si-seur**. In California,
the song can closely resemble that of the Slate-colored Fox Sparrow. The call note is a
sharp **keek**, a *Zonotrichia*-like thin, high-pitched **tseeeee**, or the characteristic cat-like
ascending **meeoow**.

Similar species
Green-tailed Towhees are distinctive, but dull individuals could be mistaken for **Olive
Sparrows**, which are smaller and lack any rusty in the crown. Juveniles of the two are
similar, but the Olive Sparrow is less extensively streaked below, more buffy in hue,
and has a buffy supercilium; the breeding ranges of the two species do not overlap.

Geographic variation None.

Distribution
Breeds from s-central and central Oregon, se Washington, s Idaho, s-central and sw Montana, Wyoming, and possibly w-central South Dakota, south through California, principally east of the Sierras, and in the mountains of sw California, Nevada, n and central Arizona, w-central and ne New Mexico, east to central and w Colorado, w Oklahoma, and sw Texas.

Winters from s California, s Nevada, central Arizona, central New Mexico, and Texas, south to s Baja California, Jalisco, Guanajuato, Querétaro, Morelos, Hidalgo, and Tamaulipas, and rarely north to their breeding range. Most common in winter in sw Texas west to s Arizona.

Migrates through California, Arizona, New Mexico, and w Texas, rarely east to sw Kansas and Manitoba. Spring migration occurs from late Feb through mid-June (mostly in late Apr to mid-May); fall migration from July through Oct (mostly Sept to early Oct).

Conservation status
Logging of forests at high elevations may increase suitable habitat for Green-tailed Towhees, but the destruction of sagebrush and reseeding with grass has destroyed their habitat in many places. Sagebrush habitats and, in winter, mesquite thickets are important for these birds. In most places, populations appear to be stable.

Molt
The complete Prejuvenal molt occurs in the nest (late May–July). The partial Prebasic I molt does not include the remiges, primary-coverts, or rectrices; it occurs July–Sept. A partial Prealternate molt, during which only the throat and head feathers are replaced, takes place Feb–May. The Definitive Prebasic molt is complete, and occurs July–Sept.

Description
Adults—*Head:* crown rusty or cinnamon-rufous; forehead, lores, and malar stripe gray to dark gray; supraloral and submoustachial stripes, and chin and throat white; face otherwise gray or greenish-gray; *back:* nape, mantle, and ***rump*** greenish-gray or greenish-brown, with centers of mantle feathers somewhat darker; *tail:* greenish, tinged with yellowish-olive; ***wing:*** greenish-olive with a yellow bend in the wing (carpal edge); ***underparts:*** chin and throat white, usually contrasting sharply with the gray breast; flanks grayish to whitish; belly white; undertail-coverts whitish beige; ***bill:*** black; base of lower bill can be white or bluish-white; ***legs*** and ***feet:*** dull brown to grayish; *iris:* dark reddish-brown.

First-winter (after Aug and Sept)—Resemble adults, but have duller crowns on average.

Juveniles (late May to Aug)—Crown, back, breast, and flanks heavily streaked with dark brown; throat whitish, and contrasts with dark brown malar stripe; tail and wings have a greenish cast.

Hybrids
Occasionally hybridizes with Spotted Towhee. Hybrids show the rufous crown and white throat of this species, and the black on the head and upper breast, grayish upper body, and rufous flanks of the Spotted Towhee.

Reference Dobbs, Martin, and Martin (1998).

5.1 Adult Green-tailed Towhee, Riverside Co., California, USA, May 1993. This fresh-plumaged individual is unlikely to be confused with any other sparrow. The striking head pattern is distinctive. The body is mostly mid-gray with contrasting yellow-green edges to wing and tail feathers (Brian E. Small).

5.2 Green-tailed Towhee, Riverside Co., California, USA, May 1997. This dull, heavily abraded individual shows extensive wear on the tertials, coverts and primary coverts and is possibly a second-year bird. Much of the greenish edges to the wing feathers is lost and shows as a panel on the primaries and a patch on the lesser-coverts (Brian E. Small).

5.3 Green-tailed Towhee, Riverside Co., California, USA, Nov 1999. This extremely fresh individual shows the subtle blend of colors and tones of the body plumage very nicely. Note the striking head pattern with the chestnut crown patch and white supraloral, submoustachial stripe and throat. Note also the gray edges to the chestnut crown feathers and the extensive brown wash to the flanks; both suggest a first-winter bird but ageing is problematic (Brian E. Small).

5.4 Green-tailed Towhee, Oregon, USA, Sept 1994. Another view of a fresh-plumaged individual. The brightness of the yellow-green edges to wing and tail feathers varies with light intensity and wear. This bird shows no gray on the crown, paler gray underparts and more green in the wing-coverts and may be an adult (Larry Sansone).

5.5 Juvenile Green-tailed Towhee, e Oregon, USA, Aug 1996. Lacks the head pattern of the adult and shows blackish streaking on otherwise buffy-gray crown, nape and ear-coverts. Upperparts similar to adult but note obscure buffy edges to wing-coverts and tertials. Underparts whitish with extensive brown wash on flanks and some narrow streaking on breast. Younger individuals can appear more streaky (Herbert Clarke).

5.6 Juvenile Green-tailed Towhee, Mono County, California, USA, 9 July 2000. This individual is younger than the bird shown in fig 5.5 (Mike Danzenbaker).

6 Spotted Towhee

(Pipilo maculatus)

Measurements
Length: 17.7–21.0 cm; 7.0–8.3 in.
    (males slightly larger than females).
Wing: 77.0–94.0 mm; 3.0–3.7 in.
    (male av. ca. 87 mm; female av. ca.
    82 mm; geographically variable).
Mass: 33.0–54.0 g.

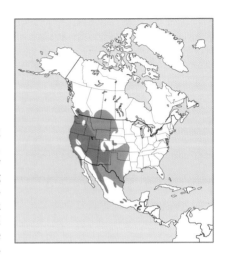

Spotted Towhees are large, long-tailed sparrows. Males have a **black head, breast, back, wings,** and **tail, rusty flanks, white belly,** and **white spotting on the mantle**; females are similarly patterned, but **brownish** or **dusky black** where the males are black. Territorial males sing persistently from a shrub. Like other towhees, Spotted Towhees 'double-scratch.' Non-singing birds can be difficult to see.

Habitat
Spotted Towhees breed in dense brush, thickets, tangles, up to a few meters tall, with or without scattered emergent trees, madrone, manzanita, chaparral, pine-oak thickets, and in the Great Plains in shrubby thickets along streams and coulees, from sea level to 2135 m. In winter they are found in shrubs and thickets.

Behavior
They hop forward during locomotion, but also hop backward when scratching for food (like other towhees they do a 'double-scratch,' in which they scratch backward with both feet to displace litter). They also run. Territorial males will sing from an exposed perch. Longer flights are steady or slightly jerky.

Voice
The song is variable both among and within populations. It consists of 1–5 notes followed by a trill that is usually on a higher pitch than the introductory notes, a ***chup chup chup zeeeeee*** or ***clip-clip-cheeee***. The song is harsher and less musical than that of Eastern Towhees. The song of west coast birds is reduced to a dry buzz, often lacking the introductory notes. The call is a catbird-like ***pshew*** or ***jereer*** or ***meaah***.

Similar species
The **Eastern Towhee** is similar, but the back lacks white streaks or spots, and there is a conspicuous white spot on the base of the primaries. Female Eastern Towhees are a richly colored brown.

Geographic variation

P. m. arcticus is the most northeastern subspecies, occurring in the Great Plains west to the Rocky Mountains. They are heavily spotted, relatively pale, with large tail spots. *P. m. montanus* occur in the s-central Rocky Mountains, from s Idaho and central Nevada south to w Chihuahua and e Sonora; it has less spotting than *P. m. arcticus*, the males are blacker, and the females more nearly resemble the males in coloration. *P. m. curtatus*, of the n-central Rocky Mountains are very similar to *P. m. montanus*; the females are grayer and paler than female *P. m. montanus*, and on average they have shorter wings. *P. m. oregonus* of the Pacific northwest, from s British Columbia south through Oregon has the least white spotting and streaking of the subspecies, and a smaller tail spot; the black and rufous on males is bright. *P. m. oregonus* intergrades into *P. m. falcifer* in s Oregon and n California, and is poorly differentiated. *P. m. megalonyx* of coastal s California and Santa Rosa and Santa Cruz islands differs from other Californian subspecies by having large feet and a longer claw on hallux. *P. m. falcinellus* of the Central Valley of California and the middle elevations of the Sierra Nevada is intermediate between coastal subspecies and interior ones. The black is darker and glossier than *P. m. curtatus*, and its rump is olivaceous rather than gray (as it is in *P. m. megalonyx* and *P. m. falcifer*). *P. m. clementae*, which is restricted to San Clemente (where extirpated) and Santa Catalina islands, California, is very like *P. m. megalonyx*, but slightly larger.

Distribution

Many populations migratory. Breeds from s British Columbia, s Alberta, s Saskatchewan south through central North Dakota, central South Dakota, n Nebraska, and Colorado, w Kansas (east to Wichita), south to w Texas, and the highlands of Mexico south to Oaxaca and s Sinaloa, and nw Baja California.

Winters from s British Columbia, Washington, Oregon (mostly in west), s Idaho, Utah, sw Wyoming, Colorado, Nebraska, Kansas, Oklahoma, and w Missouri south through Oklahoma, Texas, w Louisiana to Tamaulipas, Nuevo León, Coahuila, Chihuahua, Sonora, and Baja California. Rare but regular east to the Atlantic Coast and north to Ontario.

Migrates throughout the west and Great Plains. Spring migration takes place from early Mar to late May (most in mid-Apr to late May). Fall migration occurs 29 Aug to 17 Dec (most in mid-Sept to early Oct).

Conservation status

Spotted Towhees have been extirpated on several islands in the Pacific (e.g. Isla Guadalupe and San Clemente Is.) due to habitat destruction (browsing and over grazing); isolated populations on Santa Catalina Is. and Isla Socorro are vulnerable. When logging leads to the development of shrubby second-growth, Spotted Towhees can take advantage of that habitat while it is available.

Molt

The Juvenal plumage is acquired by a complete Prejuvenal molt that occurs in the nest. The Basic I plumage is acquired by complete body and tail molt and an incomplete wing molt that generally begins in Aug and is complete by the end of Sept. There is no separate Alternate plumage. The Definitive Basic plumage is acquired by a complete Prebasic molt that begins in July and may continue through Sept (the timing doubtless varies geographically).

Description

Adult males—Large. *Head*, nape, mantle, and *rump:* black with some white streaking on the mantle; *tail:* black with outer web of lateral rectrix white, and tips of outer three to five rectrices white; *underparts:* breast black, flanks cinnamon-rufous, belly white, undertail-coverts buffy, but the same color as the flanks in northwestern birds; *wing:* black, with edges of primaries white; scapulars and coverts boldly tipped with white, making the wings and the back appear spotted; *bill:* black, with lower bill paler in winter; *legs* and *feet:* light brownish; *iris:* bright red.

    Adult females—Similar to males, but the back of the head, throat, and breast is duller and more sooty, or in some populations (Great Plains, northwest coast) dull brownish-gray.

    First-winter males (after Aug and Sept)—Similar to adults, but duller, the dark areas being sooty gray instead of black, and primary-coverts brownish and eye color gray-brown.

    First-winter females—Similar to first-winter males, but browner.

    Juveniles (May through Aug)—Forehead and crown dark blackish-brown or brownish, inconspicuously streaked with light brown; nape and mantle colored like crown, but with more streaks; mantle dark brownish, mottled with buff or light brown, and white in the scapulars. Wings dark brown to blackish, with coverts and tertials edged in buff. Underparts buffy and streaked. Females are browner in color than males.

Hybrids

Hybridizes commonly with the Eastern Towhee in the Great Plains, and, in Mexico, with the Collared Towhee (*P. oaci*) where their ranges overlap. Rarely hybridizes with the Green-tailed Towhee (see account of that species).

Reference Greenlaw (1996a).

6.1 Spotted Towhee, *Pipilo maculatus.* Boyce–Thompson Arboretum, near Superior, Arizona, USA, Jan 1995. The distinctive white mantle and wing spotting is well shown on this adult male. This individual is probably referable to *P. m. montanus*, but because of considerable variation within named subspecies, the subspecific identification of the wintering birds is uncertain (Richard Ditch).

6.2 Adult male Spotted Towhee, Ventura Co., California, USA, Nov 1996. The obvious white spotting on the scapulars and, to a lesser degree, the mantle easily distinguish this species from Eastern Towhee. Note also the spotted white wing-bars. The bright red eye and uniform blackness of the wings indicate this is an adult bird (Brian E. Small).

6.3 First-winter male Spotted Towhee, Ventura Co., California, USA, Oct 1994. An adult male but notice the contrast between the retained juvenile flight feathers and primary coverts, which appear faded and brown, and the fresh black greater-coverts. Also, the eye color is duller orange-red (Brian E. Small).

6.4 First-winter (second calendar year) male Spotted Towhee, Durham Co., Ontario, Canada, Jan 2000. The quite extensive whitish spotting on the scapulars and mantle suggests this out-of-range bird is probably *P. m. arcticus*. The dull reddish iris, and contrast between the brownish flight feathers and fresh black tertials and greater-coverts indicate a bird in its first winter (Sam Barone).

6.5 Female Spotted Towhee, Ventura Co., California, USA, Nov 1994. Female Spotted Towhees are much more similar to males than are Easterns. The color of the hood and upperparts varies among forms, but averages sooty-brown to blackish-gray (as here). As with the male note the spotted scapulars and wing-bars. The scapular and, particularly, mantle spotting tends to be suffused with buff (Brian E. Small).

6.6 Female Spotted Towhee, s Texas, USA. Subspecific identification of Spotted Towhee is problematic due to variation. This female is possibly of the form *P. m. arcticus*. Note the grayish-brown hood and upperparts and extensive pale spotting on the scapulars extending onto the mantle. This highly migratory form shows the most sexual dimorphism within the species (Steve Bentsen).

6.7 Juvenile male Spotted Towhee, Madera Canyon, Arizona, USA, 22 Aug 1993. This individual is molting into first-winter plumage. Note the largely mottled brownish head and flanks with a few blackish and rufous feathers molting in (Greg W. Lasley).

7 Eastern Towhee

(Pipilo erythrophthalmus)

Measurements
Length: 17.3–20.6 cm; 6.8–8.1 in.
(males slightly larger than females).
Wing: 70.5–93.5 mm; 2.8–3.7 in.
(geographically variable).
Mass: 32.1–52.3 g (male av. = 42.1 g;
female av. = 39.1 g [Pennsylvania,
Mar–Oct]).

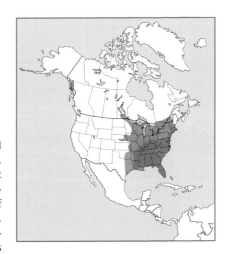

Eastern Towhees are large, long-tailed sparrows. Males have a **black head, bill, breast, back, wings,** and **tail; bright rusty flanks,** and **white bases** to the **primaries,** and in the **sides** and **corners** of the **tail**; females are similarly patterned, but a **rich light, somewhat reddish-brown** where the males are black. Males often sing from a conspicuous perch. Towhees jerk their tails in flight, and although large can be difficult to see.

Habitat
Towhees are birds of dense deciduous or mixed thickets, forest edges, and young jack pine. In winter they are found in dense brush and thickets, with dense understory, and may appear at feeders.

Behavior
Males may sing from a conspicuous perch in a bush or small tree. Females incubate closely and may run from the nest, giving a broken-wing distraction display. They usually hop (rather than run) on the ground, and use a double-scratch when foraging. Flight is variable; longer flights are usually slightly jerky or undulatory.

Voice
The song of the Eastern Towhee has an introductory note and a trill that is highly variable. It is a loud, distinctive **drink your teeeee**, or **drink teeeee**. The **'teeeee'** is generally higher than the other elements, and the **'your'** lower. The call note is an emphatic **chee-wink, joree,** or **wink**.

Similar species
The western, **Spotted Towhee** male is similar, but its scapulars and wing-coverts are tipped with white, giving the back a spotted appearance, and they lack the white at the bases of the primaries. Female Spotted Towhees are variable, dull brown, dark gray or dull black – never the rich brown of female Eastern Towhees.

Geographic variation

Four subspecies are generally recognized: *P. e. erythrophthalmus* of the northeast, west to Manitoba, and south to eastern Oklahoma, northern Arkansas, western South Carolina and central North Carolina; *P. e. canaster*, largely resident in eastern Louisiana, southern Arkansas east to northwestern Florida; *P. e. rileyi*, largely resident in coastal North Carolina, eastern South Carolina, southern Georgia, west to central Florida Panhandle, and *P. e. alleni* is resident in other parts of Florida (except for the Keys). *P. e. canaster* is similar to *P. e. erythrophthalmas*, but larger billed. *P. e. alleni* is pale-eyed, short-winged, and rather pale-plumaged, with little white on the wing and tail. *P. e. rileyi* is intermediate between *P. e. erythrophthalmus* and *P. e. alleni*, with variable, but commonly straw-colored irides.

Distribution

Partly migratory. **Breeds** from s Manitoba and probably west to se Saskatchewan, east through s Ontario, s Quebec, Vermont, New Hampshire, central Maine, s New Brunswick, Nova Scotia (rare), south through ne North Dakota, se South Dakota, central and se Minnesota, Iowa, central Nebraska, central Kansas, ne Oklahoma, Arkansas, e Louisiana, east to the Atlantic coast and south to s Florida.

Winters from e Nebraska, e Kansas, s Missouri, s Illinois, s Indiana, s Ohio, s West Virginia, and Virginia south to s Florida, the Gulf Coast, and e Texas; uncommon in winter north to Minnesota, Wisconsin, Michigan, and s New York (remains farther north in mild winters); very rare in winter in Arizona.

Migrates throughout the east. Spring migration takes place late Apr through early May; fall migration occurs mid-Sept through mid-Oct. One record for England (June).

Conservation status

As farms were abandoned in the northeast, early successional vegetation provided good habitat for towhees. However, many of these have developed into woods that are not used by this species. Urbanization has also decreased suitable habitat for towhees. Towhees are often common in thickets behind coastal dunes; as these areas are developed for cottages and recreation, towhee habitat is destroyed.

Molt

The Juvenal plumage is acquired by a complete Prejuvenal molt that occurs in the nest. The Basic I plumage is acquired by a Prebasic molt that involves all of the feathers but the secondaries, primaries, and primary-coverts; this usually begins in mid-Aug, but may begin in mid-July, and is complete by mid-Sept. There is no Alternate plumage. The Definitive Basic plumage is acquired by a Prebasic molt that takes place from early Aug though late Sept.

Description

Adult males—Large. *Head*, nape, mantle, and *rump* black; *tail:* black with outer web of lateral rectrix white, and tips of outer three rectrices white; *underparts:* throat and breast black; flanks cinnamon-rufus; belly white; undertail-coverts buffy; *wing:* black, with white bases to the primaries and white edges to the primaries; tertials broadly edged with white; *bill:* black in summer; lower mandible horn-colored in winter; *legs and feet:* light brownish, toes usually darker; *iris:* color varies geographically, ruby red in most populations, but orange or orangish-white in coastal Georgia and northern Florida, and yellowish white in Florida.

Adult females—Similar to males, but brown where males are black, and bill brownish-horn color.

First-winter males—Similar to adults, but primary-coverts brownish, contrasting with darker secondary coverts, wing feathers dark brown to blackish, and eye color gray-brown (in fall).

First-winter females—Similar to adults, but primary-coverts brownish, and eye color gray-brown.

Juveniles (May through Aug)—Forehead and crown blackish-brown, inconspicuously streaked with light brown, with brown streaking becoming more conspicuous on the nape and mantle. Ear-coverts blackish-brown, often with some brown; submoustachial stripe buff; malar stripe and throat blackish-brown. Wings black, with coverts and tertials edged with buff. Underparts buffy, with dark brown streaks. Tail blackish-brown with pale edges. The bill is dusky above and flesh-colored below, legs and feet pinkish-buff, and the iris is brown or reddish-brown. As with adults females are brown where males are black.

Hybrids
Hybridizes with the Spotted Towhee where their ranges overlap in the Great Plains.

Reference Greenlaw (1996b).

7.1 Adult male Eastern Towhee *P. e. erythrophthalmus* (at nest), Ontario, Canada, 7 July 1984. Highly distinctive with hood and back solidly black. The wings are black with white patch at base of primaries and edges to outer primaries and tertials. Underparts white with extensive rufous flanks and fulvous undertail-coverts. Eye is deep ruby-red (James M. Richards).

7.2 Male Eastern Towhee, Cape May, New Jersey, USA, Oct 1995. The brownish primary-coverts and flight feathers, and dull brownish iris indicate that this is a first winter bird (Kevin T. Karlson).

7.3 Female Eastern Towhee, Jones Beach, New York, USA, Oct 1993. Overall pattern as male but black on upperparts is replaced with brown and the tertials are edged with warm buff rather than white (Kevin T. Karlson).

7.4 Female Eastern Towhee, central Florida, USA, Mar 1996. This female shows a dull grayish-brown eye color and may be a first-winter bird. However, since eye color is so variable in the SE part of the range it is difficult to be sure. Also, because of the brown color of the upperparts, judging contrast between different ages of flight feathers and coverts is extremely difficult (Brian E. Small).

7.5 Adult male Eastern Towhee, central Florida, USA, Mar 1996. Birds resident in the southeastern portion of the range have variable eye color ranging from pale yellow to reddish-orange. This male, probably *P. e. alleni*, shows a particularly pale whitish-yellow eye color (Brian E. Small).

7.6 Female Eastern Towhee, central Florida, USA, Mar 1996. This female, also probably *P. e. alleni*, shows a yellowish eye color typical of this resident form (Brian E. Small).

7.7 Juvenile male Eastern Towhee, Jamaica Bay Wildlife Refuge, New York, USA, August 2000. Largely brown with dense dusky streaking on head and underparts. This bird shows blackish flight feathers and tail and is thus a male (Michael D. Stubblefield).

8 Canyon Towhee

(Pipilo fuscus)

Measurements

Length: 18.0–22.3 cm; 7.1–8.8 in.
  (males slightly larger in size).
Wing: 86.1–100.7 mm; 3.9–4.0 in.
  (geographically variable;
  males slightly larger).
Mass: 36.6–52.5 g, av. 44.4 g (Arizona).

Canyon Towhees are large, brown, long-tailed sparrows. They have a **rufous crown** and **pale throat, outlined with darker feathers**, a dark **chest spot**, and **buffy undertail-coverts**. Sexes are alike in coloration. Males may sing from a conspicuous perch on a rock or small shrub or tree; they run or hop, and use a double-scratch when feeding.

Habitat

Canyon Towhees inhabit scrub along dry streams, upland desert scrub, and at higher elevations dry pine-oak woodlands; they are often found in urban areas, but not in heavily settled areas.

Behavior

The Canyon Towhee varies from being a shy, difficult to see bird to a conspicuous urban species. Males advertise their territories by song, and unmated males sing almost constantly from a low tree or bush. They generally hop on the ground, and double-scratch when feeding. Flight is not rapid, but maneuverable.

Voice

The song of the Canyon Towhee is a musical tinkling, typically a series of 6 or 7 evenly spaced double syllables, *chili-chili-chili-chili-chili-chili, chur chee-chee-chee ch*, with the middle elements higher, or a thinner junco-like **chip-chip-chip-chip-chip-chip**; the song may change tempo in the middle. The call is a rough *shedup*. The locative call is a thin high-pitched *seep* or a soft *tic*.

Similar species

Canyon Towhees are like **California Towhees**, but paler, and the streaks bordering the throat are thinner, and the throat and undertail-coverts are buffy rather than cinnamon. The songs and calls differ.

Geographic variation

Only three of the 10 subspecies generally recognized are found north of Mexico. *P. f. mesoleucus*, the most widespread of these, has a darker cap and is grayer in coloration on the back, sides, and flanks, and has a shorter wing than *P. f. mesatus*, which is found in Colorado, ne New Mexico, and nw Oklahoma. *P. f. texanus*, of w and central Texas, south to n Coahuila, is like *P. f. mesoleucus*, but darker and grayer, and has a shorter tail. These forms are not safely separated in the field.

Distribution

Resident from central and se Colorado, extreme w Panhandle of Oklahoma, New Mexico (absent in e and nw), central and w Texas, central, n and e Arizona, south to Sonora (absent in nw) and in highlands to n Oaxaca.

Conservation status

Some local populations have been extirpated by rural and urban development along southwestern rivers. There is no indication that development in southern Arizona has affected numbers in any quantifiable way.

Molt

The Basic I plumage is acquired by a Prebasic molt in Oct that involves all but the secondaries, primaries, primary-coverts and usually the rectrices. There is no Alternate plumage. The Definitive Basic plumage is acquired by a complete Prebasic molt that takes place in the late fall.

Description

Adults—Large. ***Head:*** brown, with rusty brown crown; lores and supraloral spot buffy; ear-coverts brown, flecked with buff; post-auricular stripe buffy; submoustachial stripe and throat buffy; malar stripe thin and brown; ***back*** and ***rump:*** brown and unmarked; ***underparts:*** chin and throat pinkish-buff, sometimes slightly flecked with brown, a crescent-shaped necklace of brown spots extending from the malar stripe across the upper breast; breast brown, flecked with beige and darker brown, often with a central spot; flanks brown; belly beige, becoming pinkish-beige posteriorly; undertail-coverts rufous-beige; ***wing:*** brown; ***tail:*** brown, with rectrices (especially outer ones) indistinctly tipped with buff; tail darker than rump and back; ***bill:*** brownish, lower mandible paler; ***legs*** and ***feet:*** light brownish, toes usually darker; ***iris:*** brown.

First-winter (after Oct)—Like adults, but juvenal wing and tail feathers retained.

Juveniles (Apr through Oct)—Like adults, but crown lacks rust; throat, breast, and flanks brown spotted, and edges of coverts tipped with pinkish-buff, forming one or two indistinct wing-bars.

Hybrids None described.

Reference Johnson and Haight (1996).

8.1 Adult Canyon Towhee *P. f. texanus*, Davis Mountains, Texas, USA, May 1997. Essentially grayish, tinged brown, with contrasting pale buffy eye-ring, throat and richer buff undertail-coverts. Note the dull rufous crown patch and fine dark streaking bordering the throat (Brian E. Small).

8.2 Adult Canyon Towhee *P. f. mesoleucus*, Portal, Arizona, USA, Mar 1995. Note the overall grayness of the plumage compared with California Towhee. The streaking on the sides of the throat forms a reasonably distinct malar stripe. Note how obscure the dull rufous crown patch appears on this bird (Brian E. Small).

8.3 Adult Canyon Towhee *P. f. mesoleucus*, Sulphur Springs Valley, Arizona, USA, Feb 1999. A nice view of a fresh individual showing the head pattern well. Note the pale buffy eye-ring, submoustachial, throat and streaks on ear-coverts. The crown is dull rufous with gray edges to feathers (Jim Burns/Natural Impacts).

8.4 Adult Canyon Towhee *P. f. texanus*, Big Bend, Texas, USA, 22 May 1995. This worn individual appears quite dingy and shows even paler buffy areas on head. Note the bold dark streaks bordering the lower edge of the pale throat (James M. Richards).

9 California Towhee

(Pipilo crissalis)

Measurements
Length: 20.9–24.1 cm; 8.2–9.5 in.
   (males slightly larger than females).
Wing: 85–104 mm; 3.3–4.1 in.
Mass: 37.0–61.7 g, av. 41.5–-55.8 g
   (geographically variable).

California Towhees are large, long-tailed sparrows that are nearly **uniformly brown**, with a **rusty brown face, throat**, and **undertail-coverts**, and an orangish iris. Juveniles are lightly streaked below. Members of a pair often occur together, foraging on the ground; they scratch less vigorously than Spotted Towhees.

Habitat
The California Towhee is typically a bird of brushy hillsides, shrubby thickets, streamside thickets and dry upland chaparral, and parks and gardens with suitable cover. In some areas (Argus Mountains) they are found in willow thickets.

Behavior
Males sing infrequently, and after they are mated mostly in the evening. Persistently singing birds are probably unmated males. They run and more commonly hop on the ground; members of a pair commonly forage together. They scratch less vigorously than do Spotted Towhees.

Voice
The song is a series of staccato notes, getting faster toward the end, *tss tss tss tsurr tsurr*, or *tic-tic-tic-ti-ti-ti-ti-ti-ti*, all on the same pitch. Some sing *tss tss it tss chi chi chi chi chuchu chee tsee tsee* on different pitches, first falling then rising. The first notes are soft and can be heard only at a short distance. The call notes are a high-pitched, sharp *tsip* or *chip*, or an emphatic *chink*.

Similar species
Canyon and **Abert's towhees** are similar in size and coloration. Canyon Towhees generally have shorter tails, are paler, and grayish-brown on the head and underparts, and have a necklace of brownish spots and a faint central breast spot and pale rusty crown. Abert's Towhees are washed with cinnamon-brown and have a black face that contrasts with their light-colored bill. Juveniles of these species are similar to adults, but faintly streaked below.

Geographic variation

Six subspecies of California Towhees are generally recognized from north of Mexico. Geographic variation is clinal, and these are poorly differentiated. *P. c. bullatus* is found in sw Oregon and in the Shasta valleys of n-central California. These are relatively large and large-billed, and average darker on the crown and back, and grayer on the flanks than California Towhees from central California. *P. c. carolae* is found in California, east of the humid coastal region, and is grayer on the back than the north coastal California Towhees, *P. c. petulans*, and are slightly larger than the coastal *P. c. crissalis* of the central coast, south to Santa Barbara. *P. c. crissalis* has a slightly paler cap and is slightly browner in color. *P. c. senicula* from southwestern coastal California is relatively small, and darker and browner in color than other subspecies. The isolated *P. c. eremophilus* of the Argus Mountains is intermediate in size and coloration between *P. c. senicula* and *P. c. carolae*; the total population of *P. c. eremophilus* is small. None of these subspecies can be safely identified in the field except on geographic grounds.

Distribution

Resident from se Oregon, n-central California and nw California south through w California (absent from San Joaquin Valley) and Baja California.

Conservation status

Although much of their original habitat has been destroyed, California Towhees have been able to adjust to a certain extent to exotic vegetation, and throughout most of their range they are reasonably common.

Molt

The Basic I plumage is acquired by a partial Prebasic molt, June–Nov, that does not include the primary-coverts, secondaries, and primaries; sometimes the rectrices are molted. There is no Alternate plumage. The Definitive Basic plumage is acquired by a complete Prebasic Molt, June–Oct.

Description

Sexes similar—Large. *Head:* crown dark cinnamon-brown; side of face brown, with buff in front of eye, and indistinctly around eye; submoustachial area buffy, thinly streaked with brown; malar stripe thin and brown; ***back*** and ***rump:*** dark brown, contrasting slightly with crown, and unstreaked; ***underparts:*** chin and throat cinnamon-brown, with a thin crescent-shaped necklace of brown spots; breast and flanks buffy cinnamon-brown to grayish olive-brown; belly pale olive-brown, becoming buffy cinnamon posteriorly; undertail-coverts cinnamon-brown; ***wing:*** brown and unmarked; *tail:* long, brown, and unmarked, with thin cinnamon-brown tips to outer 2 or 3 rectrices; *bill:* brown, lower bill paler; *legs* and *feet:* pale brownish; *iris:* orangish-brown.

First-winter (after Oct)—Like adults, but they usually retain the juvenal wing and tail feathers, which are duller in color.

Juveniles (Apr–Aug)—Like adults, but have indistinct streaking on the underparts and pale buff lores and throat.

Hybrids None reported.

References Pyle (1997), Rising (1996).

9.1 California Towhee *P. c. crissalis*, Ventura Co., California, USA, Nov 1997. Generally warm brown on the head and upperparts with contrasting buffy eye-ring and throat. The throat is bordered with dark streaks on the lower edge. The grayish underparts are heavily suffused with brown on the flanks and highlighted by the bright rusty undertail-coverts. This bird shows some wear on the wing-coverts and tertials, but cannot be safely aged (Brian E. Small).

9.2 Adult California Towhee *P. c. crissalis*, Ventura Co., California, USA, July 1994. This molting and heavily abraded mid-summer individual appears paler than would a bird in fresh plumage although the overall impression remains the same (Brian E. Small).

9.3 California Towhee *P. c. crissalis*, Ventura Co., California, USA, Oct 1999. Another fresh individual. Note the prominence of the buffy-cinnamon eye-ring and mottling on face (usually paler on Canyon Towhee). This bird exhibits some wear on the wings and the tertials and visible primaries are certainly quite brown indicating the possibility of a first-winter bird. Accurate ageing usually is not possible (Don Des Jardin).

10 **Abert's Towhee**

(Pipilo aberti)

Measurements
Length: 21.2–23.1 cm; 8.3–9.1 in.
Wing: 78–98.1 mm; 3.1–3.9 in.
   (geographically variable;
   males slightly larger).
Mass: 38.9–55.6 g (male av. = 47.5 g;
   female av. = 44.7 g [Arizona,
   Mar–Aug]); 42.5–54.9 g
   (male av. = 49.4 g; female av. = 46.6 g
   [Arizona, Oct–Feb]).

Abert's Towhee is a large, long-tailed,
brown sparrow with a **black face** and
pale bill. The undertail-coverts are dark
rust. It runs or hops, and, like other
towhees, scratches for food.

Habitat
Historically, Abert's Towhees were found in cottonwood-willow woodlands with
dense shrubby understory, and mesquite woodland along the Colorado River and its
perennial tributaries; today they are found in remnants of this vegetation, shrubs,
exotic vegetation (e.g. salt cedar), and in cities (Phoenix, AZ) in exotic habitats.

Behavior
Because Abert's Towhees live on permanent territories they can be secretive, but in
cities can be quite easily observed. They sing rather infrequently and fly only short
distances. They hop or run on the ground, and double-scratch for food.

Voice
The song of Abert's Towhee is a rather sharp series of notes, a *peep peep chee-chee-chee,*
sleep sleep cha cha, or *chi chi chi chur chur chur chz*. The song tends to accelerate at
the end, often ending in rapid notes on a lower pitch. Mated males sing little, and the
song is apparently not used in territorial defense. The commonest vocalization is the
'squeal duet', given by members of a pair when they rejoin or are engaging in territorial disputes. It is a *sleep sleep cha cha cha*. The locative call is a thin, high-pitched *seep*.

Similar species
Canyon and **California towhees** are also brown, long-tailed sparrows, but have
rather pale throats, edged with darker feathers, rusty caps, and are not dark around
the bill as Abert's Towhee is.

Geographic variation
Three subspecies, *P. a. aberti*, *P. a. dumeticolus*, and *P. a. vorhiesi* have been recognized.
P. a. dumeticolus, of se California, is said to be somewhat paler on the back than the

others. However, the variation is clinal, and there is variation in all populations, probably reflecting real variation as well as wear and sun-bleaching. Their ranges are a matter of dispute, and they cannot be separated in the field. However, *P. a. vorhiesi* is probably a synonym of *P. a. aberti*.

Distribution
Resident from sw Utah and se Nevada (Virgin River Valley), south through western Arizona and se California (lower Colorado River and Imperial and Coachella valleys), and extreme northern Sonora, east across s-central Arizona along the Gila River drainage basin to w New Mexico.

Conservation status
Widespread destruction of its favored riparian habitat for agriculture, grazing, urban developments, and golf courses has substantially reduced population densities. Exotic habitats, such as salt cedar, and exotic plantings in cities have created new habitats for the species, but have not adequately replaced the habitat lost.

Molt
The Basic I plumage is acquired by a partial Prebasic molt that occurs June–Oct that involves all of the body plumage and sometimes the rectrices; some birds replace some or all of the remiges in the Prebasic I molt. There is no Alternate plumage. The Definitive Basic plumage is acquired by a Prebasic molt, June–Oct.

Description
Adults—*Head:* brown, with blackish lores, supraloral spot between the eye and the bill, and anterior forehead forming a black mask; ***back*** and ***rump:*** brown, contrasting little in color with crown; ***wing:*** brown and unmarked; ***underparts:*** chin and throat brown, tinged with cinnamon and thinly streaked with dark brown; breast and flanks brown; belly buffy-brown, tinged with cinnamon or brownish-pink; undertail-coverts dark rust or cinnamon-brown; ***tail:*** brown and unmarked; ***bill:*** pale grayish-brown; ***legs*** and ***feet:*** pale brownish with toes darker; ***iris:*** tan.

    First-winter (after Oct)—Like adults, except that juvenal wing and tail feathers are retained through the first year.

    Juveniles (Apr–Sept)—Like adults, but somewhat paler in color, with thin streaks on the flanks and belly, and with cinnamon-brown coverts.

Hybrids None reported.

References Hubbard (1972), Tweit and Finch (1994).

10.1 Abert's Towhee, Salton Sea, California, USA, Oct 1993. Overall warm brown, slightly paler and more buffy on underparts becoming bright cinnamon on undertail-coverts. Note the blackish supraloral area extending under eye and onto malar and chin (Brian E. Small).

10.2 Abert's Towhee *Pipilo aberti.* Salton Sea, Imperial Co., California, USA, Oct 2000. A nice view of the head pattern showing the extent of black on the face. Note the streaky effect on the throat and malar region. The eye-ring is dull brown and not especially noticeable. The pale pinkish-horn bill contrasts with the blackish face (Michael D. Stubblefield).

10.3 Abert's Towhee, Salton Sea, California, USA, Jan 1996. A rear view showing the contrast between the brown upperparts and blackish tail and flight feathers (Brian E. Small).

11 Rufous-winged Sparrow

(Aimophila carpalis)

Measurements
Length: 12.3–13.6 cm; 4.8–5.4 in.
Wing: 53–65 mm; 2.1–2.6 in.
Mass: 12.5–17.5 g, av. = 15.3 g
(sexes similar).

The Rufous-winged Sparrow is a medium-sized sparrow of mixed bunch-grass and thornbrush. It has **rusty lateral crown and eye-stripes**, and **dark moustachial and malar stripes**; resembles *Spizella* sparrows; males often sing from a bush not far from the ground, and they are rather easy to see.

Habitat
Rufous-winged Sparrows are found in flat desert grassland in desert scrub, with desert hackberry, chollas, mesquite, and palo verde, usually along washes.

Behavior
They hop when feeding, when they generally pick food from the ground, and run if pursued. When flushed, they may fly from grass cover to a small tree; they have a periodic dip in flight.

Voice
The song is variable. Sometimes it is a series of rapid notes, often with 2–4 introductory notes, followed by a trill, a series of *chip* or *tsip* notes, such as *chip burr chip-ip-ip-ip-ip-ip-ip*, or *tsee chip-ip-ip-ip*, the first note higher than the following trill, resembling the song of Canyon or Abert's towhees. Also an accelerating series of abrupt, down-slurred notes, *cha cha cha chi chi chi ci ci ci c c c c* that may remind one of the song of the Field Sparrow. The call note is a distinctive high-pitched *tzeet*, *seep*, or *tzlip*. Only the males sing, and they sing throughout the year, although especially during the breeding season, which occurs after the summer rains have begun.

Similar species
The Rufous-winged Sparrow does not closely resemble other sparrows, although it is vaguely similar to the slimmer adult **Chipping Sparrow**. The rusty secondary-coverts are evident only in the hand. **Rufous-crowned Sparrows** are darker, especially on the neck, throat, and breast, which tend to be brownish in Rufous-crowned Sparrows and grayish in Rufous-winged Sparrows.

Geographic variation

Only *A. c. carpalis* occurs north of Mexico; the two additional subspecies occur in Mexico. These subspecies are poorly differentiated; *A. c. carpalis* in Arizona is somewhat larger than Mexican birds.

Distribution

Resident from s-central Arizona and se Arizona, south through central and se Sonora and central Sinaloa.

Conservation status

Rufous-winged Sparrows were extirpated or at least greatly reduced in numbers in Arizona by over-grazing, and there were only scattered records for the state until the mid-1950s. Today they seem to be found in areas that were never heavily grazed.

Molt

The Prejuvenal molt, which probably occurs in the nest, is complete. The Basic I plumage is acquired by a partial Prebasic molt that occurs in Aug–Nov and includes all body feathers, median-coverts, and 8–10 inner greater-coverts, and sometimes the 1–3 innermost primary-coverts. Primaries 1–3 are molted in some birds and 0 to all 12 of the rectrices may be molted. There is partial Prealternate I molt that occurs Apr–June, and includes body feathers, sometimes greater wing-coverts, 1–3 tertials, and occasionally some secondaries and 2–12 rectrices. The Definitive Basic plumage is acquired by a complete Prebasic molt that occurs Aug–Nov.

Description

Adults—*Head:* broadly streaked with rufous, sometimes with an indistinct median crown-stripe; supercilium buffy gray; lores and eye-stripe rusty; ear-coverts buffy gray; moustachial and malar stripes dark brown; submoustachial stripe and chin pale buffy gray; ***back:*** including uppertail-coverts and tail brownish-gray or light grayish-brown, the mantle and scapular feathers with dark brown oblong centers, giving a streaked appearance; ***wing:*** brown, with rusty lesser coverts; median and greater coverts edged with buff, forming one or two indistinct wing-bars; ***underparts:*** grayish-white, with breast slightly darker and flanks buffy gray; undertail-coverts light buff; ***bill:*** upper mandible brown; lower mandible flesh-colored with a dusky tip; ***legs*** and ***feet:*** brownish; ***iris:*** light brown.

First-winter (Aug–Nov)—Similar to adult; wing and tail feathers are usually retained from juvenal plumage.

Juveniles (May–June)—Crown and back light brown, heavily streaked with dark brown; submoustachial stripe suggested; underparts whitish with brown spotting on throat and breast, and flanks streaked with brown; margins of coverts buff.

Hybrids None described.

References Howell and Webb (1995), Lowther *et al.* (1999), Phillips *et al.* (1964).

11.1 Adult Rufous-winged Sparrow *A. c. carpalis*, Tucson, Arizona, USA, May 1997. Rather smaller than other *Aimophila* within its range but with a moderately stout bill and slight crested appearance. The rufous lesser-coverts are visible here but are often hidden by the scapulars. Otherwise note the pale buffy upperparts finely streaked darker and mostly pale gray head with contrasting rufous crown and blackish moustachial and malar stripes. Apart from some slight wear on the tertials this bird is in fresh plumage (Brian E. Small).

11.2 Adult Rufous-winged Sparrow *A. c. carpalis*, Florida Wash, Arizona, USA, Aug 1996. A nice view of the head pattern and uniform pale gray underparts. Note the chestnut crown and post-ocular stripe and the blackish loral, moustachial and malar stripes. The moderately stout bill is largely pinkish with a dark culmen. The slim '*Spizella*-like' shape is quite evident here (Brian E. Small).

11.3 Juvenile Rufous-winged Sparrow *A. c. carpalis*, Aug 1996. The whitish underparts are boldly streaked across the breast and the malar is less well defined than an adult. The head is mostly buffy-brown streaked with dusky with ill-defined paler supercilium and neck sides. From what little we can see of the upperparts they appear buffy-brown with dusky streaking (Mike Danzenbaker).

12 Cassin's Sparrow

(Aimophila cassinii)

Measurements
Length: 13.1–14.7 cm; 5.2–5.8 in.
Wing: 56–68 mm; 2.2–2.7 in.
   (males slightly larger).
Mass: 17.8 g (males, Kansas, June);
   males 16.0–19.5 g, av.=17.8 g;
   females 16.0–21.5 g, av.18.1 g
   (se Arizona).

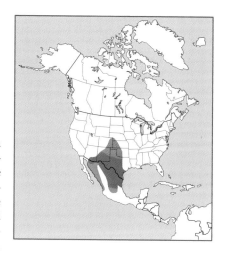

Cassin's Sparrow is a fairly large, grayish sparrow of dry grasslands that lacks conspicuous markings. In flight, the **white tips to the tail feathers** may be apparent. It has **streaks on the flanks**, and the **central two tail feathers are pale, and barred**. Territorial males sit in low bushes, commonly sage, juniper, or mesquite, or on the ground, to sing. They often give a spectacular flight song. Both the song and the flight display are distinctive.

Habitat
In the central plains, Cassin's Sparrows live in shortgrass interspersed with sagebrush and rabbitbrush. In the south and southwest they are found in shortgrass interspersed with mesquite, hackberry, yucca, oaks, cactus, ocotillo and other bushes. Along the Texas coast they live in bunch grass.

Behavior
Territorial males sit in low bushes, commonly sage, or on the ground to sing; also, they often give a spectacular flight-song. When flushed, they may fly to a nearby fence or bush, or drop back into the grass.

Voice
The song is a clear, usually descending sweet, liquid trill, followed by 2 notes, the second usually higher than the first; this is preceded by 2 soft notes that are seldom heard: *ti ti tzeeeeeeee tay tay*. The song is often given in flight, as the male flies into the air to a height of about 6 m, sets his wings, and floats back to a low bush. There is also a *chitter* flight song that is a series of rapid *chips* that become a warbler sound at the end. *Chip* calls are given by adults when around young; soft *sip* notes are given by young. Singing may commence on warm days in Feb, and may persist through Sept. Males commonly sing at night.

Similar species
Botteri's Sparrow is similar and in Texas and Arizona can be found in the same habitat. See the account of that species.

Geographic variation None.

Distribution
Breeds from central Wyoming (perhaps west to sw Idaho), sw South Dakota, sw Nebraska, w Kansas, and e and central Colorado south through w-central Kansas and central Oklahoma, and e New Mexico to s Texas, s Arizona, and n Sonora, and south on the Mexican Plateau through Chihuahua, Durango, and Tamaulipas, to s Tamaulipas, and San Luis Potosí; territorial males have been reported in s California.

Winters from se Arizona, central New Mexico (rare), and w and s-central Texas, south to s Nayarit, Guanajuato, San Luis Potosí, and Tamaulipas.

Migrates rarely through California (May to mid-July) and e Nevada.

Conservation status
Since the 1930s, Cassin's Sparrow has increased in abundance in Texas as a consequence of clearing brush to establish grasslands in the western part of the state. In many parts of its range, numbers fluctuate substantially from year to year.

Molt
Young birds molt twice in the first 6 months after fledging: After fledging there is an incomplete Presupplemental molt that lasts up to 2 months, followed by a complete Prebasic I molt in Sept–Nov. There is a partial prolonged Prealternate molt in Feb–Aug; in most or all first year birds there is a Presupplemental molt that takes place on the breeding grounds during which the body plumage is replaced. The Definitive Basic plumage is acquired by a complete Definitive Basic molt Aug–Nov. There is a partial prolonged Definitive Alternate molt (mostly of body contour feathers) from mid-Feb–Aug that may be delayed by breeding.

Description
Adults—*Head:* brown streaked with gray and dark brown; supercilium buff; thin dark brown submoustachial stripe; *back:* mantle and scapulars brown, feathers with dark brown subterminal spots and edged with buff, giving a scaly appearance; *rump:* and uppertail-coverts with brown spots; *wing:* brown, with secondary coverts edged in buff, forming an indistinct wing-bar; alula pale yellow; *tail:* middle rectrices light brownish-gray with narrow brown bars; lateral two rectrices edged and tipped with white (indistinct in worn individuals); *upperparts:* chin, throat, and breast gray; flanks gray with black streaks posteriorly; belly whitish; undertail-coverts sometimes buffy; *bill:* brownish-gray, with upper mandible darker, and a pale bluish-gray tomial edge and lower mandible; *legs* and *feet:* light brownish or dark pinkish-flesh; *iris:* dark brown.
First winter (July–Mar)—Like adult, but some with dark spots on breast.
Juveniles (May-Aug)—Similar to adults, but back brown, feathers with buffy tips and darker central streaks, greater-coverts edged with white, and light streaking on the breast and throat.

Hybrids None described.

References Dunning *et al.* (1999), Hubbard (1977), Pyle (1997), Rising (1996), Willoughby (1986), Wolf (1977).

12.1 Adult Cassin's Sparrow, Falcon Dam, Texas, USA, Mar 1995. Overall structure is similar to Botteri's but the bill is less stout, the crown more rounded (sometimes with a slight crested appearance, as here) and the body somewhat slimmer. This fresh individual exhibits many features different from Botteri's of any form. Note especially the centers to the scapulars and uppertail-coverts which are largely chestnut-brown with thin black shaft-streak and anchor-shaped subterminal line (Kevin T. Karlson).

12.2 Adult Cassin's Sparrow, Falcon Dam, Texas, USA, Mar 1996. This fresh-plumaged individual should present few identification problems. The upperparts and crown are gray with chestnut and black streaking. The underparts are pale grayish with blurred, though obvious, brown streaks on the lower flanks. The wing-coverts are edged and tipped pale grayish-buff forming obscure wing-bars. On fresh birds the supraloral is pale buffy-yellow (Kevin T. Karlson).

12.3 Adult Cassin's Sparrow, Florida Grasslands, Arizona, USA, Apr 1998. The tail on this moderately fresh individual shows the classic Cassin's pattern. Notice the jagged edge to the black central streak, creating a barred effect. This feature usually holds good on all but the most worn birds (Jim Burns/Natural Impacts).

12.4 Adult Cassin's Sparrow, Portal, Arizona, USA, Aug 1995. This heavily worn late summer individual could cause problems but close inspection reveals many Cassin's features. The pattern on the scapulars and uppertail-coverts is still distinctive with the subterminal mark appearing as a spot. The streaking on the lower flanks, though much abraded, is still evident (Brian E. Small).

12.5 Adult Cassin's Sparrow, Portal, Arizona, USA, Aug 1995. Another view of a scruffy and abraded late summer bird. The upperparts are extremely worn and have lost all gray and buff edges but still appear slightly spotty due to the blackish subterminal (now terminal!) marks on the scapulars and uppertail-coverts (Brian E. Small).

12.6 Juvenile Cassin's Sparrow, Tucson, Arizona, USA, Nov 1988. Similar to juvenile Botteri's Sparrow. Differs in being somewhat whiter on the underparts with very fine and sparse streaking across breast. The wing-coverts tend to be tipped whiter, forming more obvious wing-bars (Rick and Nora Bowers).

12.7 Juvenile Cassin's Sparrow, Tucson, Arizona, USA, Nov 1988. Another view, showing the extent of fine streaking on the breast. On this bird the pale eye-ring is quite marked on an otherwise streaky head. The pale grayish-white tip and edge to the outermost tail feather can be seen (lacking on Botteri's) (Rick and Nora Bowers).

13 **Bachman's Sparrow**

(Aimophila aestivalis)

Measurements
Length: 12.4–15.2 cm; 4.9–6.0 in.
(males slightly larger).
Wing: 56–65 mm; 2.2–2.6 in. (males);
54–63 mm; 2.1–2.5 in. (females).
Mass: av. 20.8 g (Arkansas).

Bachman's Sparrow is a fairly large, large-billed, round-tailed sparrow with **reddish-brown lateral crown-stripes**, **streaked scapulars** and **back**, gray chin and throat, and **unstreaked, buffy breast**. Males often sing from a conspicuous perch, but otherwise individuals are often difficult to find.

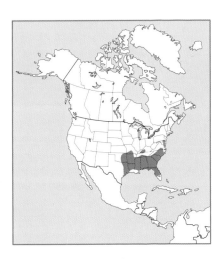

Habitat
At all seasons, Bachman's Sparrows are characteristically birds of open native pine woods with fairly dense grassy understory; they are also found in oak savannah in tallgrass prairie. They are also found in open grassy areas where intrusion of forbs is limited by poor soils. In the north, they are found in degraded pastures and abandoned fields.

Behavior
During the breeding season, males sing persistently and often all day from an exposed perch, generally less than 3 m from the ground. Otherwise, Bachman's Sparrows are secretive and difficult to see. When flushed, they generally drop again into the understory vegetation, and they do not respond to 'spishing.'

Voice
The song is melodious, highly variable, but distinctive. It generally consists of a long, sweet note followed by a clear trill; sometimes there is a third element. Each individual sings several different songs differing in pitch or tempo, often repeating one several times, then switching to another. The song is similar to that of the Eastern Towhee, with the second element – the trill – often like Swamp Sparrow, but shorter and less emphatic. Birds sing all day, and counter singing is common. A bubbling, exuberant flight-song has also been described. The call note is a thin, high **chip** or **pseet**, much like that of the Chipping Sparrow.

Similar species
Botteri's Sparrow is very similar in appearance, and both vary geographically. The very different habitat preferences and songs facilitate field identification of these two, which have non-overlapping ranges. Western Bachman's Sparrows have a distinct

brown eye-stripe, and are more rufescent in color than eastern Botteri's Sparrows. Botteri's Sparrows may have rusty crown-stripes. The two central tail feathers of **Cassin's Sparrows** are pale brown, contrasting with the others, which are dark, and distinctly barred; the lateral tail feathers are edged and tipped with dull white. Cassin's Sparrow is grayer in appearance.

Geographic variation

Three subspecies are recognized, *P. a. bachmani,* which breeds from Virginia south to South Carolina and Alabama, *P. a. aestivalis,* which breeds from s South Carolina, Georgia, and Peninsular Florida, and *P. a. illinoensis* which breeds in Indiana, Illinois, and Missouri, south to Louisiana and e Texas. *P. a. illonensis* is doubtfully distinct from *P. a. bachmani.* Geographic variation is clinal, and reliable subspecific identification probably is not possible.

Distribution

Breeds from s-central Missouri, e and central Oklahoma (west to Osage, Creek and Pontotoc counties), e Texas, Arkansas, se Illinois, s-central Indiana, sw Kentucky, and West Virginia (formerly?), s-central Virginia, south to the Gulf Coast and s-central Florida. *Winters* from se North Carolina south to the Gulf States, and s Florida.

Bachman's Sparrows formerly rarely but regularly wandered north to southern Ontario in spring.

Conservation status

Bachman's Sparrows are strongly affected by forestry practices. Their numbers increase when understory vegetation is burned every third year or so, discouraging the growth of woody plants, and encouraging the growth of grasses. The species has declined in numbers in the northern parts of its range (Illinois, Indiana, Kentucky, West Virginia, and Virginia). The causes for this are unclear.

Molt

In hatch year birds, there is a complete Prebasic molt that occurs July–Dec; there is a Presupplemental molt in most hatch year birds, with the body feathers being replaced from June–Sept, then again, along with the remiges from Sept–Dec (this may occur either on the summer or winter grounds). There is a complete Prebasic molt in adults that occurs June–Nov, and a partial Prealternate molt, Feb–July; the adult Prebasic molt occurs principally on the wintering grounds.

Description

Adults—Fairly large and round-tailed. *Head:* median crown-stripe buffy gray; lateral crown-stripes dull rusty; supercilium and side of head buffy gray, with a narrow rusty post-ocular stripe; nape buffy gray, narrowly streaked with chestnut or chestnut-brown; *back:* streaked with chestnut or chestnut-brown, the feathers often with blackish centers; *rump:* grayish brown with chestnut-brown centers; *tail:* dark brown, rounded, and slightly longer than wing; may show pale tips and faint bars, central ones paler than others; *wing:* coverts chestnut-brown, without conspicuous wing-bars; marginal coverts pale yellow; *underparts:* chin and throat very pale dull gray or buffy white, deepening on chest, sides and flanks, surrounding paler buffy white belly; females may have small black spots on breast; a dusky submaler streak sometimes present; *bill:* stout, upper mandible dusky, lower mandible paler; *legs* and *feet:* pale brownish-buffy or dull yellow; *iris:* brown.

First-winter (Sept–Feb)—Resemble adults, but are less rufous on the back, and the breast often has blackish spots.

Juveniles (May–Sept)—Crown and back dark brown or black, with mantle and scapulars edged with buffy or reddish-brown, but less rufous than adults, and heavily streaked with brown; greater-coverts edged with rust to form a slight wing-bar; underparts whitish or cream; chin, sides of neck, throat, breast, and flanks streaked with brown.

Hybrids None described.

References Dunning (1993b), Pyle (1997), Willoughby (1986).

13.1 Adult Bachman's Sparrow *A. a. illinoensis*, e. Texas, USA, May 1995. A chunky, stout-billed *Aimophila*. The buffy breast is sharply demarcated from the whitish belly and the crown is largely chestnut, both features are characteristic of this form. Note also the warm buffy suffusion on the face and the chestnut post-ocular stripe (Brian E. Small).

13.2 Adult Bachman's Sparrow *A. a. illinoensis*, Poyen, Arkansas, USA, Apr 1993. The upperparts on this bird show broad chestnut streaking and the wings appear more uniformly chestnut due to extensive edges, especially on the coverts. Note also the almost solid chestnut crown and buffy (pale on this individual) breast. Compare these features with Fig. 13.3 (Jim Burns/Natural Impacts).

13.3 Adult Bachman's Sparrow *A. a. aestivalis*, Florida, USA. On this form the ground color of the upperparts is gray with sharply defined black and chestnut-brown streaking on mantle and crown. The wings show an obvious chestnut panel created by broad edges to the bases of the secondaries and primaries. The underparts are whitish with a grayish-buff suffusion across the breast. Note the short-winged, longish-tailed aspect of this species (Greg W. Lasley).

13.4 Adult Bachman's Sparrow *A. a. aestivalis*, USA, May. Another view of a nominate adult showing the rather uniform grayish underparts and the bold chestnut streaking on the crown and mantle (Erik Breden).

13.5 Juvenile Bachman's Sparrow *A. a. aestivalis*, South Carolina, USA, July 1990. The rather buffy ground color to the upperparts (generally lacking chestnut tones) and blurry dusky streaking across the breast are obvious juvenile characteristics. Note also the pale buffy eye-ring and narrow buff edges and tips to the wing-coverts (Rick and Nora Bowers).

14 Botteri's Sparrow

(Aimophila botterii)

Measurements
Length: 12.9–16.1 cm; 5.1–6.3 in.
    (males slightly larger).
Wing: 59–71 mm; 2.3–2.8 in.
    (larger in Texas than Arizona).
Mass: 15.7–25.5 g; male av. 19.7 g,
    female av. 21.0 g (breeding season,
    Arizona).

Botteri's Sparrow is a fairly large, rather flat-headed, **large-billed**, and **round-tailed** sparrow without conspicuous markings. Territorial males sit in low bushes or trees to sing, but otherwise they spend most of their time on the ground, and can be difficult to see.

Habitat
In Arizona, Botteri's Sparrows are found in fairly tall grass (especially sacaton), mixed with mesquite, ocotillo, and oaks. In Texas, they are found in saltgrass mixed with mesquite, palo verde, yucca, and prickly pear, or in bunchgrass, growing among scattered huisache or mesquite bushes.

Behavior
Territorial males sit in low bushes or on a fence to sing, but otherwise Botteri's Sparrows spend most of their time on the ground and can be difficult to see. When flushed, they may drop back into the grass, or fly to the nearest bush. They occasionally sing in horizontal flight.

Voice
The song is loud, clearly whistled, repetitive, slightly canary-like, and characteristically consists of two *che-lick* elements (like Horned Lark flight calls, or Western Kingbird calls), followed by a variable series of notes, ***wit-wit-wit-wit-t-t-t-t-tseeoo wit wit***, becoming more rapid, like a bouncing ball; or *che-lick che-lick wit wit* (lower pitch) ***wit-wit-wit-wit-t-t-t-t***, sometimes dropping in pitch at the end. The song is highly variable; individuals often vary their songs. The song carries well, and can probably be heard up to 200 m. The call note is a *chip*, *pit*, or *tsip*.

Similar species
Botteri's Sparrow is very similar in size and coloration to **Bachman's Sparrow**. Western Botteri's Sparrows may appear slightly warmer rusty buff ventrally than eastern Bachman's Sparrows, and Bachman's Sparrows usually show some rusty on the crown; western Bachman's Sparrows are more rufescent in color than eastern ones, and have a

distinct brown eye-stripe. The ranges of Bachman's and Botteri's sparrows do not overlap, and their songs are distinctive. Eastern Botteri's Sparrows are paler and grayer in overall color than western ones, and may show some rust in the crown. Botteri's Sparrow can be told from the similar **Cassin's Sparrow**, which are often found in the same fields as Botteri's, in several ways: the central two tail feathers of Cassin's Sparrows are pale brown (contrasting with the others, which are darker), with distinct barring, and the lateral ones are edged and tipped with dull white (which may not be evident on worn birds), whereas the tails of Botteri's and Bachman's sparrows are brown with the edges of the feathers paler brown; the mantle and scapular feathers of Botteri's and Bachman's sparrows are brown with the edges of the feathers paler brown; the mantle and scapular feathers of Botteri's Sparrows are brown with dark brown centers, whereas the back feathers of Cassin's Sparrows are paler brown with subterminal dark spots, and pale fringes, giving them a scaly appearance (except in worn birds); overall, Cassin's Sparrow has a grayer appearance than Botteri's especially western Botteri's. There are distinct dark brown spots on the lower flank of Cassin's Sparrow.

Geographic variation
Of the several subspecies described, only two occur north of Mexico, *A. b. texana*, of se Texas, and *A. b. arizonae*, of se Arizona and sw New Mexico. *A. b. texana* is generally pale and gray, with a whiter belly than *A. b. arizonae*, which, in contrast, appears to be pale reddish. Individuals from Texas average slightly larger in wing length than those from Arizona.

Distribution
Breeds from se Arizona, sw New Mexico, south to Chiapas and locally to Costa Rica, and north along the Gulf Coast of eastern Mexico into coastal s Texas (lower Rio Grande Valley), and w Texas (Presidio County – records for one year).

Winters probably from n Mexico south through its breeding range.

Conservation status
Botteri's Sparrows require substantial ground cover and are sensitive to grazing; they were formerly more widespread in Arizona than today. In southeastern Texas, habitat degradation has resulted in a decrease in range (they were formerly found north to Corpus Christi), and a decrease in numbers, but they remain common where suitable habitat exists. Much of their remaining habitat in Texas is now protected.

Molt
The molts of Botteri's Sparrow are not well known, but probably they are similar to those of Cassin's and Bachman's sparrows, which are closely related.

Description
Adults—Fairly large. ***Head:*** brown, with centers of crown feathers dark brown; supercilium and lores pale buffy brown, and eye-stripe somewhat darker; ***back:*** brown, with centers of mantle and scapular feathers dark brown; ***tail:*** brown, with darker centers; ***wing:*** brown with yellowish alula and lesser coverts, and edges of median and greater-coverts somewhat lighter; ***underparts:*** chin, throat, breast, and flanks buffy brown, somewhat paler on belly; undertail-coverts buffy brown with dark brown centers; ***bill:*** brownish-gray, upper bill darker than lower bill, with pale bluish-gray tomial edge; ***legs*** and ***feet:*** dull pinkish; ***iris:*** dark brown. Females may have more streaking on the crown and neck, and perhaps faint streaking on flanks.

First-winter (July–Dec)—Similar to adult, but sometimes with light brown spots on breast.

Juveniles (June–Aug)—Crown, back, and rump feathers with large dark centers; underparts dull white to buffy on breast, heavily streaked on throat, breast, and flanks; edges of greater-coverts rusty and tipped with buff; undertail-coverts buffy orange without dark centers.

Hybrids None reported.

References Adams and Byon (1999), Pyle (1997), Webb and Bock (1996).

14.1 Adult Botteri's Sparrow *A. b. arizonae*, Florida Wash, Arizona, USA, Aug 1996. A chunky, short-winged and rather longish-tailed *Aimophila*. The stout bill is accentuated by the rather flat crown profile. Overall rather drab buffy-gray but note chestnut tones on the crown, post-ocular stripe and scapulars characteristic of this form. Clearly visible here are the thin black shaft-streak centers to the scapulars and uppertail-coverts (Brian E. Small).

14.2 Adult Botteri's Sparrow *A. b. arizonae*, Florida Wash, Arizona, USA, Aug 1995. On this moderately worn individual concentrate on the overall structure of the bird, noting especially the stout bill profile. The underparts are uniform pale grayish-buff lacking any streaking on the lower flanks. Just visible are the black shaft-streaks on the scapulars (Brian E. Small).

14.3 Adult Botteri's Sparrow *A. b. arizonae*, Florida Wash, Arizona, USA, June 1993. On this fresh-plumaged individual note the overall uniform grayish-buff appearance with chestnut tones on crown, post-ocular stripe and scapulars. The very narrow black shaft-streaks are barely visible. The head shows a broad, though obscure, grayish supercilium that is whiter on the supraloral area (Brian E. Small).

14.4 Adult Botteri's Sparrow *A. b. arizonae*, Florida Grasslands, Arizona, USA, July 1998. This moderately worn individual captures the feel of the species very well. Notice the black shaft-streaks on the scapulars and uppertail-coverts, the uniform underparts lacking any streaking on the lower flanks, and whitish supraloral (Jim Burns/Natural Impacts).

14.5 Adult Botteri's Sparrow *A. b. arizonae*, Florida Grasslands, Arizona, USA, Aug 1998. On fresh and moderately worn birds the shape of the blackish center to the tail feathers can be a useful distinction from Cassin's. On this Botteri's notice the uniformly smooth edge to the black central streak. Also obvious here are the black shaft-streaks on the uppertail-coverts and lack of streaking on the lower flanks (Jim Burns/Natural Impacts).

14.6 Juvenile Botteri's Sparrow *A. b. arizonae*, Madera Canyon, Arizona, USA, June 1987. The fine dusky streaking across the breast and buffy edges and tips to the wing-coverts are characteristic of juvenile plumage. Botteri's Sparrow has a flatter crown and stouter bill than Cassin's Sparrow. To distinguish from a similarly plumaged Cassin's the overall structure, especially the stout-billed, flat-crowned aspect, is useful to note (Rick and Nora Bowers).

14.7 Adult Botteri's Sparrow *A. b. texana*, Kenedy Co., Texas, USA, June 2000. The upperparts and head are distinctly grayer than on *arizonae* and lack the reddish and buffy tones characteristic of that form in fresh plumage. Overall the basic pattern is similar on both subspecies (Greg Lasley).

14.8 Botteri's Sparrow *Aimophila b. texana*, Kenedy Ranch, Kenedy Co., Texas, USA, May 1999. Another view of a fresh plumaged adult. Notice that the chestnut tones are limited to the head stripes and the lower scapulars (Michael L. Gray)

15 Rufous-crowned Sparrow

(Aimophila ruficeps)

Measurements
Length: 12.7–15.5 cm; 5.0–6.1 in. (males somewhat larger).
Wing: 55.6–72.5 mm; 2.2–2.9 in., males slightly larger.
Mass: 16.0–23.3 g; male av.=19.3 g, female av.=18.1 g (Arizona) males 17.0–20.6 g (av. 18.8 g, n = 11); females 16.7–19.7 g (av. 18.4 g, n = 10) (Santa Barbara, Co., California).

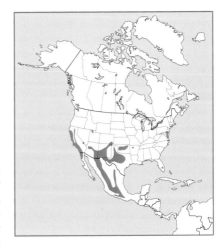

The Rufous-crowned Sparrow is a fairly large, round-tailed sparrow with a **rusty crown, gray supercilium, distinct dark malar stripe, rather prominent eye-ring**, and **unmarked grayish or buffy gray underparts**. Territorial males will often sing from a fairly exposed perch in bushes or on a rock, but they spend most of their time on the ground.

Habitat
Rufous-crowned Sparrows are characteristic of dry rocky hillsides and canyons, with rocks interspersed with shrubs and grass. They live in hilly semi-arid grasslands interspersed with small junipers, piñon, oaks, acacias, or other shrubs. Along the coast, they are found in sage scrub, but avoid dense, continuous chaparral.

Behavior
Territorial male Rufous-crowned Sparrows often sing from fairly exposed perches in bushes, but they spend most of their time on the ground, often running rather than flying from one patch of cover to another. During the nesting season, territorial individuals chase other Rufous-crowned Sparrows from their territories. Many individuals will respond to 'spishing.'

Voice
The song is variable, but generally a series of 6–9 jumbled bubbling or staccato notes, resembling the song of House Wren, a *tchee-dle tchee-dle tchee-dle tchee-dle tchee-dle tchee-dle*, often slightly ascending then slightly descending; sometimes the song is followed by a series of *chur* notes. The call note is a distinctive, scolding nasal *dear*, nearly always a series of *dear dear* notes; the alarm call is an upward-slurred *tzit*.

Similar species
No other sparrow closely resembles the Rufous-crowned Sparrow. **American Tree Sparrows** are somewhat smaller, with a yellow lower bill and a distinct breast spot,

and lack the brown malar stripe. **Chipping Sparrows** are slimmer, and have a white supercilium and black eyeline stripe. Juveniles resemble juvenile **Botteri's Sparrows**, but are somewhat darker in color. Juvenile Rufous-crowned Sparrows have pale brownish underparts, and a streaked back that distinguish them from juvenile **Rufous-winged Sparrows.**

Geographic variation

Several subspecies have been named. *A. r. ruficeps* is resident on the w slopes of the Sierra Nevada in central California; *A. r. canescens* is resident from Santa Barbara, California, south into Baja California; *A. r. obscura* is resident on Santa Cruz, Anacapa, and formerly Santa Catalina islands, California; *A. r. eremoeca* breeds in the s Great Plains south to ne Mexico and west to sw New Mexico, where it is replaced by *A. r. scottii*, which is found west to e California. *A. r. ruficeps* is similar to *A. r. scottii*, but the back colors and tail are darker and more rufous, ear-coverts, side of neck and underparts are brown rather than gray-brown or gray; *A. r. ruficeps* average smaller than *A. r. scottii*. *A. r. obscura* is larger-billed, and is said to be darker (buffy-gray) and less rufescent than the mainland California forms, *A. r. canescens* and *A. r. ruficeps*, which are similar to each other; *A. r. ruficeps* overall is lighter in color, with back chestnut with dark buff streaking, with less of a grayish wash. *A. r. eremoeca* has a relatively olive or brownish-gray back, with brown rather than rufous centers to mantle and scapular feathers, which are characteristic of *A. r. scottii*, and the crown averages more brightly colored than *A. r. scottii*; there appears to be clinal variation, with birds from central Texas and Tamaulipas being relatively grayer, and those from Arizona and New Mexico being more rufous on their backs, with a rusty crown, often with little trace of gray in the median crown-stripe; coloration may be significantly affected by dust bathing; the backs of *A. r. scottii* and *A. r. eremoeca* are less streaked than those of the California subspecies.

Distribution

Resident from coastal California and Santa Cruz and Anacapa islands, se California (in mountains), s Nevada (in mountains), extreme sw Utah, nw and central Arizona, and central and ne New Mexico, northeast to se Colorado, sw and s-central Kansas (Comanche Co., local), e-central e Oklahoma, central and w Oklahoma Panhandle, and w-central Arkansas (local), south through central Texas to n Baja California, and the Cape Region of Baja California Sur, and south in Mexico on both slopes to Oaxaca and w-central Veracruz. Although northern populations show slight range shifts during winter in response to severe weather, they show no regular migration. Recorded in central Kansas, w Arkansas, and coastal se Texas. They are casual in winter and early summer in ne Kansas.

Conservation status

Although there are few data on changes in the abundance of Rufous-crowned Sparrows, in most parts of their range their preferred habitat has not been greatly affected by human activities. In southern California, urban development and planting of irrigated orchards has destroyed habitat, and fire control has allowed chaparral and coastal sage scrub to grow into dense stands that are unsuitable for the species. In recent years, there has been an increase in the number of records from western Kansas and w-central Arkansas; whether this reflects a true increase in numbers or better coverage of these areas is uncertain.

Molt

The Basic I plumage is acquired by an incomplete Prebasic I molt in June to Nov that involves the body plumage, some of the tertials, usually the median and greater-coverts, sometimes the 5th and 6th secondaries, and none to all of the tail feathers. There is no Prealternate molt. The Definitive Basic molt is acquired by a complete molt that occurs after the breeding season, in Aug to Sept.

Description

Adult—Medium-sized. ***Head:*** crown rusty, thinly outlined with black above the bill, sometimes with an indistinct gray median crown-stripe and with a thin median stripe just above the bill; supercilium gray posteriorly, becoming brighter or white between the eye and bill and narrowly edged with black; eye-stripe gray; eye-ring white; sub-moustachial stripe thin and dark; lores dark gray; ***back:*** grayish-brown, with rusty or brownish centers of mantle and scapular feathers; ***rump:*** and uppertail-coverts brown and more or less unmarked; ***tail:*** brown with faint darker brown barring; ***underparts:*** unmarked gray-brown, paler on belly than on breast and flanks; ***wing:*** brown, with centers of greater-coverts dark brown, and no wing-bars; ***bill:*** upper mandible dusky brown becoming pale yellow on tomium; lower mandible pale yellow; ***legs*** and ***feet:*** pale brownish or dull yellow; ***iris:*** brown or tan.

  First-fall (June–Nov)—Resemble adults, but are more buff-colored.

  Juveniles (May–Oct)—Crown brown with brown streaks; side of face brown without distinctive markings, but distinct dark brown malar stripe; breast and flanks thinly streaked with dark brown; belly perhaps with some streaking.

Hybrids None reported.

References Collins (1999), Hubbard (1975), Oberholser (1974), Pyle (1997), Wolf (1977).

15.1 Rufous-crowned Sparrow, Ventura Co., California, USA, Nov 1994. Typical *Aimophila* shape with short wings and longish, rounded tail. The head pattern is distinctive with rufous crown and post-ocular stripe and bold whitish eye-ring. This individual, probably *A. r. ruficeps*, is rather dull and brownish with bold dusky streaking on the upperparts (Brian E. Small).

15.2 Adult Rufous-crowned Sparrow, Portal, Arizona, USA, Mar 1995. This individual, probably *A. r. scottii*, is noticeably paler and grayer than *A. r. ruficeps*. On the head notice the bold whitish forehead streak, supraloral, eye-ring and throat contrasting with the otherwise gray face and breast (Brian E. Small).

15.3 Adult Rufous-crowned Sparrow, Bitter Springs, Arizona, USA, Jan 1997. Another view of a probable *A. r. scottii* showing the overall grayness of the plumage. Apart from the obviously rufous crown, note the contrasting whitish supraloral and submoustachial stripe and dark gray lores highlighting the whitish eye-ring (Jim Burns/Natural Impacts).

15.4 Adult Rufous-crowned Sparrow, Kickapoo Cavern State Park, Texas, May 1998. This bird is very pale and gray with dull rufous centers to the back feathers and is probably (by range) *A. r. eremoeca*. Again note the contrasting gray and white head pattern with the rufous crown and post-ocular and blackish malar stripe (Dr. George K. Peck).

15.5 Adult Rufous-crowned Sparrow, Davis Mountains, Texas, USA, Aug 1997. In worn plumage many birds, as here, can appear very dull with abraded feather edges and sun-bleached wings and tail. On such individuals the crown and post-ocular stripe should still show some dull rufous and the eye-ring will stand out of the rather plain face (Greg W. Lasley).

16 Five-striped Sparrow

(Aimophila quinquestriata)

Measurements
Length: 13.0–14.5 cm; 5.1–5.7 in.
(males slightly larger).
Wing: 64–74 mm; 2.5–2.9 in.
Mass: Male av. 19.3 g (17.1–21.7 g, n = 23); female av.=18.8 g (17.9–19.5 g; n = 4).

The Five-striped Sparrow is a dark gray sparrow with a dark, **rusty brown back** and **white superciliary and submoustachial stripes**, and **bold black malar stripes**, outlining the throat – the fifth stripe. A black central breast spot is not conspicuous, but the white belly stands out.

Habitat
Five-striped Sparrows are found on steep hillsides, or either side of a wash, with water present year round. The hillsides are covered with fairly dense vegetation, including hackberry, ocotillo, yuccas, acacias, mesquite, and trumpet bush, and at higher elevations, oak and juniper. In Arizona, they are found from 1000–1200 m altitude. They are difficult to find in winter, but some are probably present all year.

Behavior
In the breeding season, males sing persistently from the top of an ocotillo, mesquite, or other plant. They make short flights from plant to plant, and on the ground make short hops. In winter they may form small, loose flocks.

Voice
The song is staccato and brief, lasting just over a second, and is usually composed of an introductory note followed by several note complexes, each usually repeated two or three times, ***tsi-gp tsi-gp twsee tweep***, or ***chip chip chip pt pt pt***, the second series of elements higher or lower in pitch than the first. Calls are described as ***chuck, pip***, and ***seet***.

Similar species See Sage Sparrow.

Geographic variation
Only one subspecies, *A. q. septentrionalis,* is found north of Mexico. It is larger than the nominate subspecies, which is found in Jalisco, Aguascalientes, and Zacatecas.

Distribution
Resident in the Sierra Madre Occidental of n and w Mexico and se Arizona (Pajarito

and Santa Rita mountains; Sonoita Creek) and ne Sonora, south through sw Chihuahua, e Sinaloa, and w Durango. A southern population is found in n Jalisco, s Zacatecas, and w Aguascalientes. Arizona birds may move south in some winters.

Conservation status
Little information. The populations in Arizona are small, but appear to be stable and well established; breeding was first documented there in 1969.

Molt
Not well known. There is a partial Prebasic I molt that takes place mid-Aug–Oct; this involves the entire body plumage, except for the yellowish body feathers, and perhaps some of the remiges and coverts. The Definitive Basic plumage is acquired by a complete Prebasic molt that occurs mid-Aug to early Oct; there appears to be a limited Prealternate molt in some individuals.

Description
Adults—Medium-sized; adults similar. ***Head:*** crown, nape, and side of face brownish-gray; supercilium, submoustachial stripe, eye-ring, and throat white; malar stripe wide and black; ***back:*** dark rusty gray, without conspicuous marking; ***rump:*** brownish; ***tail:*** dark brown, with light edges; ***wing:*** dark brown, with paler edges to coverts and scapulars; ***underparts:*** chin and throat white; breast and flanks dark gray, with a black breast spot; belly white; undertail-coverts gray with pale edges; ***bill:*** blackish, with lower mandible paler bluish-gray; ***legs*** and ***feet:*** dull pinkish-flesh; ***iris:*** dark.

First-winter (Oct–May)—Resemble adults, but retain some juvenal wing and tail feathers and coverts; belly yellowish.

Juveniles (July–Sept)—Crown and back brown, spotted with darker brown, lower back and rump without streaking, tail dark with tips of lateral rectrices white; underparts yellowish and brownish; wings dark, with primaries edged whitish, and secondaries and coverts edged with rust; undertail-coverts brown, tipped yellowish.

Hybrids None reported.

References Groschupf (1992), Wolf (1977).

16.1 Adult Five-striped Sparrow *A. q. septentrionalis*, California Gulch, Arizona, USA, July 1989. This dark and richly colored sparrow should not be confused within its limited US range. Note the coppery-brown upperparts, gray head, breast and flanks and white head stripes, throat streak and belly (Rick and Nora Bowers).

16.2 Adult Five-striped Sparrow *A. q. septentrionalis*, California Gulch, Arizona, USA, July 2000. Concentrating on the striking head pattern, note the narrow white supercilium, lower eye-crescent and submoustachial stripe. The very broad black malar stripe contrasts with the narrow white throat stripe. The underparts are mostly gray with contrasting white belly and black spot on the center of the breast (Larry Sansone).

16.3 Adult Five-striped Sparrow *A. q. septentrionalis*, California Gulch, Arizona, USA, July 2000. Another view showing the black breast spot and the extent of white on the belly. The tail shows white outer webs and tips to the outermost feathers (Larry Sansone).

17 American Tree Sparrow

(Spizella arborea)

Measurements
Length: 13–15 cm; 5–6 in.
   (males slightly larger).
Wing: 60–82 mm; 2.4–3.2 in.
Mass: 12.6–27.7 g (male av. = 18.6 g;
   female av. = 17.1 g).

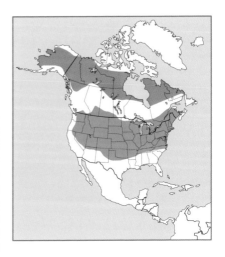

The American Tree Sparrow is a medium-sized sparrow with a **rufous crown**, a **black spot** in the center of its unstreaked grayish breast, a rusty shoulder, a rusty line back from the eye, and a **yellow lower mandible**. Territorial males sing from an exposed perch in a small bush; in winter, they are generally found in loose flocks. When flushed from the ground they usually fly up and perch in a conspicuous place.

Habitat
On the breeding grounds, they are found in open shrubby vegetation, especially deciduous vegetation (birches, willows, sweet gale), but occasionally in dwarf conifers. In winter they are found in weedy fields, hedgerows, low brush, and woodland edge; they readily come to feeders.

Behavior
On the breeding grounds, males sing from an exposed perch in a dwarf birch, willow, or small conifer, usually less than 1 m above the ground. They sing persistently through the day, but night singing is infrequent. In winter they are commonly found in loose flocks, sometimes in mixed species flocks. When flushed from the ground, they fly up into a nearby tree where they can easily be seen. They respond readily to 'spishing.'

Voice
The song is a clear, sweet and musical *tsee tsee-a tsi tsi tsi* or *tsee-a tsee tsi tsi tsi*, with the '*a*' and the final '*tsi*' lower in pitch than the other elements. The American Tree Sparrow rarely sings in mid-winter, but singing increases in frequency by Feb. The call notes, *tseet*, and in feeding flocks a musical *teedle eet*, are distinctive.

Similar species
The **Chipping Sparrow** also has a rusty cap, but is slimmer and smaller, with a black beak, white supercilium, and no breast spot. The **Rufous-crowned Sparrow** is browner, with a black malar stripe. **Field Sparrows** have pink bills and no breast spot. First year **White-crowned Sparrows** superficially resemble Tree Sparrows, but are larger.

Geographic variation

Geographic variation is weak and clinal, with two subspecies generally recognized. The western *S. a. ocracea*, which breeds in Alaska, Yukon, and nw Mackenzie south to nw British Columbia averages slightly, but not significantly larger and paler, especially on the nape, than the eastern *S. a. arborea*.

Distribution

Breeds from the Alaska Peninsula east across Yukon, perhaps on Banks Island, n Mackenzie, central Keewatin, n (and perhaps central) Alberta, n Manitoba and Ontario, n Quebec and Labrador south to s Mackenzie, extreme nw Alberta, n Saskatchewan, n Manitoba, n Ontario, central Quebec, and s Labrador.

Winters from s British Columbia, s Alberta, sw Saskatchewan, s Ontario, sw Quebec, New Brunswick, Prince Edward I., and Nova Scotia south to North Carolina, Tennessee, Arkansas, n Texas, central New Mexico, n Arizona, and (rarely) s California. Especially abundant in winter in central Plains states.

Migrates throughout North America, to the southern edge of its breeding range. Peak of fall migration is mid-Sept (central Ontario) and mid-Oct through early Nov; spring peak is mid-Mar through early Apr.

Conservation status

The breeding habitat of Tree Sparrows has been little affected by human activities, and the destruction of forests in eastern North America has probably increased suitable wintering habitat in that part of the continent, although the increased clearing and cultivation of the prairies may have decreased suitable wintering habitat in the mid-west.

Molt

The Basic I plumage is acquired by a partial Prebasic molt of only contour feathers; this occurs in late Aug–Sept. The Definitive Basic plumage is acquired by a complete Prebasic molt in late mid-July–Sept on the breeding grounds (may be completed on wintering grounds) limited Prealternate molt that occurs late Feb–Apr.

Description

Adults—Medium-sized. *Head:* cap rusty, often with a grayish median crown-stripe; supercilium gray; eyeline rusty; lores gray; malar stripe thin; *back:* rusty brown with dark streaks; *rump:* brown; *wing:* brown with rusty brown coverts and two distinct wing-bars; *underparts:* chin, throat and upper breast gray; breast with a distinct rusty spur that extends down on the breast just anterior to the bend of the wing, with lower flanks and belly fading to a warm rusty beige; upper belly white with a conspicuous black central spot next to the gray chest; *tail:* brown, with outer feathers somewhat paler; *bill:* upper mandible dark; lower mandible yellow with a dusky tip; *legs* and *feet:* brown; *iris:* dark brown.

Young in fall (July–Oct)—Similar to adults, but may have streaks on their crown, nape, and upper breast, traces of which may remain through Oct.

Juveniles (June–Sept)—Resemble adults, but have streaked brown (perhaps tinged with rusty) crown, nape, and side of neck; underparts (except for lower belly) heavily streaked with blackish-brown, often with a distinct breast spot. Most resemble adults by fall migration, although hints of the streaking may remain.

Hybrids None reported.

References Naugler (1993), Pyle (1997), Willoughby (1991).

17.1 American Tree Sparrow *S. a. arborea,* Ontario, Canada, Dec 1995. Larger than other *Spizella* sparrows with distinct rufous crown and bicolored bill. Upperparts buffy with black and chestnut feather centers. Pale gray underparts show buffy-brown flanks and distinct rusty wedge on side of breast (Mike McEvoy).

17.2 American Tree Sparrow *S. a. arborea,* Amherst Island, ON, 26 Feb 2001. The dusky smudge on the center of the breast is a variable feature, but is usually distinct (as here) and is unique amongst *Spizella* (Kevin Karlson).

17.3 American Tree Sparrow *S. a. arborea,* Durham Co., Ontario, Canada, Jan 1995. Concentrating on the head, notice the grayish-buff central crown-stripe which tends to be more prominent on winter birds. The rusty post-ocular stripe flares to form a wedge behind the eye (Sam Barone).

17.4 First-winter American Tree Sparrow *S. a. arborea*, Thunder Cape, Ontario, Canada, Oct 1991. By October first-year birds are virtually identical to winter adults and can be told apart in the hand only by checking skull ossification, as was the case here. Note the contrast between the replaced central tail feathers (fresh and rounded) and the rest (relatively abraded and tapered) (David D. Beadle).

17.5 Adult American Tree Sparrow *S. a. ochracea*, Nome, Alaska, USA, June 1998. This western form is very similar to the *S. a. arborea*, but tends to be somewhat paler overall with broader pale buff edges to mantle feathers and whiter underparts (Brian E. Small).

18 Chipping Sparrow

(Spizella passerina)

Measurements
Length: 12–14 cm; 4.7–5.5 in.
(males slightly larger).
Wing: 62–77 mm; 2.5–3.0 in.
Mass: 10.5–14.6 g; male av.=12.0 g;
female av.=12.2 g (Pennsylvania).

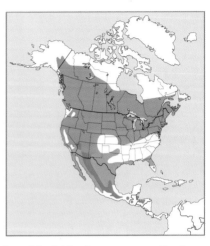

The Chipping Sparrow is a small slim sparrow with a long notched tail; adults have a **rusty cap, white superciliary stripe, black line through the eye,** and a gray rump. In the first fall, the cap may be brown, and the superciliary stripe is less distinct; the grayish rump is a good mark. Juveniles have a streaked breast.

Habitat
Chipping Sparrows are characteristically found in fairly dry, open woodlands or woodland edge with grassy understory, parks and other urban settings, and orchards; they occur in coniferous, mixed, or deciduous woods.

Behavior
In spring and summer, males sing persistently from a tree. They feed both in trees and on the ground; in migration, they are often found in rather large, loose flocks, feeding in mowed grass. Their flight is fairly strong, fast, and direct.

Voice
The song is a dry rattle or trill on one pitch, often much like the songs of the Pine Warbler or Dark-eyed Junco, lasting 2–3 s. Chipping Sparrows have a 'dawn song,' given from the ground, that consists of a series of short trills, lasting less than 1 s each. The note is a thin, clear *tseep* or a dry *chip*.

Similar species
American Tree Sparrows also have a rusty cap, but are noticeably larger, and the head is not so strikingly marked. As well, American Tree Sparrows have a yellow lower mandible, and a central breast spot.

Clay-colored and **Brewer's sparrows** are similar in size and shape, but lack the rusty cap, white superciliary and black eyeline stripes; juveniles and first-year birds are very similar, but Chipping Sparrows have a somewhat more distinct eyeline stripe that goes to the bill, and a grayish-brown rump; all three have striped crowns, but Clay-colored has a more distinct median crown-stripe. See Appendix 1 for more details.

Other sparrows with rusty crowns (**Rufous-crowned** and **Swamp**) are larger and not so slim, and lack the distinct superciliary and eyeline stripes.

Geographic variation

Three subspecies of Chipping Sparrow from north of Mexico are generally recognized, the eastern *S. p. passerina*, western *S. p. arizonae*, and Canadian *S. p. boreophila*. *S. p. boreophila*, which breeds in the north and northwest east to Manitoba and w Ontario, is supposedly larger and more grayish than *S. p. passerina*, but differences, if any, are slight. *S. p. arizonae* is slightly larger and paler than *S. p. passerina*, but the differences cannot be safely determined in the field.

Distribution

Breeds from e-central and se Alaska and central Yukon east to Great Bear Lake and southeast to n Saskatchewan, Manitoba, n Ontario, central Quebec, and sw Newfoundland (rarely north to Goose Bay, Labrador), south to central and sw Georgia, the Panhandle of Florida, Louisiana, ne and central Texas, central Oklahoma, central Kansas, Nebraska, and in the west, south through British Columbia to n Baja California, and in the highlands of central Colorado and central New Mexico south to n-central Nicaragua, e Guatemala, and Belize.

Winters from central California, s Nevada, central Arizona and New Mexico, n Texas, s Oklahoma, Arkansas, Tennessee, Virginia, Maryland, rarely north to southern Canada and south to Cuba.

Migrates throughout North America. Spring migration mostly in late Apr and May; fall migration mostly in Aug through early Oct.

Conservation status

Although still a common species, the Chipping Sparrow apparently is not as common as it was in colonial times. Not a bird of deep woodlands, Chipping Sparrows doubtless benefited from the clearing of the eastern deciduous forests. Today, they are probably declining in places where forest is regenerating.

Molt

The Basic I plumage is acquired by a partial Prebasic molt in July–Nov, that occurs on either the breeding grounds or on the winter grounds, or both. There is a limited Prealternate molt that occurs Mar–Apr, and involves only head feathers. The Definitive Basic plumage is acquired by a complete Prebasic molt that occurs Aug–Oct.

Description

Adults (sexes similar)—Small and slender. *Head:* crown rusty or chestnut, with a small medial pale spot above the bill; forehead black; supercilium and supraloral spot white; eye-stripe and lores black; *back:* brown with dark brown streaking; *rump:* gray; *wing:* greater and middle-coverts rusty, edged with white or beige, forming one or two wing-bars; *tail:* moderately long, notched and brown; *underparts:* gray; breast and flanks gray or grayish-brown and unstreaked; belly dull white; *bill:* conical, small, black in breeding individuals, pale brownish lower mandible in non-breeding individuals; *legs* and *feet:* straw-colored or light brown; *iris:* black. *In fall and winter* (Aug–Mar) adults with duller colors, the chestnut of the cap being partially or wholly obscured by buffy feathers.

First fall and winter (June–Aug in east; Aug–Mar in west)—Resemble non-breeding adults, but cap is dark beige, finely streaked with dark brown or black, especially late in the season, with some rusty in the cap; the thin, dark eyeline goes all the way to the bill; rump is grayish washed with brown and finely streaked at first.

Juveniles (June–Oct)–Have a brown crown, with thin dark streaks; buffy throat and breast with thin, dark brown streaks on the throat and flanks; back brown with dark brown streaks; tertials edged rusty; lower mandible pale yellow. Western birds are paler than eastern ones. The first prebasic molt occurs later in western birds than eastern ones, sometimes following migration.

Hybrids Chipping Sparrows are known to have hybridized once with both Clay-colored and Brewer's sparrows.

References Kaufman (1990), Middleton (1998), Rising (1996), Willoughby (1991).

18.1 Adult Chipping Sparrow *S. p. passerina*, New York City, New York, USA, Apr 1999. The rusty crown, narrow white supercilium and black eye-line are distinctive on this familiar *Spizella*. Note also the sharp black streaking on the buffy back and the pale gray face and whitish underparts. The bill is mostly black with a pale base to the lower mandible (Michael D. Stubblefield).

18.2 Adult Chipping Sparrow *S. p. arizonae*, Mount Pinos, California, USA, June 1996. Concentrating on the head, note the white forehead stripe edged with black. The face is pale gray with whiter lower eye-crescent, submoustachial stripe and throat. This individual is quite worn and has lost much of the edges of the buffy feather on the back and wings (Brian E. Small).

18.3 Adult Chipping Sparrow *S. p. passerina*, Ontario, Canada, Oct 1989. Winter adults are duller than breeding birds and closely resemble first-winter birds. The crown of this bird clearly shows some rusty color and the black eye-line is sharply defined. Note also the very fresh and broadly rounded tail feathers (Dr. George K. Peck).

18.4 Chipping Sparrow *S. p. arizonae*, central Oregon, USA, Sept 1993. This fresh fall individual differs from breeding adult in lacking chestnut on crown which instead is brown streaked with black. The face and breast are suffused with buffy-brown and the dusky malar stripe is quite distinct. The bill is mostly flesh-pink with a darker culmen. Ageing fall individuals in the field is difficult, although the lack of obvious chestnut in the crown suggests a first-winter bird (Brian E. Small).

18.5 Juvenile Chipping Sparrow *S. p. arizonae*, White Mountains, California, USA, Aug 1996. The dusky streaking on head, neck and underparts is generally more extensive than on other *Spizella* sparrows. Note the brownish suffusion on the ear-coverts and sides of breast. The black centers to the median and greater wing-coverts cut though the pale tips forming spotted wing-bars (Brian E. Small).

18.6 Juvenile Chipping Sparrow *S. p. arizonae*, Mount Pinos, Kern County, California, USA, June 1993. Note the fine dusky streaking within the supercilium and on neck sides, breast and flanks. The brown crown is paler on the central forehead and evenly streaked with blackish. Notice the grayer fringes to the uppertail-coverts contrasting with the buffy ground color of the back (Larry Sansone).

19 Clay-colored Sparrow

(Spizella pallida)

Measurements
Length: 12.5–14 cm; 5.0–5.5 in.
  (males slightly larger).
Wing: 56–67 mm; 2.2–2.6 in.
Mass: 9.8–14.5 g.

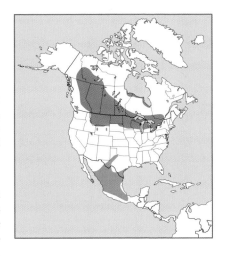

The Clay-colored Sparrow is a small, slim sparrow with a long, notched tail, unstreaked breast, **buffy brown ear-coverts**, **broad white supercilium**, and **whitish median crown-stripe**.

Habitat
Clay-colored Sparrows breed in open uncultivated brushy areas where bushes are interspersed with grassy areas. In the northern prairies, where they breed commonly, they are often found in rose, snowberry, or wolfberry thickets, commonly along a stream or near the edge of a pond. They also occur in alder, willow, birch, or poplar parkland. Where Clay-colored and Brewer's sparrows occur together, Clay-colored Sparrows appear to occupy denser and more diverse vegetation. On migration they occur in mesquite and other desert shrubs, thickets, weed patches, and open woodlands and parks. In the Canadian prairies they have moved into urban parkland habitats.

Behavior
In spring and summer males often sing persistently, and may be easily approached; they generally sing from a perch 0.3–2 m high, but occasionally up to 6 m. They sometimes sing at night. Clay-colored Sparrows forage on the ground; they hop, but do not run.

Voice
The song is a series of 2–8 (usually 2–3) short (about 2 s each), low-pitched, loud insect-like buzzes, *zee-zee-zee* or *buzz-buzz-buzz* or *bzztt-bzztt-bzztt*. The call note is a sharp *seep* or *chip*, or a weak *tsip-tsip*.

Similar species
The light brown ear-coverts, distinctly outlined by a dark brown fringe, relatively bright whitish buff supercilium, and thin pale central crown-stripe usually separate the Clay-colored Sparrow from the similar **Brewer's Sparrow**; overall, Clay-colored Sparrows are more colorful than Brewer's Sparrows, which appear to be plain-faced. Juvenile and first-winter Clay-colored, Brewer's, and Chipping sparrows are similar (see Appendix 1). The facial pattern of the juvenile Clay-colored Sparrow is generally

more distinct than that of Brewer's; the supercilium of Brewer's Sparrow is grayish whereas it is buffy on Clay-colored; the moustachial stripe and outline of the ear-coverts are less distinct on Brewer's than on Clay-colored. Juvenal **Chipping Sparrows** usually lack rufous in the crown, but have a distinct, thin stripe from the eye to the bill; juvenal Clay-colored Sparrows have an indistinct median crown-stripe.

Geographic variation None described.

Distribution

Breeds from w-central and s Mackenzie, e British Columbia, Alberta, nw and central Saskatchewan, across Manitoba and Ontario (irregularly north to James and Hudson bays) and into s Quebec, s New Brunswick, south to New York, w Pennsylvania, Michigan, s Wisconsin, and locally to n Indiana and n Illinois, Minnesota, n Iowa, ne South Dakota, south to Nebraska, and west to Montana and e Washington.

   Winters from s Texas south to Veracruz, Oaxaca, Chiapas, and rarely to Guatemala and to w Mexico and uncommonly to Baja California; very rare in Cuba.

   Migrates primarily through the Great Plains from the Rocky Mountains east to the Mississippi Valley; regular in s California in the fall, and in the east (most records in the fall). Most spring migration takes place in mid- to late May; fall migration peak is in late Sept to mid-Oct.

Conservation status

Clay-colored Sparrows have recently expanded their breeding range east through central Ontario into southern Quebec, western Pennsylvania, and New York and the northeast, where they are often found in abandoned fields with shrubs or small trees, or in young conifer plantations. Intensive fires that burn off shrubs have a negative effect on the species. The species formerly bred in northwestern Iowa, but the conversion of brushy prairie into cropland has destroyed most of the suitable habitat there, and there are few modern breeding records; however, recently they have been found in increasing frequency.

Molts

The Basic I plumage is acquired by an incomplete Prebasic molt that involves all of the body feathers, wing-coverts (except for primary-coverts), some secondaries, and perhaps some rectrices; this takes place July–Sept. The Prealternate I and Definitive Prealternate molts are similar and partial, and involve most of the body feathers and some secondaries and rectrices. The Definitive Basic plumage is acquired by a complete Prebasic molt, usually completed on the breeding grounds, July to as late as mid-Nov.

Description

Adult (sexes similar)—Small and slim. *Head:* streaked, dark brown crown with a distinct pale central stripe, a broad, brownish or grayish-white supercilium, pale lores that contrast little with the supercilium, brown ear-coverts that are distinctly outlined by a thin, dark brown fringe and a dark brown moustachial stripe, thin but distinct moustachial and malar stripes; side of neck gray; *back:* brown with distinct dark brown stripes; *rump:* brown; *wing:* brown with middle and lesser-coverts edged in beige forming two indistinct wing-bars; *tail:* long, thin, notched, unstreaked; *underparts:* chin and throat unstreaked, white; breast and flanks pale, warm beige; belly whitish; *bill:*

upper mandible brownish-black, darker at tip; lower mandible light reddish-brown; *legs* and *feet:* light brown or brownish-flesh; *iris:* dark reddish-brown.

First-winter (Aug–Apr)—Resemble adults, but buffier, brown streaks on crown thinner making the central stripe less distinct; nape gray; some may retain some flank streaking.

Juveniles (July–Sept)—Similar to adults, but crown streaked with blackish and median stripe buffy; nape gray; throat and flanks with distinct brown streaks; supercilium indistinct, but pale dull buff, the dark fringe around the ochre-brown ear-coverts and richer brown color separate it from Brewer's Sparrow; both species molt before they migrate.

Hybrids Hybridization with Brewer's, Chipping, and Field sparrows has been reported. Hybrids with Field Sparrows at least sometimes sing intermediate songs.

References Dechant *et al.* (1998a), Garrido and Kirkconnell (2000), Hoag (1999), Kaufman (1990), Knapton (1994), Rising (1996), Willoughby (1991).

19.1 Adult Clay-colored Sparrow, s Texas, USA, Apr. The striking head pattern, gray neck-sides, pale lores, and buffy body plumage are distinctive. Note the pale central crown-stripe and the mostly pink bill (Steve Bentsen).

19.2 Adult Clay-colored Sparrow, Florida, USA, Apr 1996. Concentrating on the head, note especially the whitish central crown-stripe, supercilium and submoustachial stripe contrasting with the warm brown, dark-framed ear-coverts. The lores are buffy. The lateral crown is streaked with black and there is a thin, but distinct blackish malar stripe (Kevin T. Karlson).

19.3 Adult Clay-colored Sparrow, Florida, USA, May 1992. The underparts are mostly pale gray with whiter throat and a buffy wash on the breast sides and flanks. Note the uniform gray neck contrasting with the striking head pattern and boldly streaked back (Herbert Clarke).

19.4 First-winter Clay-colored Sparrow, Furnace Creek, California, USA, Jan 1969. The strong buffy suffusion on the breast sides and flanks suggest this individual is in its first winter. There is also a hint of some retained juvenile streaking on the breast and some of the inner greater-coverts show the typical juvenile shape to the black centers (Herbert Clarke).

19.5 First-winter Clay-colored Sparrow, Thunder Cape, Ontario, Canada, Oct 1991. As in Fig. 19.4 note the buffy suffusion on the breast with some very faint dusky streaking just visible on the breast sides. This bird was positively aged as a first-winter in the hand by incomplete skull ossification (David D. Beadle).

20 Brewer's Sparrow

(Spizella breweri)

Measurements

Length: 12–13 cm; 4.7–5.1 in.

Wing: males 61.5–66.2 mm, av. = 64.1 mm (2.5 in.); females 60.0–62.0 mm, av. = 60.7 mm (2.4 in.) (nw Canada, *S. b. taverneri*). Males 60.5–64.5 mm, av. = 61.8 mm (2.4 in.); females 57.5–60.0 mm, av. = 59.2 mm (2.3 in.) (Nevada, *S. b. breweri*). Males 60.5–66.0 mm, av. = 61.9 mm (2.4 in.), n = 38; females 58.5–62.0 mm, av. = 60.0 mm (2.4 in.), n = 8 (n-central Washington, *S. b. breweri*).

Mass: 10.9 g (Idaho; sexes combined); 11.1 g (*S. b. breweri*); 11.7 g (*S. b. taverneri*). Males 11.1 g (n = 38); females 10.7 g (n = 8) (n-central Washington, *S. b. breweri*).

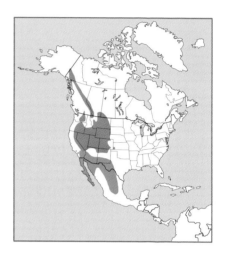

Brewer's Sparrow is a small, slim sparrow with a long, notched tail. The **finely streaked, brown crown, dull gray or beige supercilium, obvious thin white eye-ring**, and generally duller coloration (brown on back), separate Brewer's Sparrow from the similar Clay-colored Sparrow. Brewer's Sparrows are gregarious when not breeding.

Habitat

Brewer's Sparrows breed in a variety of habitats, but in the southern parts of their range they prefer big sagebrush and silverberry in short grass. They are also found in mountain mahogany, rabbitbrush, or piñon-juniper woodlands; the northern population is found in subalpine fir and krummholz, and less commonly in balsam-willow or dwarf birch habitat, at or above timberline. In migration they occur in a variety of habitats, including weeds and brush, agricultural, and urban areas. In winter they can be found in creosote bush deserts, mesquite grassland, and in other low, xeric vegetation.

Behavior

When not breeding, Brewer's Sparrows are usually gregarious and can be found in fairly large and noisy flocks. They forage on or near the ground. On the breeding grounds, they can be inconspicuous, and do not easily flush from the nest. They are perhaps loosely colonial. Males often incubate, which makes them difficult to find. In winter, they may occur in huge flocks.

Voice

There are two distinct categories of songs: the long song is varied and sustained with a variety of buzzing, bubbling, wheezing, and a 'canary-like' trilling on different pitches; the short song varies from single trills to three or four part songs; it is a *bzzzzzzz chip-chip-chip-chip* . . ., the trill on a slightly lower pitch than the buzz. The first part of the song is like that of a Clay-colored Sparrow. Unpaired males sing one or rarely two individually distinctive short songs. In winter and spring, individuals often engage in flock singing, especially on the breeding grounds, but even in migration and in winter. The call note is a weak, high *chip*, a *tsip*, or *seep*. Brewer's Sparrows also have an aerial predator alarm call, and give a single *pit* call when a predator approaches the nest.

Similar species

See **Clay-colored Sparrow**, and Appendix 1. Juveniles less rufous in scapular region than **Chipping Sparrow**.

Geographic variation

Two subspecies are generally recognized: Brewer's Sparrow (*S. b. breweri*) and the 'Timberline' Sparrow (*S. b. taverneri*). The Timberline Sparrow, which breeds in the mountains from se Alaska, Yukon, and nw British Columbia south locally to s Alberta, nw Montana, and e British Columbia, is slightly larger (see measurements above) and darker and grayer than *S. b. breweri*, although the differences are subtle and it is not yet clear whether or not they can be consistently separated in the field; the facial feathers of the former are more distinct than those of the latter, and the eye-ring is more distinctive. Where their ranges overlap in latitude, *S. b. breweri* breeds at lower elevations, in sagebrush. There are winter specimens of Timberline Sparrows from s California, Arizona, New Mexico, and w Texas; they probably principally winter in Mexico.

Distribution

Breeds from extreme e-central Alaska, sw Yukon, the interior of nw British Columbia, and w Alberta, and from central Alberta southeast to sw Saskatchewan and sw North Dakota, and south through se British Columbia, sw Saskatchewan, and nw North Dakota, w South Dakota, w Nebraska, w Kansas, w Oklahoma, Colorado, nw New Mexico, and Utah, to central Arizona, e and s California, and n Baja California.

Winters from central and s interior California, s Nevada, central Arizona, and central and w Texas south to s Texas, and in the highlands to Jalisco and Guanajuato, and in the Pacific lowlands of central and n Mexico and s Baja California.

Migrates throughout the west (rare on the coast north of Mexico). Spring migration is primarily from mid-Apr through May; arrive in Alaska in early June. Fall migration occurs from Aug through late Oct.

Conservation status

Numbers have dropped by about 60% since 1961; the reasons for this are unclear, but reflect habitat destruction, as schrubland is grazed and removed for agriculture, and invaded by exotic plants.

Molt

The Basic I plumage is acquired by a partial Prebasic molt that occurs Sept–Mar; the primary-coverts, inner and middle secondaries, primaries, and rectrices are not molted. The Definitive Basic is acquired by a complete Prebasic molt, July–Oct; there is a partial Prealternate molt Mar–Apr.

Description

Adults—Small and slim; sexes similar. *Head:* the streaked, brown crown lacks a distinct pale central stripe (although some birds appear to have a hint of a stripe); supercilium pale dull gray to dull whitish (usually not as bright as in Clay-colored); lores pale; eye-ring thin and white; ear-coverts brown, not outlined by a dark fringe; moustachial and malar stripes thin and brown; side of neck grayish-brown or brownish and faintly streaked; *rump:* brown with dark brown streaks or rows of spots; *wing:* brown, median and greater-coverts edged with buff forming two poorly defined wingbars; *tail:* long, notched and brown; *underparts:* throat pale and unstreaked; breast and flanks dingy gray, sometimes lightly streaked under the wing; belly dull white; *bill:* conical, small, pale brown with a dusky tip; *legs* and *feet:* pale pinkish or pale horn color; *iris:* dark.

    First-fall (June–Aug)—Similar to adults, but less sharply streaked above, buffier above, and wing-bars buffy and more distinct.

    Juveniles (July–Aug)—Similar to adults, but less streaked above and with breast and flanks narrowly streaked with black triangular marks. Chest, upper belly and flanks of 'Timberline Sparrows' (see below) heavily streaked, making these separable from other juvenile Brewer's Sparrows.

Hybrids Brewer's Sparrows hybridize with both Chipping and Clay-colored sparrows.

References

Doyle (1997), Kingery (1998), Klicka *et al.* (1999), Pinel *et al.* (1993), Pyle (1997), Rising (1996). Rotenberry *et al.* (1999), B. L. Walker (unpub. data), Willoughby (1991).

20.1 Adult Brewer's Sparrow *S. b. breweri*, Riverside Co., California, USA, May 1997. Overall somewhat grayer than other *Spizella* sparrows with evenly streaked gray-brown crown and less distinct head pattern. The whitish eye-ring is quite bold and stands out from the relatively plain face. On this slightly worn individual the warmest brown color is on the lower scapulars and edges to the inner (replaced) tertials and secondaries (Brian E. Small).

20.2 Adult Brewer's Sparrow *S. b. breweri*, near Beatty, Nevada, USA, Apr 1998. Another slightly worn individual showing the grayish tone of the upperparts. The underparts are pale gray with whiter throat and slight buffy wash on the lower flanks. Note how the whitish eye-ring stands out from the grayish face. The abraded and rather pointed central tail-feathers suggest this bird is in its second year (Larry Sansone).

20.3 Adult Brewer's Sparrow *S. b. breweri*, near Beatty, Nevada, USA, Apr 1998. Compared with other *Spizella* the grayish collar on Brewer's shows fine, though distinct, dark streaking and thus contrasts less with the head and back (Larry Sansone).

20.4 First-winter Brewer's Sparrow *S. b. breweri*, central Oregon, USA, Sept 1996. Most first-winter birds are identical to winter adults and could only be told in the hand. This individual shows some retained juvenile streaking on the breast sides and shows contrast on the greater-coverts with the middle feathers older and paler and with the distinctive juvenile black center pattern visible on the upper feathers (Brian E. Small).

20.5 Juvenile Brewer's Sparrow *S. b. breweri*, central Oregon, USA, Aug 1994. Overall buffer than adult with extensive dusky streaking on head and breast. The median and greater-coverts show the typical juvenile shape to the black centers forming spotted wing-bars (Brian E. Small).

20.6 Juvenile Brewer's Sparrow *S. b. breweri*, central Oregon, USA, Sept 1997. A more advanced individual with much of the dusky streaking already molted out from the head and breast. The juvenile wing-coverts are retained (Brian E. Small).

20.7 Adult Brewer's Sparrow *S. b. breweri*, Sulphur Springs, Arizona, USA, Feb 1999. The cold-looking grayish tones of this fresh-plumaged adult are quite distinct from other *Spizella*. The head pattern, though quite distinct, does not look as bold as that of Clay-colored and the bill is marginally smaller and shorter (Jim Burns/Natural Impacts).

20.8 Adult 'Timberline' Sparrow *S. b. taverneri*, Teton Co., Montana, USA, July. This form is very similar to *breweri* and is probably only safely identified within its montane breeding habitat. It tends to be slightly 'colder gray' in tone with broader blackish streaking on the back. The head pattern is slightly better defined and the eye-ring less obvious than *breweri*. However, most of these features are somewhat variable and caution is advised (Milo Burcham).

20.9 Adult 'Timberline' Sparrow *S. b. taverneri*, Teton Co., Montana, USA, July. Another view of a moderately worn adult in the hand. Note particularly the thick blackish streaking on the crown and mantle (Milo Burcham).

21 Field Sparrow

(Spizella pusilla)

Measurements
Length: 12.0–14.0 cm; 4.7–5.5 in.
Wing: 59–70 mm, male av. = 66.1 mm,
   female av. = 62.4 mm; 2.3–2.8 in.
Mass: males 11.5–14.3 g (av. = 13.1 g);
   females 11.4–14.0 g (av. = 13.0 g)
   (breeding birds, Pennsylvania).

The Field Sparrow is a small, slim sparrow with a long, notched (or double rounded) tail. The **dull pinkish-rust markings on the head, pink bill**, and **thin, but distinct, eye-ring** separate it from the other *Spizellas* (except for Worthen's, which see).

Habitat
Field Sparrows breed in old fields with scattered bushes, blackberry tangles, sumac, deciduous thickets, and small trees (commonly hawthorn and pines), and brushy fencerows, with fairly tall grass and dense litter. In the mid-west, Field Sparrows are particularly common in all seasons in broomsedge fields interspersed with small trees.

Behavior
On the breeding grounds males sing persistently, often from an exposed perch in a bush. In winter, they are solitary or occur in small flocks (often of mixed species composition). They generally are not difficult to see, and respond to 'spishing'.

Voice
The song is a series of from 2 to several clear, plaintive, run-on whistles that accelerate and ascend into a trill, and can be written *swee-swee-swee-swee-wee-wee-wee-wee*. The call note is a *tsip*, *zweep*, or a sharp *chip*.

Similar species
Worthen's Sparrow is similar (especially to western Field Sparrows), but lacks the eye-ring and any rust on the upper flank, near the bend of the wing; there is no rust in the post-ocular stripe or ear-coverts of Worthen's, but this can be faint in western Field Sparrows. Worthen's has darker, usually blackish, legs. **American Tree Sparrows** are larger, have a more distinctly patterned face, a dark upper mandible and yellow lower mandible, and a distinct central breast spot. Adult **Chipping Sparrows** have a darker rusty crown, and distinct white supercilium and eyeline stripe. Juveniles can be separated from other *Spizellas* by their pink bills.

Geographic variation

Two subspecies are generally recognized: *S. p. pusilla*, which breeds west to the Great Plains, and *S. p. arenacea*, which breeds east to Minnesota, central Kansas, and Oklahoma. *S. p. arenacea* is similar to *P. p. pusilla*, but the wings and especially the tail are longer, the coloration grayer, the cap usually has a median stripe, the rusty eyeline usually is lacking or less obvious, and the rusty colors are paler. The variation is clinal, and many birds from the Great Plains are intermediate.

Distribution

Breeds: from s Manitoba, e Montana, s Saskatchewan (local), s Alberta (not confirmed) central Minnesota, Michigan, s Ontario, sw Quebec, and s New Brunswick south to Georgia, n Florida, the Florida Panhandle, the Gulf Coast, west to central Texas, Oklahoma, e Colorado and South Dakota.

    Winters from Massachusetts, s Ontario (rare), s Michigan, s Wisconsin, Ohio, Indiana, Illinois, Missouri, and Kansas south through Texas, se New Mexico to Coahuila, Nuevo León, Tamaulipas, the Gulf coast, and central Florida, and rarely to southern Arizona and southern California.

    Migrates east of the Rocky Mountains.

Conservation status

Field Sparrows were probably most abundant in the late 19th Century, following the clearing of the forests for fields. In recent years, their numbers have declined somewhat, probably because many marginal farms have reverted to forest, but they can still be common where there is suitable habitat. They will occupy burned areas so long as there is woody vegetation present.

Molt

There is a partial Presupplemental molt in late June to late Aug that involves the replacement of some of the back plumage. The Basic I plumage is acquired by a Prebasic molt in mid-Aug to late Oct. This involves all body plumage and usually all of the wing feathers. The Basic I plumage is similar to the Definitive Basic plumage except that some slight streaking may persist on the underparts. There is no Prealternate molt in the species.

Description

Adults—Small and slim; sexes similar. *Head:* pinkish-rusty cap, sometimes with a faint, grayish median stripe (more prominent in west); side of head light gray with a white eye-ring and a small rusty eye-stripe (less prominent in west); *back:* pinkish-rusty nape; back rusty brown with darker brown streaking; *rump:* unstreaked or slightly streaked with light-brown; *wing:* brown, rusty coverts and two whitish wing-bars; *tail:* moderately long, dark brown and notched, and edged with light gray; *underparts:* gray, with rufous wash on breast and flanks (rufous less prominent in west); *bill:* pink; *legs* and *feet:* pale brown or pinkish-yellow; *iris:* brown.

    First fall (July–Oct)—Resemble adults, but usually with indistinct streaking on the breast and sides.

    Juveniles (May–Oct)—Similar to adults without rusty colors. Crown dull gray to brown, and breast and flanks with light dusky streaks.

Hybrids

There is a record of a nest attended by two Field Sparrows and a Clay-colored Sparrow, with one of the Field Sparrows and the Clay-colored doing most of the work. In northern Vermont a hybrid Clay-colored X Field Sparrow sang an intermediate song and mated with a field sparrow.

References Dechant *et al.* (1999a), Carey *et al.* (1994), Hoag (1999), Pyle (1997), Rising (1996), Willoughby (1991).

21.1 Field Sparrow, s Texas, USA. A slender *Spizella* with a pink bill and obvious whitish eye-ring. Note the rather plain buffy-gray face with contrasting dull rufous crown and post-ocular stripe (Steve Bentsen).

21.2 Adult Field Sparrow *S. p. pusilla*, New York City, New York, USA, Apr 1998. The face and underparts are mostly pale gray with a slight brownish suffusion on the sides of the breast and flanks. Note the gray neck collar contrasting with rufous lower scapulars (Michael D. Stubblefield).

21.3 Field Sparrow *S. p. pusilla*, New York City, New York, USA, Oct 1998. Fresh fall birds (adults and first-winter birds are virtually identical) tend to be a little buffier overall than spring individuals. Note the two whitish wing-bars (most obvious on the median-coverts). The dull rufous crown has a contrasting grayish central stripe (Michael D. Stubblefield).

21.4 Field Sparrow, Jones Beach, New York, USA, Oct 1991. The mild-mannered look due to the bold whitish eye-ring set in a rather plain face is well shown on this fresh fall bird.
Note the contrast between the streaked buffy back and the plain gray rump. The central tail feathers have been replaced and are thus fresher than the rest (Kevin T. Karlson).

21.5 Field Sparrow, Kickapoo Caverns, Texas, USA, May 1996. This individual is very pale on the head and underparts with dull rufous on the post-ocular reduced to a small wedge and is probably of the western form *S. p. arenacea*. The eye-ring, although whitish, stands out less due to the paler gray face (Rick and Nora Bowers).

22 Worthen's Sparrow

(Spizella wortheni)

Measurements
Length: 13–14 cm; 5.1–5.5 in.
Wing: 65–70 mm; 2.6–2.8 in.
Mass: No information.

Worthen's Sparrow is a small, slim sparrow with a **pink bill**, light **rusty crown**, no wing-bars, and a gray, unpatterned side of face, breast, flanks, belly, and **dark legs**.

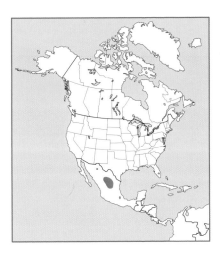

Habitat
This little-known sparrow apparently breeds in weedy, overgrown fields and in open, dry shrubby desert, from 1200 to 2450 m. In Zacatecas it is found in mesquite grassland near the edge of the pine-oak forest, and in Coahuila it is found in fairly tall grassland interspersed with Yucca and small junipers, and in Nuevo León in saltbush.

Behavior
The species is not well studied, but probably is behaviorally like the Field Sparrow.

Voice
The song is a **peee churrrr**, with the initial note slurred and generally, but not always, on a lower pitch; they also give a Chipping Sparrow-like dry rattle.

Similar species
See **Field Sparrow**.

Geographic variation
None described. Worthen's Sparrow is considered to be a subspecies of Field Sparrow by some.

Distribution
Resident in Coahuila, Nuevo León (Las Esperanzes), Chihuahua, sw Tamaulipas, and Zacatecas; also recorded from San Luis Potosí, Puebla, and Veracruz. Although there is some post-breeding wandering, Worthen's Sparrows probably are not migratory but may form small flocks in winter.

Conservation status
No information available for our area. In Mexico, the species seems to be suffering range contraction because of the destruction of its mesquite or yucca-juniper habitat. Recent records are all from se Coahuila and w Nuevo León.

Molt
Not described.

Description
Adults—Small and slim; sexes similar. *Head:* crown rusty; forehead gray or rusty gray; side of face gray, with a thin white eye-ring; *back:* pale brown with dark brown streaking; *rump:* brownish-gray, with centers of some feathers light brown; *wing:* brown, with two indistinct buffy wing-bars; *underparts:* breast light gray with rust anterior to the bend of the wing; throat and belly whitish; *tail:* brown, edged with pale gray; *bill:* pinkish-orange; *legs* and *feet:* black or dark horn-colored (perhaps seasonally variable); *iris:* dark.

First-winter—Probably like adults.

Juveniles—Similar to juvenal Field Sparrows, but have a prominent pale buffy eye-ring; their post-ocular stripe is buffy.

Hybrids None reported.

References Behrstock *et al.* (1998), Rising (1996), Wege *et al.* (1993).

22.1 Adult Worthen's Sparrow *S. w. wortheni*, Las Esperanzes, Nuevo León, Mexico, 18 June 1994. This worn individual is quite similar to a Field Sparrow, but note the gray forehead and lack of any rufous on the post-ocular area. Although heavily abraded, the wing-bars are almost non-existent (Greg W. Lasley).

22.2 Adult Worthen's Sparrow *S. w. wortheni*, Las Esperanzes, Nuevo León, Mexico, 18 June 1994. The head is mostly pale gray with an obvious white eye-ring and contrasting dull rufous cap. Note the gray forehead above the pinkish bill. The underparts are uniform pale gray, whiter on the throat and with a slight brownish wash on the flanks. The legs and feet are dark (pinkish on Field Sparrow) (Greg W. Lasley).

22.3 Worthen's Sparrow *S. w. wortheni*, Tanaye de Emergencia, Coahuila, Mexico, 5 Oct 1990. This fresh fall bird is much buffier overall than mid-summer birds and would probably cause more of an identification challenge. However, note the grayish forehead, lack of brownish post-ocular stripe (although the ear-coverts are washed with buffy-brown) and the rather uniform pale underparts. The wing-bars are more obvious in fresh plumage especially the median one (Greg W. Lasley).

23 Black-chinned Sparrow

(Spizella atrogularis)

Measurements
Length: 12.5–15.0 cm; 4.9–5.9 in.
Wing: 58–68 mm; 2.2–2.7 in.
   (males slightly larger).
Mass: 9.0–14.8 g.

The Black-chinned Sparrow is a small, slim, **dark gray** sparrow with a long tail, **striped brown back**, and (in breeding males) **pinkish bill**.

Habitat
Arid brushland, commonly in tall (1–2 m high) and fairly dense sagebrush, and dry chaparral, often in rocky areas, from sea level to 2700 m.

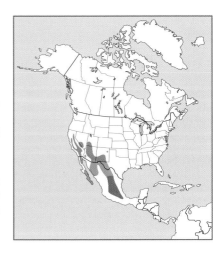

Behavior
The Black-chinned Sparrow is usually not a conspicuous bird, although territorial males sing persistently from an exposed perch. They feed both on the ground and in bushes, and their flight is generally near the ground.

Voice
The song consists of 1–5 introductory notes followed by 3–5 slurred notes and sometimes 1–2 terminal notes, an upslurred trill, *sweet-sweet-te-te-te-tt-tt-t-t-t*, or a downslurred *dear-dear-dew-dew-dew-de-de-d-d-d*. The call is a *seep* or *chip*.

Similar species
Black-chinned Sparrows do not closely resemble any other sparrows; they look like slim '**Gray-headed Juncos**,' without white in the tail.

Geographic variation
North of Mexico, three subspecies are generally recognized. *S. a. caurina* breeds in the coastal ranges of central western California; *S. a. cana* breeds in the mountains of s-central and sw California, south to northern Baja California; *S. a. evura* breeds east of the Sierra Nevada south and east to southern Arizona and New Mexico and w Texas. *S. a. evura* averages larger than the Pacific coastal forms, which are little different from each other. None of these subspecies can be reliably differentiated in the field.

Distribution
Breeds from central California (rarely north to n Oregon), the s Sierra Nevada south to n Baja California, and east across s Nevada and Utah, central and se Arizona, central New Mexico, and w Texas, south in the Mexican highlands to Guerrero, Oaxaca, and Puebla.

Winters from extreme se California, s Arizona and New Mexico, w Texas, and Nuevo León south to the highlands of Mexico.

Migrates through southwest. In spring migrates late Mar through early Apr (peak mid-May); in fall migrates from late Aug through early Nov.

Conservation status

Black-chinned Sparrows are declining in southern California and because of degradation of habitat by mining, overgrazing, trail bikes and other off-road vehicles.

Molt

The Prebasic I molt is partial, involving body plumage, primary and secondary-coverts, and rarely some wing and tail feathers, and takes place primarily on the breeding grounds, July to Aug. The Alternate I plumage is acquired by a partial Alternate I molt, primarily in Mar, that involves mostly face, chin, throat, crown and upper breast feathers. The Definitive Basic plumage is acquired by a complete Definitive Basic molt in July to Sept, and there is a limited Definitive Alternate molt that is like the Alternate I molt.

Description

Small and slim; sexually dimorphic in color. **Adult males—*Head:*** gray, with black around the base of the bill; ***back:*** rusty or cinnamon-rufous brown, streaked with black; ***rump:*** gray or olive-gray; ***tail:*** long, dark grayish-brown and unpatterned; ***wing:*** brown or rusty brown with indistinct wing-bars; ***underparts:*** gray, with dull white belly; ***bill:*** cinnamon, with the tip darker; ***legs*** and ***feet:*** brown; ***iris:*** auburn.

Adult females—Like adult males, but usually with the black of the chin less extensive, duller, or missing.

First fall and winter (Aug–Mar)—Like adult females, but the chin and throat without black, not contrasting with the breast and often brownish-gray instead of gray, and with streaks on the back narrower and less sharply defined; edges of wing-coverts more rusty, and underparts paler, indistinctly streaked with light gray.

Hybrids None reported.

References Rising (1996), Tenney (1997).

23.1 Adult male Black-chinned Sparrow *S. a. cana*, Baldwin Lake, California, USA, June 1995. Typical *Spizella* shape, but mostly mid-gray head and underparts unique. This male shows distinct sooty-black lores and throat highlighting the bright pink bill. The lower belly and undertail-coverts are whiter (Brian E. Small).

23.2 Adult male Black-chinned Sparrow *S. a. evura*, Portal, Arizona, USA, July 1995. The gray head and neck contrasts with the bright pale rusty back. The wings are rather dark with narrow pale fringes to the coverts though not forming obvious wing-bars (Brian E. Small).

23.3 Adult Female Black-chinned Sparrow *S. a. evura*, Panamint Mountains, California, USA, Aug 1996. Similar to male, but with slightly darker gray shading on the face where male shows black. Note the contrasting bright pale rusty back which is narrowly streaked black. Legs are dark. Note that this bird is in active tail molt (Herbert Clarke).

23.4 Juvenile/First-winter Black-chinned Sparrow, s California, USA, Sept 1994. Similar to female but with some brown suffusion on ear-coverts, breast and flanks. The throat and malar area are whitish and the lores show no darker gray or blackish shading. The buffy edging to the wing-coverts is a little broader, forming more obvious wing-bars (Herbert Clarke).

24 **Vesper Sparrow**

(Pooecetes gramineus)

Measurements:
Length: 13.5–15.0 cm; 5.3–5.9 in.
Wing: 74–87 mm; 2.9–3.4 in.
 (males somewhat larger than females).
Mass: 21.3–28.9 g (Saskatchewan and
 North Dakota).

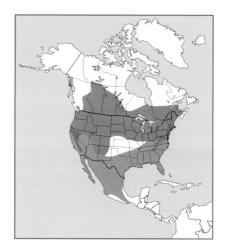

Vesper Sparrows are fairly large, have a **streaked breast**, notched tail with **distinct white edges to the outer tail feathers**, a rusty shoulder, conspicuously streaked back, and a thin, but distinct eye-ring.

Habitat

In the east, Vesper Sparrows are found in sparse pastures and cultivated land, well drained areas, and fairly dry pastures. Suitable singing perches appear to be an important part of a territory. In the west, they are characteristic of dry sagebrush-grass associations, dry, open ponderosa pine parkland, and sometimes in sagebrush in piñon-juniper, and alpine and sub-alpine shortgrass meadows. In winter, they are found in weedy or grassy pastures, prairies, old burned areas, or woodland clearings.

Behavior

Although territorial males sometimes sing from the ground, they usually seem to prefer a high perch, often in a tree near the edge of a field, or at the top of a shrub. Vesper Sparrows run or hop on the ground, and sometimes use a towhee-like double scratch when feeding. Females incubate closely and often perform a broken-wing distraction display when flushed from the nest. Vesper Sparrows are usually found in small, loose flocks of up to 10 individuals. When flushed, they typically fly to a nearby tree or bush and perch in the open. They commonly take dust baths.

Voice

The song of the Vesper Sparrow is sweet and musical, generally starting with two long clear notes, often downward slurs, followed by shorter flutelike trills, often rising then falling in pitch; sometimes the long notes at the beginning are the highest, with the remainder of the song declining in pitch. The song reminds one of Song Sparrow, but is sweeter and more plaintive. Rarely a flight song is given. The call note is a sharp *chirp*.

Similar species

Savannah Sparrows are smaller, shorter-tailed, and have a distinct median crown-stripe, a yellow supercilium, and lack the eye-ring, rusty shoulder (not always visible on Vesper Sparrows), and distinct white in the tail. **Baird's Sparrows** have conspicuous yellow-ochre head markings, and appear to be flat-headed. Juvenile **Grasshopper** and **Le Conte's sparrows** are streaked below, but much smaller, and have short tails that lack the white. Wintering **Lapland** and **Smith's longspurs** have white edges to the lateral tail feathers. Longspurs are chunkier, shorter-tailed than Vesper Sparrows, and unlike Vesper Sparrows are often found in flocks (often with Horned Larks and Snow Buntings). **Song Sparrows** are usually much more heavily streaked, have a central breast spot, and a long, rounded tail that lacks white.

Geographic variation

Three subspecies are often recognized. *P. g. gramineus* occurs in the east. *P. g. confinis* and *P. g. affinis* occur in the west, the latter in the Pacific northwest. *P. g. confinis* is slightly larger than *P. g. gramineus*, with a narrower bill, paler and grayer back, and reduced and thinner ventral streaking. *P. g. affinis* is like *P. g. confinis*, but smaller, with ground coloration tending to be buffy brown rather than grayish-brown. These subspecies cannot be identified in the field, and probably not reliably in the hand.

Distribution

Breeds from central and s British Columbia, s Mackenzie, Alberta, Saskatchewan, central Manitoba, central and s Ontario, s Quebec, New Brunswick, Prince Edward Island, central and s Nova Scotia south to s California, central Nevada, Utah, central and ne Arizona, central New Mexico, w and central Colorado, w and ne Kansas, Nebraska, n Missouri, Illinois, Indiana, Ohio, n-central Kentucky, West Virginia, w Virginia, e Tennessee, w North Carolina, Maryland, and Delaware.

Winters se Oregon, sw Utah, central and s Arizona, s New Mexico, Texas, s Oklahoma, s Missouri, Arkansas, Kentucky, and Maryland south to Florida, Guerrero, Oaxaca, n Veracruz, and s Baja California.

Migrates throughout the United States. Spring migration begins in late Feb, with a peak of activity mid- to late Apr; fall migration occurs in Aug through Oct, with a few remaining in the north through Nov.

Conservation status

Vesper Sparrows have declined in numbers in the east because of changes in farming practices: during the 19th and early 20th centuries the practice of leaving one-quarter of the fields fallow each year would have created good habitat for Vesper Sparrows as they readily nest in short fields. As well, the abandonment of marginal, sandy farmlands has resulted in the loss of shortgrass suitable for them. In Saskatchewan, they are commonest one to two years after a burn. Today, the species is endangered in Rhode I. and New Jersey.

Molt

The Prebasic I molt is partial, takes place on the breeding grounds, July to Oct, and includes the body-feathers, coverts, but not the tertials or rectrices. There is no Prealternate molt, and the Definitive Basic molt is complete, and takes place on the breeding grounds.

Description

Adults—Fairly large; sexes similar in color. *Head:* crown and nape grayish-brown, conspicuously streaked with dark brown; supercilium and submoustachial stripes grayish or buffy, paler than other facial markings, but not distinct; thin white eye-ring; ear-coverts pale in center, but dark toward the back; moustachial and malar stripes brown; throat pale, with indistinct spotting; ***back:*** nape and mantle grayish-brown, with dark centers to feathers, making the back conspicuously streaked; ***rump:*** less conspicuously streaked than back; ***tail:*** brown, with outer web and tip of outer-most (6th) rectrix white, 5th variable, but usually with some white in the outer web; ***wing:*** brown, with tips of the median and greater-coverts, and tertials edged buffy or buffy white, forming one or two indistinct wing-bars; lesser-coverts rusty; ***under-parts:*** throat buffy or buffy white and indistinctly spotted; breast and flanks narrowly streaked with brown; belly white; undertail-coverts whitish; ***bill:*** upper mandible dusky brown; lower pinkish or flesh-colored; ***legs*** and ***feet:*** pinkish or flesh-colored; ***iris:*** light brown or brown.

Hybrids A hybrid reported with Field Sparrow is based on a sight record, and is almost certainly not valid.

References Dechant *et al.* (2000), Rising (1996).

24.1 Adult Vesper Sparrow, s Texas, USA, Feb. This chunky, streaky-looking sparrow is relatively featureless. The characteristic white outer tail feathers and rufous lesser-coverts, obvious in flight, are rarely visible on a perched bird. However, note the bold white eye-ring and the whitish submoustachial stripe and ear-covert spot (Steve Bentsen).

24.2 Adult Vesper Sparrow *P. g. gramineus*, Algonquin Prov. Park, Ontario, Canada, June 1968. During the breeding season worn adults (as here) can appear very drab. Pale wing-bars and edges to mantle feathers are lost due to abrasion. The best features to concentrate on are the whitish eye-ring and surroundings to the ear-coverts. Note the very short primary projection (compare with female longspurs) (Dr. George K. Peck).

24.3 Adult Vesper Sparrow *P. g. affinis*, central Oregon, USA, Aug 1994. This late summer adult (still in active wing molt) shows a hint of the rufous lesser-coverts which are usually hidden by overlapping scapulars and breast feathers. Note also the fairly obvious buffy wing-bars formed by the broad tips to the median and greater-coverts. The stout bill is mostly pinkish with dusky culmen. As with many perched birds, the white outer rectrices are barely visible (Brian E. Small).

24.4 Adult Vesper Sparrow *P. g. confinis*, Lake Co., Montana, USA. A fine study of a breeding adult. The rufous lesser-coverts (usually hidden by the overlapping scapulars) are just visible here (Milo Burcham).

24.5 Juvenile Vesper Sparrow *P. g. affinis*, central Oregon, USA, Aug 1994. Differs from adult in appearing decidedly more buffy overall with pale fringes to back feathers creating a slightly scalloped effect. Note the typical juvenile shape to the black centers to the median and greater-coverts with the broad shaft streak invading the buff tip (Brian E. Small).

25 Lark Sparrow

(Chondestes grammacus)

Measurements
Length: 14–18 cm; 5.5–7.0 in.
   (males slightly larger).
Wing: 73–97 mm; 2.9–3.8 in.
Mass: 24.7–33.3 g, av. 29.0 g.

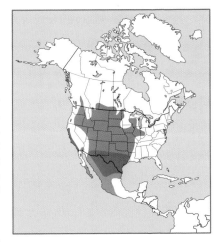

The Lark Sparrow is a fairly large sparrow with a **brightly colored chestnut, black, and white face**, conspicuous **white in the tail**, and an unstreaked breast with a **prominent breast spot**, and a long rounded tail. They are often found in flocks when not breeding. Hops and runs on the ground.

Habitat
Lark Sparrows breed in open, dry woodlands, often open cottonwood woodlands, especially along rivers, scrubland, mesquite or oak savannah, and piñon-juniper woodlands, and ponderosa pines interspersed with bunch grass. In winter they may be found in agricultural areas or large suburban gardens, oak woodlands, chaparral, mesquite and acacia mixed with grassland, or grassy desert scrub.

Behavior
Lark Sparrows are easily flushed and often will fly to a fence or to a low branch; they may fly high and for long distances. Territorial males sing persistently from an exposed branch, often from a cottonwood tree in a field or at the edge of woods. During courtship, males strut with their tail upright, showing the white tail spots. Lark Sparrows walk or hop. In winter they occur in loose flocks, often comprised of only Lark Sparrows.

Voice
The song is musical and variable, a broken series of clear notes, *twee twee trerere trerere twee twee twee*, introduced with 1 or 2 clear *twee* notes, followed by some gurgly and rough buzzy notes, and 1 to 3 more clear notes. An individual singing bird may vary his song in a singing bout. There is soft singing in spring migratory flocks. The call note is a sharp, distinctive, warbler-like *tsip*, or a metallic *cheep*, often given in flight.

Similar species
This is a distinctive sparrow. The head patterning somewhat resembles **Sage Sparrow**, which also has some white in the tail, and a central breast spot, but lacks the rusty or chestnut facial markings and the obvious white in the tail. Young Lark Sparrows have a slightly streaked breast and flanks, but have a white throat and conspicuous white in the corners of the tail.

Geographic variation

Two subspecies are generally recognized, the eastern *C. g. grammacus* and the western *C. g. strigatus*. The eastern birds are slightly darker in coloration, with darker chestnut markings on the head, and wider streaks on the back. The two subspecies are very similar, and cannot be separated in the field, and probably not in the hand.

Distribution

Breeds from w Oregon, e Washington, s interior of British Columbia, se Alberta, Saskatchewan, s Manitoba, w Minnesota, e-central and se Minnesota, w and central Wisconsin, s Michigan, sw Ontario, and formerly east to Pennsylvania, Maryland, w Virginia, and probably North Carolina, south to West Virginia, nw and w-central Alabama, nw and n-central Louisiana, Texas, n Tamaulipas, Nuevo León, Zacatecas, Durango, s Chihuahua, ne Sonora, and s California. Breeding east of the Mississippi Valley, where the species is declining, is local and irregular.

Winters from sw Oregon, California, s Nevada, central and s Arizona, s Utah, s New Mexico, Oklahoma, central and e Texas, south through Mexico to s Baja California and Chiapas, and along the Gulf Coast south to Veracruz, and rarely along the Atlantic Coast from Virginia southward.

Migrates regularly, but uncommonly along the Atlantic Coast, especially in the fall; it is very rare along the coast of British Columbia, north to Alaska, the Maritime Provinces, and south to Yucatán, Guatemala, El Salvador, Honduras, Cuba, and the Bahamas. Recorded twice in England (May, June). Fall migration Sept through Oct (mostly in Sept).

Conservation status

In pre-colonial times, the Lark Sparrow was strictly a western bird. However, with the clearing of forests, they extended their range eastward, and became common in many places east of the Allegheny Mountains by the 20th Century. Recently, as marginal forests in the east have reverted to second-growth woodlands, Lark Sparrows have declined in number, and today they are rare and local in the east, and their numbers are declining there. However, they are still common in the west, especially in the Great Plains and central Texas, where their numbers are stable. Burning is usually beneficial, and in Arizona their numbers increase two years after a burn. They are common in southern Baja California in winter.

Molt

There are partial Prebasic I and Presupplemental molts from June to Nov; these are variable and involve the body feathers, coverts, and usually some of the wing feathers. The Prealternate molt is absent or limited, and takes place in Feb to Apr. The Definitive Basic molt is complete and takes place on the breeding grounds, from June to Oct.

Description

Adults—Fairly large; sexes similar. *Head:* white or light beige median crown-stripe, rusty or chestnut lateral crown-stripes, becoming blackish near bill; white supercilium; thin black eyeline stripe; wide white crescent under eye; chestnut ear-coverts with a white spot at the posterior; white submoustachial stripe; prominent black malar stripe that becomes broader toward the neck, and a white throat; *back:* nape warm brown, slightly streaked with darker brown; mantle brown with conspicuous brown stripes; *rump:* brown and unstreaked; *tail:* brown with outer 3–5 rectrices boldly tipped with white and outer two edged laterally with white; *wing:* brown, with bases of primaries conspicuously whitish (producing a rather distinct band); primary-coverts dark; median coverts dark brown, boldly tipped in white, forming a wing-bar; *underparts:* throat white; breast pale beige with a bold, brown breast spot; flanks pale beige; belly dull white; undertail-coverts dull white, slightly spotted with light brown; *bill:* brownish to blackish as the tip, yellowish, or pinkish gray, paler below; *legs* and *feet:* dull flesh color; *iris:* sepia or brown.

First-fall (July–Nov)—Resemble adults but head marking duller, and brown streaking on the breast and flanks.

Juveniles (May–July)—Underparts heavily streaked; head has brown, not rusty, lateral crown-stripes and ear-coverts, and whitish submoustachial stripes.

Hybrids None described.

References
Dechant *et al.* (1999b), Garrido and Kirkconnell (2000), Martin and Parrish (2000), Pyle (1997), Rising (1996).

25.1 Adult Lark Sparrow, Concan, Texas, USA, May 1995. The striking chestnut, black and white head pattern and the white-tipped tail are distinctive. Note also the stout horn-colored bill and the contrast between the streaked back and the uniform brown rump and uppertail-coverts. The tail feathers have broad rounded tips typical of adult birds (Brian E. Small).

25.2 First-winter Lark Sparrow *C. g. strigatus*, White Mountains, California, USA, Aug 1994. This very fresh fall individual has quite a dull head pattern compared with an adult with brownish rather than chestnut lateral crown-stripes and ear-coverts. The creamy supercilium and crown-stripe show some retained juvenile streaking and the inner greater-coverts show the typical juvenile shape to the black centers. The tail feathers are relatively pointed compared with the adult in Fig. 25.1 (Brian E. Small).

25.3 Juvenile Lark Sparrow *C. g. strigatus*, White Mountains, California, USA, Aug 1994. The dull head pattern with obvious streaking within the supercilium and malar area easily identify this individual as a juvenile. Note also the bold blackish streaking across the breast and the shape of the centers to the median and greater-coverts creating spotted buff wing-bars (Brian E. Small).

25.4 Juvenile Lark Sparrow *C. g. grammacus*, Cape May, New Jersey, USA, Sept 1988. This bird has molted out most of the blackish streaking on the breast, but still shows some speckling within the pale supercilium. The head pattern is dull, lacking the chestnut tones on the ear-coverts typical of adults. On the visible greater-coverts notice the thick black central streak which cuts through the buff tip, typical of many juvenile sparrows (Kevin T. Karlson).

(Amphispiza bilineata)

Measurements
Length: 12–14 cm; 4.7–5.5 in.
　(males slightly larger).
Wing: 60–66 mm; 2.4–3.0 in.
Mass: 10.2–16.4 g, av.=13.5 g.

Black-throated Sparrows are smallish to medium-sized sparrows with a prominent **white supercilium, white malar stripe,** and a **black throat and breast.** Their back and wings are sandy brownish, tail brownish-black with white tips to the outermost feathers (in unworn individuals), and belly grayish to pale grayish-brown.

Habitat
The Black-throated Sparrow is a bird of sparse xeric shrubs, commonly found on hillsides where ocotillo, cactus, mesquite, cat-claw and other thorny plants predominate, or in saltbush, greasewood, canotia, and creosote, interspersed with taller plants. In some areas they are found in sagebrush, antelope brush, and rabbit brush, perhaps interspersed with piñon-juniper. They occur from below sea level to over 2200 m, but below 1500 m in the northern parts of their range. In winter, can be found in riparian areas.

Behavior
Males sing from an exposed perch in a low shrub, and chases are common when territories are being established. On the ground, Black-throated Sparrows move with short hops, and occasionally run. They are not difficult to see. In winter, they gather in small flocks, commonly with other sparrows.

Voice
The song is a short, pleasant, tinkling, rapidly repeated *tchi-tchi-twirr* or *tsp tsp tsp tsp churrrrrr*, with the initial notes quick and distinct and the last a prolonged trill, often on a different pitch. There is a great deal of variability in the song, both within populations and in the repertoire of a single individual. The call note is a low *chip* or tinkling notes.

Similar species
The bold, black throat and breast separate the Black-throated Sparrow from others; the white markings on the face are more extensive than those of **Sage Sparrows**, and the supercilium on the Black-throated Sparrow is longer, extending well behind the eye. The crown is not spotted or streaked, and the crown and back are somewhat darker than in Sage Sparrows.

Geographic variation

North of Mexico, three subspecies are generally recognized. *A. b. bilineata* is found from central Texas south into Mexico, *A. b. deserticola* is found from Oregon and w Colorado south into Mexico, and *A. b. opuntia* is found from w Oklahoma, s Colorado, south through w Texas and New Mexico into Mexico. *A. b. bilineata* may have a white tip to the outer 2 rectrices, whereas others have a white tip only on the outermost rectrix. These subspecies are not well marked, and need more study.

Distribution

Breeds from central Washington (local), s-central and se Oregon, Idaho, sw Wyoming south to nw and s Colorado, w Oklahoma, Texas, and through e California to s Baja California, central Sinaloa, Hidalgo, Querétaro, Guanajuato, and n Jalisco.

Winters from s California, sw Utah, central Arizona, s New Mexico, Oklahoma (very rare), and central and s Texas south through the breeding range, and rarely to coastal s California. Most common in winter from s Texas, s New Mexico, central and s Arizona, and se California, southward.

Conservation status

The clearing of brush on rangeland has decreased the abundance of this species, and numbers declined both in Texas and the southwest during the 1970s. Nonetheless, it is widespread, and one of the commonest of desert birds.

Molt

The Basic I plumage is acquired by an incomplete Prebasic I molt in June to Nov that involves body feathers, coverts, rectrices and some of the wing feathers; this molt is probably completed on the wintering grounds. There is no Prealternate molt. The Definitive Basic molt is complete, and takes place on the breeding grounds.

Description

Adults—Fairly small in size; sexes similar in coloration. *Head:* crown and ear-coverts brown or grayish-brown; supercilium long, extending to nape, and white, sometimes partially thinly bordered with black above; lores and throat black; malar stripe white, with a thin white crescent under the eye; *back:* sandy brownish, becoming grayish-brown toward the nape; *rump:* brownish; *tail* blackish, with the tips of the outermost rectrix white (often inconspicuous in worn individuals), and outer webs of lateral feathers whitish; *underparts:* chin, throat, and breast black, with the black terminated in a black 'v' on the breast, the black bordered by grayish-white, becoming darker and browner on the flanks and belly; undertail-coverts light beige and unpatterned; *wing:* brown, with feathers edged with pale brown, coverts, scapulars, and tertials edged with buff; *bill:* dark gray, with lower mandible a paler bluish-gray; *legs* and *feet* dark gray; *iris:* dark brown.

First-fall (Apr–Nov)—Similar to adults, but without any distinct black markings on the head, the supercilium, chin, and throat white, the throat sometimes flaked with grayish, the breast more or less distinctly streaked, the coverts and tertials edged with buffy brownish, and the back with obscure dusky streaks. First-year birds apparently migrate before completing their prebasic molt.

Juveniles (Mar–July)—Crown dark gray-brown, lores and ear-coverts gray, partial white eye-ring, supercilium white, not extending to nape, nape and upper back tinged with brown-gray, rump grayish or brownish-gray; uppertail-coverts brown, darker than back; rectrices black, outer ones tipped with white and white on outer webs; throat mottled with gray; breast, upper belly, and flanks finely streaked with gray; lower belly and undertail-coverts light buffy; wings blackish (not as dark as tail), with coverts and tertials edged with light rusty brown.

Hybrids None reported.

Reference Rising (1996), Smith *et al.* (1997).

26.1 Adult Black-throated Sparrow *A. b. deserticola*, Portal, Arizona, USA, May 1997. The bold gray, black and white head pattern and the subtle, airbrushed quality of the body plumage render this adult bird unmistakable (Brian E. Small).

26.2 Adult Black-throated Sparrow *A. b. deserticola*, Portal, Arizona, USA, May 1997. The white supercilium and submoustachial stripe contrast with the gray crown and ear-coverts and the striking black throat. The black extends onto the upper breast as a point. The undertail is black with white outer webs and tips to the outer feathers (Brian E. Small).

26.3 Adult Black-throated Sparrow, Falcon Dam, Texas, USA, March 1995. Geographical variation within the species is subtle and it is generally not possible to subspecifically identify most birds except by range. The shade of the grayish-brown mantle and size of the white tail spots (not visible here) are difficult to assess in the field. This bird is probably, by range, *A. b. bilineata* (Kevin T. Karlson).

26.4 Juvenile Black-throated Sparrow *A. b. deserticola*, se Arizona, USA, Aug 1993. Differs primarily from adult in having a whitish throat and a band of dusky streaks across the breast. Overall plumage generally paler and buffier than adult. The wing-coverts show blackish shaft streaks and broken buff tips forming spotted wing-bars (Brian E. Small).

26.5 Juvenile Black-throated Sparrow *A. b. deserticola*, Ventura County, California, USA, Oct 1999. Upperparts are paler and browner than adult with fine dusky streaking on mantle. The wing-coverts and tertials show quite pronounced buffy-brown tips and edges. Best told from juvenile Sage Sparrow by rather plain crown and sharply defined whitish supercilium (Don Des Jardin).

Bell's Sparrow

(Amphispiza belli)

Measurements
Length: 12.5–14.5 cm; 4.9–5.7 in.
(males slightly larger).
Wing: 65–68 mm (avs. for 7 populations
from California 2.6 in.) (males).
Mass: 14.4–15.6 g (males; avs. for 7
populations from California).

Bell's Sparrow is a medium-sized sparrow
with a conspicuous **white supraloral
spot and submoustachial stripe**, a
broad black malar stripe, and a conspicuous **black breast spot**.

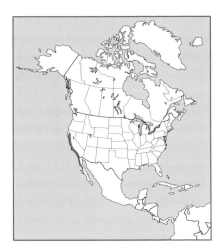

Habitat
Bell's Sparrows are generally found in
chaparral dominated by dense chamise
(greasewood), but may be found in bac-
charis and coastal sagebrush, and in brush in arid washes.

Behavior
Hops or walks on the ground, running through open areas with its tail cocked.

Voice
The vocalizations of Bell's Sparrows are similar to those of Sage Sparrows, but persons
familiar with them can detect differences. The song is a thin, tinkling, but musical
tweesitity-slip, twesitity-slip, swer or a sing-song *chappa-chee, chip-chippa-chee*,
with the song lasting 2–3 s. The call note is a high, thin *tik* or *tik-tik*.

Similar species
The **Sage Sparrow** is like Bell's Sparrow in general pattern and coloration, but paler.
The back of Bell's Sparrow is deep gray-brown, contrasting little with the tail, whereas
the tail of Sage Sparrow is noticeably darker than the back. The dorsal striping of Bell's
Sparrow is indistinct; it is more conspicuous on Sage Sparrow. The facial markings are
blackish and more striking, and the flank and breast streaking generally somewhat
less extensive on Bell's Sparrow. Bell's Sparrow is also smaller than Sage Sparrow, and
this can sometimes be detected in the field.

Geographic variation
Three subspecies, two found north of Mexico, are recognized. The San Clemente Sage
Sparrow *A. b. clementeae*, found only on San Clemente I., is poorly differentiated, but
has a longer bill and lighter juvenal plumage than *A. b. belli*, which is found in
California. In Baja California, it is replaced by *A. b. cinerea*, which is similar in size,
but paler in color.

Distribution
Resident in California and Baja California from the inner Northern Coast Range south to coast in Marin Co., and along coast and in foothills south to Bahia Ballenas, Baja California; also in western Sierra Nevada from El Dorado Co. south to Mariposa Co. An isolated population on San Clemente I., California. Some wander in winter, rarely to se California.

Conservation status
The population on San Clemente I. was threatened because of habitat destruction by goats, but the goats have been removed, and the habitat suitable for Bell's Sparrows is recovering.

Molt
Probably like that of Sage Sparrow.

Description
Adults—Sexes similar. *Head* and *nape:* gray-brown; crown faintly streaked; supraloral spot and eye-ring white; lores dark; ear-coverts gray; moustachial stripe dark brown; submoustachial stripe pale buff to whitish; malar stripe dark; *back:* mantle brownish, with obscure streaking; *rump:* brown; *tail:* dark brown, with outer web and tip of lateral rectrices white in unworn individuals; *wing:* brownish, with scapulars, tertials, and greater-coverts broadly edged in buff; *underparts:* throat buffy white; breast slightly darker, often with a necklace of thin, dark stripes; breast spot dark brown; flanks buffy white and streaked; belly dull white; *bill:* dark brown, paler below; *legs* and *feet:* dark yellow brown; *iris:* dark brown.

First-fall and winter (June–Aug)—Resemble adults.

Juveniles (Apr–July)—Are similar to Sage Sparrows, but darker.

Hybrids None reported.

References Martin and Carlson (1998), Rising (1996).

27.1 Bell's Sparrow *Aimophila bellii,* coastal California, USA, April 1997. Bell's Sparrows show much stronger head pattern than Sage Sparrows, and they are much more richly colored overall. Mantle streaking is often restricted to the lower scapulars (Mike Danzenbaker).

27.2 Adult Bell's Sparrow, San Diego Co., California, USA, Feb 1998. The striking head pattern, shared only with Sage Sparrow, is distinctive. Otherwise the upperparts are brownish with obscure dusky streaking. The white underparts are suffused with buffy-brown on the flanks with narrow, though distinct, dusky streaking from sides of breast to lower flanks (Rick and Nora Bowers).

27.3 Adult Bell's Sparrow, San Diego Co., California, USA, Feb 1998. Concentrating on the mostly gray head, notice the sharply demarcated white supraloral, broken eye-ring, submoustachial stripe and throat contrasting with the black lores and broad malar stripe. There is a variable blackish smudge on the center of the breast (Rick and Nora Bowers).

28 Sage Sparrow

(Amphispiza nevadensis)

Measurements
Length: 13.5–16.0 cm; 5.3–6.3 in.
(males slightly larger).
Wing: 68.7–77.3 mm (averages of 14
populations; males only); 2.7–3.0 in.
Mass: 16.1–18.7 g (averages of 14
populations; males only).

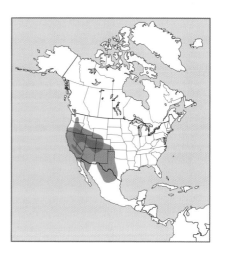

The Sage Sparrow is a medium-sized sparrow with a gray-brown head, sandy brown back, with faint streaking on the back and flanks, and **a bold white supraloral spot, white eye-ring**, and a **conspicuous white submoustachial stripe, often outlined with a dark malar stripe** – which is usually much darker in birds from the interior of California than those from the Great Basin – and a **dark breast spot**. Often run rapidly on the ground with their tail cocked.

Habitat
Sage Sparrows breed in cold desert (saltbush) or semi-desert (sagebrush) where they are characteristically found in sagebrush, saltbush, antelope brush, and rabbit brush from sea level to nearly 2000 m, generally in places where sagebrush or saltbush are dominant, and some places where sagebrush is interspersed with scattered juniper or piñon. After breeding some move to higher elevations. In winter northern birds move south into sagebrush grasslands, and coastal chaparral. In se California, in winter, they are commonly found in weedy scrub (esp. *Suaeda*), often near water.

Behavior
In the Great Basin, Sage Sparrows often arrive on their breeding grounds paired. Males sing from the top of bush, twitching their tails while singing. When not singing, they may be difficult to see as they forage on the ground. Characteristically, they run along the ground with their tails cocked. Females are difficult to flush from the nest, and then tend to run from the nest. Post-breeding birds tend to form small flocks, and may move to higher elevations.

Voice
The song is a weak, plaintive, high-pitched series of tinkling notes, lasting 3–4 s: *tsit tsit, tsii you, tee a-tee*, or *tsit-tsoo-tseeetsay*, the third note high and accentuated, or *chip-si ship-si-do chip-si-do shu-zup*, with the *do* and *zup* slightly lower. Individual males tend to sing only a single song pattern. Calls are a rapidly repeated, high *te te te te*, or *tse tse tse*. The alarm note is a thin *tsip*, similar to that of juncos, but weaker.

Similar species
See **Bell's Sparrow**. The **Five-striped Sparrow** of s Arizona is similar in pattern, but darker, with a wide black malar stripe, and unstreaked gray breast and flanks. Juveniles can be told from juvenile **Black-throated Sparrows** by their less distinct supercilium, pale or white only in front of the eye, and streaked crown.

Geographic variation
Two subspecies are commonly recognized, *A. n. nevadensis* and *A. n. canescens*. *A. n. canescens* is confined to central California, and is smaller and generally more richly colored than *A. n. nevadensis*. These cannot be safely differentiated in the field; they probably intergrade in the Owens Valley in e-central California. In spite of their similarities, some research (some of it unpublished) suggests that these two should be separated at the species level. Bell's Sparrow (*A. belli*) is often treated as conspecific.

Distribution
Breeds from east of the Cascade range in e-central Washington and west of the Rocky Mountains in s Idaho, s-central and sw Wyoming, south to w Colorado, nw New Mexico, ne Arizona, Utah, and west to e-central California and c California.

Winters rarely from sw Kansas, w Oklahoma, s Colorado, and uncommonly from w Texas north to Utah, central Nevada, south to n Chihuahua, n Sonora, and n Baja California.

Migrates throughout the west and w Texas; very rare in spring north to British Columbia.

Conservation status
Sage Sparrows are sensitive to habitat destruction, and converting sagebrush grasslands to grasslands doubtless depress populations. They are not threatened, however.

Molt
The Prebasic I molt is incomplete and does not include the juvenal remiges or rectrices; occurs in June through Aug. There is no Prealternate molt. The Definitive Basic plumage is acquired by a complete molt beginning in June and finishing by mid-Sept.

Description
Adults—Medium-sized; sexes similar. *Head* and *nape:* gray-brown; crown faintly streaked; supraloral spot and sometimes some of the supercilium white; eye-ring white; lores dark; ear-coverts gray; moustachial stripe dark brown; submoustachial stripe pale buff to whitish; malar stripe dark; *back:* mantle pale brownish with thin dark brown streaking; *rump:* brown; *tail:* dark brown, with outer web and tip of lateral rectrices white in unworn individuals; *wing:* brownish, with scapulars, tertials, and greater-coverts broadly edged in buff; *underparts:* throat buffy white; breast slightly darker, often with a necklace of thin, dark stripes; breast spot dark brown; flanks buffy white and thinly streaked; belly dull white; *bill:* dark brown, paler below; *legs* and *feet:* brownish; *iris:* dark brown.

First winter (after Aug)—Resemble adults; some tertials and often some secondaries replaced, and these contrast in color with others.

Juveniles (May–Sept)—Grayish-brown, heavily streaked with brown on crown, nape, and mantle, and undersides, with pale white supraloral spot, and buffy wing-bars.

Hybrids None reported.

References
Johnson and Marten (1992), Martin and Carlson (1998), Pyle (1997), Rising (1996).

28.1 Adult Sage Sparrow *A. n. canescens*, White Mountains, California, USA, Aug 1994. Similar to Bell's Sparrow and with it shares a distinctive head pattern. Overall slightly paler and less richly colored than Bell's with grayer malar stripe and distinctly paler buffy flanks which are lightly streaked dusky (Brian E. Small).

28.2 Adult Sage Sparrow *A. n. canescens*, White Mountains, California, USA, Aug 1994. The upperparts are grayish-brown with obscure dusky streaking on the scapulars. The wings show broad buffy tips to the median and greater-coverts forming two reasonably distinct wing-bars. Notice the sparse streaking on the breast-sides and flanks (Brian E. Small).

28.3 Juvenile Sage Sparrow *A. n. canescens*, Panamint Mountains, California, USA, Aug 1996. Much paler and buffier overall than adult with fine dusky streaking on head, breast and mantle. The head pattern is muted with the pale eye-ring standing out of the rather plain face. The wing-coverts show pale buffy tips broken by narrow black shaft-streaks forming spotted wing-bars. Best told from juvenile Black-throated Sparrow by streaked crown and ill-defined supercilium (Herbert Clarke).

28.4 Adult Sage Sparrow *A. n. nevadensis*, Salome Highway, Arizona, USA, Dec 1995. *A. n. nevadensis* is similar to *A. n. canescens*, but is even paler with more distinct, though narrow, streaking on back and a weaker malar stripe (Jim Burns/Natural Impacts).

28.5 Adult Sage Sparrow *A. n. nevadensis*, June 2000. The weak, grayish malar stripe is well shown here. Notice also the grayish breast smudge and the buffy flanks which are finely streaked dusky (Mike Danzenbaker).

28.6 Adult and juvenile Sage Sparrows, Mono Lake, Mono Co., California, USA, August 1987. Birds breeding in Mono Co. are probably *A. n. nevadensis* (although intergrades with *A. n. canescens* might occur there). The adult is in very worn plumage and appears very drab. Note the grayish head with contrasting whitish eye-ring and submoustachial stripe. The juvenile also shows the bold eye-ring but is obviously streaked on the upperparts and breast (Mike Danzenbaker).

29 Lark Bunting

(Calamospiza melanocorys)

Measurements
Length: 14.0–18.0 cm; 5.5–7.1 in.
(males slightly larger).
Wing: 85–92 mm; 3.3–3.6 in. (average
88 mm; 3.5 in., males); 82–85 mm;
3.2–3.3 in. (average 83 mm; 3.3 in.,
females).
Mass: 29.5–51.5 g (average 37.6 g; sexes
combined) (Arizona); breeding males
36.9–42.3 g (average 39.6 g), breeding
females 31.8–38.9 g (average 36.4 g)
(Saskatchewan).

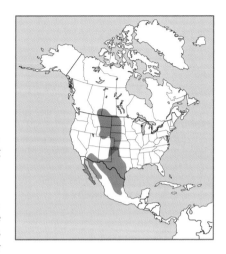

In summer, male Lark Buntings are **large,
black sparrows**, with conspicuous **white
patches in the wing**, and **white corners
to the tail**. Females are large, **heavily
streaked with chocolate-brown**,
whitish buff in the wings, and **white or whitish-buff tips to the corners of the tail**.
Males in winter resemble females, but with black and white on wings, and usually
some black on the throat and breast. Note the **large conical bill**.

Habitat
Lark Buntings breed in shortgrass prairie with bare ground, sometimes interspersed
with sage and other shrubs, as well as stubble fields and alfalfa. In winter they are
found in brushless, weedy dry grassland, desert scrub, and open farmland.

Behavior
On the breeding grounds, these are conspicuous birds, with males frequently giving a
stiff-winged flight display, rising to 10 m, then floating back to the ground, singing.
The birds forage on the ground, and males follow females as they forage when they
are off the nest; they hop, walk, or 'gallop' on the ground. They often seem to breed
in loose colonies in dry grasslands. Locally, their numbers fluctuate greatly from year
to year, and in dry years they may nest commonly east of their usual breeding range.
In winter, they are usually found in flocks, often large ones.

Voice
The song is a musical mixture of short notes and slurred phrases, *kazee kazee kazee
kazee, ziziziziz zoo quit quit quitquit trrrr too wewewewewew tur tur quit quit quit
quit*, or *sweet sweet sweet sweet sweet sweet toot toot toot toot toot chug chug chug
tr-r-r-r-r-r*, often given in a stiff-winged display flight. The call note is a gentle *who-
ee-ee, whee-ta-wer* or *hoo-ee*.

Similar species

No other species resembles a breeding male Lark Bunting. At all seasons, it may be found in the same fields as **McCown's** or **Chestnut-collared longspurs**, and female or young longspurs resemble female or young Lark Buntings, Both longspurs, especially the Chestnut-collared, have noticeably smaller bills. The patterns of white in the tail differ: Lark Buntings have light or white tips to some tail feathers, whereas these two longspurs have whitish bases to some rectrices. Other longspurs have whitish edges to the lateral tail feathers. Female Lark Buntings may remind one of a Song Sparrow, or female Purple Finch.

Geographic variation

None described.

Distribution

Breeds from s Alberta, s Saskatchewan, sw Manitoba, and sw Minnesota (rare), south through South Dakota, Nebraska, central and w Kansas, w Oklahoma, nw Texas, and e New Mexico, and through central Montana, e Idaho, south through Wyoming to nw Colorado and se Utah; has bred in wet years in e California.

Winters: from s Nevada, s California, central Arizona, and s New Mexico, and s and e Texas, regularly north to sw Kansas and se Colorado, south to Tamaulipas, Jalisco, and Baja California.

Migrates through the Great Plains and California (mostly in fall); most common in migration in w Kansas, e Colorado, and w Texas. In Mexico, spring migration begins in Feb and peaks in the United States in mid-Mar through early May. Some depart the breeding grounds in July with large flocks leaving by late July, and a peak in southern Texas early Sept. Wanders west to Washington and east to Quebec.

Conservation status

The numbers of Lark Buntings may vary greatly from year to year, both in summer or winter, presumably reflecting local fluctuations in the climate. It is thus difficult to assess their status, but there does seem to have been a small long-term increase in their number. They have expanded their wintering range northward in recent years. They avoid areas where brush cover has been eliminated, and spraying to control grasshoppers destroys an important source of their food. The species would benefit from efforts to preserve native shortgrass and bunch grass prairies.

Molt

The Prejuvenal molt occurs June–Aug. The Basic I plumage is acquired by a partial Prebasic Molt that involves the innermost secondaries, the outermost primaries, all of the tail feathers, but not the medium or greater-coverts. This molt takes place July–Sept, and commences on the breeding grounds and is completed during stopovers on migration or on the wintering grounds. There is a partial Prealternate I Molt, Jan–Apr, that involves the greater-coverts and tertials, outer secondaries, and sometimes the central rectrices; this molt is variable. The Definitive Prebasic molt is complete (?), and the timing is like the Prebasic I molt. The adult Prealternate molt is like the Prealternate I molt, but does not involve the greater-coverts.

Description

Adults—Large and robust; sexually dimorphic in color. **Males in summer:** *Head, back,* and *underparts:* black, sometimes flecked with white on the belly; *wing:* black, with primaries narrowly edged with white, secondaries tipped in white, and tertials boldly edged in white; coverts white; *tail:* outer web white, inner webs of outermost five rectrices tipped with white; *bill:* large, conical and bluish, paler below; *legs:* brownish; *feet:* darker; *iris:* reddish-brown.

Adult females—*Head:* crown and nape brown, streaked with darker brown; supercilium and lores pale brown; ear-coverts brown, but paler in the center, and with a pale spot on the back edge; moustachial and malar stripes dark brown; submoustachial stripe and throat pale brown; *back:* brown and streaked with darker brown; *underparts:* pale brown, broadly streaked on the neck and flanks; *tail:* brown, with all but central rectrices tipped with dull white, especially on the inner webs; undertail-coverts pale brown, with dark brown centers; *bill:* dark horn-colored; *legs* and *feet* horn-colored.

Adult males in winter (Aug–Mar)—Like adult females, but with varying amounts of white in the face, throat, breast, and belly, remiges, and coverts, and scapulars with broad, whitish edges.

First-winter (Aug–Mar)—Similar to adult females; hatching year males obtain some black feathers in a Prealternate Molt starting in Jan or Feb.

Juveniles (June–Aug)—Similar to adult females, but with a yellowish cast, and broad, buffy edges to the neck and back feathers, and scapulars, giving a scaly impression; large, pale buffy patch evident on the wings.

Hybrids None reported.

References Dechant *et al.* (1999e), Pyle (1997), Rising (1996), Shane (1972, 1996, 1998, 2000), Shane and Seltman (1995).

29.1 Adult male Lark Bunting, Texas, USA, May 1995. Essentially black with a large white wing patch. No other North American sparrow resembles the adult male in breeding attire. This bird is in fresh plumage and still retains some buffy fringes on the head and lesser-coverts. The ample, deep-based bill is bluish-gray (Brian E. Small).

29.2 Adult male Lark Bunting, e Colorado, USA, July 1992. This mid-summer male is completely velvety black (all buffy edges worn away) with the contrasting white wing panel. Note the narrow whitish edges to the inner greater-coverts and tertials (Herbert Clarke).

29.3 Adult male Lark Bunting, Whitewater Draw National Wildlife Refuge, Arizona, USA, Nov 1997. Adult males in winter show heavy black streaking on the underparts and exhibit variable blackish mottling on the throat. Both features are clearly visible here as well as the large whitish wing panel (Jim Burns/Natural Impacts).

29.4 Lark Bunting, Whitewater Draw National Wildlike Refuge, Arizona, USA, Nov 1997. This fresh-plumaged bird resembles a female but might in fact be a first-winter male. The blackness of the centers to the tertials, wing-coverts and tail together with the bold black malar stripe are suggestive of this (Jim Burns/Natural Impacts).

29.5 First-winter male Lark Bunting Arizona, USA, Jan 1998. Resembles female but with blacker centers to wing-coverts and tertials and bolder black streaking on back and underparts. The malar stripe is thicker and blacker than on female and often, as here, extends onto the throat (Herbert Clarke).

29.6 Female Lark Bunting, Arizona, USA, Jan 1998. Brown upperparts, streaked darker contrast with whitish submoustachial stripe and underparts which are boldly streaked with brown on the breast and flanks. Recognized from other streaky sparrows by hefty size, deep-based bill and virtually no primary projection (Herbert Clarke).

29.7 Female Lark Bunting, Cape May, New Jersey, USA, Sept 1993. The cream-colored wing patch is diagnostic. Concentrating on the head pattern, note the whitish supercilium, lores, ear-covert patch and submoustachial stripe with contrasting brown ear-coverts and crown (Kevin T. Karlson).

(Passerculus sandwichensis)

Measurements
Length: 11.4–15.4 cm; 4.5–6.1 in. (males
    slightly larger; largest on Sable
    Island, NS, and Aleutian Islands, AK).
Wing: 64–84 mm; 2.5–3.3 in.
Mass: 15.6–32.5 g (breeding birds).

Savannah Sparrows are brown or dark
brown, **streaked** on both their back and
breast, have **pink legs**, a **yellow supercilium**, whitish or buffy median crown-
stripe, and a medium to rather short,
notched tail with no white. Their flight
is direct, and they generally are not difficult to see. Geographically variable.
Juveniles are heavily streaked with blackish-brown; *first fall* birds are buffier than
adults. Geographically variable.

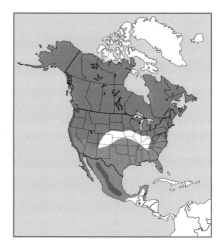

Habitat
Savannah Sparrows are birds of open country. They typically are found in grassy
meadows, cultivated fields (especially alfalfa), lightly grazed pastures, roadside edges,
coastal grasslands, sedge bogs, and in saltmarshes and tundra; they prefer habitats
with short to intermediate vegetation height, and a well developed litter layer.
Although Savannah Sparrows avoid woodlands, they are generally found in fields
with some herbaceous vegetation, and at the northern edge of their range are often
found in open scrub willows or birches; in the more arid parts of their range they are
usually found around the grassy margins of ponds. Resident populations along the
coast of California, from Morro Bay south into Baja California, and along the coast
of Sonora and Sinaloa, are found in saltmarshes where *Salicornia* (pickleweed),
Allenrolfea, Sueda (sea blight), *Atriplex,* and *Distichlis* (saltgrass) are dominant plants.
Non-breeding large-billed Savannah Sparrows (see below) can be found in a variety
of habitats in s California, including beaches, wharves, and city streets, in addition
to marshes.

Behavior
On the breeding grounds, males sing persistently, generally from an exposed perch.
Chases are common. Incubating females may flush directly from the nest, or may perform a 'rodent-run' distraction display. Savannah Sparrows generally feed on the
ground, but will glean larval insects from branch tips. In the breeding season they feed
alone or in pairs, but in the winter are often found in loose flocks; they are not usually
in mixed flocks. They (especially 'Ipswich' Sparrows) sometimes feed at the tide line on

sandy beaches and among beach wrack. They generally are not difficult to see; their flight is strong and direct, and they will often alight in a small tree or bush.

Voice
The typical song of the Savannah Sparrow is a lisping **tzip-tzip-tzip ztreeeeeeeeeee-ip**, usually uttered from a perch, but sometimes in flight. At a distance, the **'tzip'** notes may not be audible, and the terminal **'ip'** is often not given. During the breeding season, they may sing at night. The call is a thin **seet**, **chip**, or **tzip**; sometimes an emphatic **chip chip chip** is given by the female around the nest; a **buzt buzt buzt** may be given by a subordinate in an aggressive encounter.

Similar species
Song Sparrows are larger, with a longer, rounded tail and larger bill; the crown-stripe is less distinct, and it lacks yellow in the supercilium (as do some Savannah Sparrows). Both species, however, are highly variable, and habitat and behavior are useful aids to identification. Savannah Sparrows are found in open fields or the edges of fields, and when flushed their flight is direct. Song Sparrows are found in edge or brush habitats, and when flushed their flight is slightly undulating, with their long tail flopped slightly to one side. The central breast spot, often given as a good field mark for Song Sparrows, is often present on Savannah Sparrows. **Vesper Sparrows** are larger and longer-tailed, with a thin, but conspicuous eye-ring, no median crown-stripe or yellow in the supercilium, and they have rusty shoulders (lesser coverts). In flight, they show conspicuous white in their outer tail feathers. **Baird's Sparrows** appear flat-headed and large-billed; the entire head is washed with yellow ochre, and with a buffy ochre crown-stripe; territorial Baird's Sparrows are rather easy to see, but otherwise they are secretive and hard to flush, unlike Savannah Sparrows. **Grasshopper Sparrows** have an unstreaked breast and are short-tailed and flat-headed; juvenile Grasshopper Sparrows have streaked breasts, but otherwise are shaped like adults.

Geographic variation
As many as 12 subspecies from the United States and Canada have been recognized. Of these, two, *P. s. beldingi* and *P. s. alaudinus* are resident or partially migratory in coastal saltmarshes in California. Birds resident from Humboldt Bay south to Morro Bay have been called *P. s. alaudinus*, whereas *P. s. beldingi* are resident from Santa Barbara south to nw Baja California. The birds from Morro Bay are little different from those farther south, and we feel that they should be placed in the same subspecies.

Large-billed Savannah Sparrows (*P. s. rostratus*) are easily identifiable in the field. They breed along the coast of Sonora, Mexico, are now uncommon to fairly common in winter in s California.

The large, pallid Ipswich sparrows (*P. s. princeps*) are also readily identifiable in the field. They breed on Sable I., Nova Scotia, and winter along the Atlantic Coast from Massachusetts south to s Georgia.

Variation among populations of typical Savannah Sparrows is clinal. Birds from Labrador and the Hudson Bay lowlands average darker on the back, with darker ventral streaking than other birds; the names *P. s. labradorius* and *P. s. oblitus* have been used for these. South of these, the eastern birds are called *P. s. savanna*. *P. s. sandwichensis* from the Aleutian Islands and the Alaskan Peninsula are similar to other typical Savannah Sparrows in coloration, but substantially larger. There is clinal variation in size from west to east along the Alaskan Peninsula with the birds at the western end being nearly as large as those on the Aleutian Is., and those at the eastern end nearly as small as birds from the Alaskan mainland; these latter birds are called *P. s. anthinus*, which breed from Alaska east across the Yukon and Northwest Territories. South of these are *P. s. nevadensis*, which average paler than other Savannah Sparrows. *P. s. rufofuscus* of Arizona and New Mexico are very similar. The name *P. s. brooksi* has been applied to the birds breeding from Vancouver I. south along the coast to nw California. Except for the large size of *P. s. sandwichensis*, which often enables identification in the hand, these subspecies are poorly differentiated, and we do not think that any of these subspecies can be identified in the field.

Distribution

Widespread. **Breeds** from the northern limit of the mainland of Canada (rarely to Victoria I.) and the United States south to Pennsylvania and central New York and in the mountains to n Georgia, central Ohio, Indiana, Illinois, and Iowa, n Nebraska, w Colorado and New Mexico, and south in mountains to s Mexico (and perhaps Guatemala), and west to the Aleutian Is., Alaska, south to California, and along coast to Baja California (south to Bahia Magdalena).

Winters south of breeding range and at lower elevations from Massachusetts, w Tennessee, s Missouri, s Kansas, Oklahoma, New Mexico, Arizona, s Nevada, and s California south to s Mexico and Honduras and rarely to the Bahamas and Cuba. Resident along the coast of California and Baja California.

Migrates throughout North America. Spring migration is mostly in Apr and May; fall migration mostly Aug through Oct (peak early Oct). There are two records for the British Isles: one *P. s. princeps* (Apr), and one typical (Sept); there is a probable record for Korea (Dec).

Conservation status

Abundant in many places where they occur. Clearing of woodlands in the east has doubtless increased habitat for Savannah Sparrows, and consequently their numbers in that region. In the prairies, transformation of grassland to crop land has destroyed extensive areas of suitable habitat for Savannah Sparrows, but they are still abundant where appropriate habitat exists. They are most likely to thrive in large tracts of grassland that are burned occasionally and lightly grazed to reduce woody vegetation. It is best if these areas are not grazed, burnt, or mowed during their breeding season, roughly May through July. Along the coast of California and Baja California the destruction of saltmarshes for marinas and other developments have extirpated many populations, and others are threatened.

Molt

The Prebasic I molt may begin before the juvenal plumage is fully acquired, and juvenal wing and tail feathers are retained. The Prealternate molt is incomplete and occurs in Feb. The Definitive Basic molt is complete and takes place July to early Sept.

Description

[There are four major groups of this geographically variable species. We shall describe them separately.]

Typical Savannah Sparrow (most of North America): Adults—Medium sized (largest on Sable I., NS, and the Aleutian I., AK). *Head:* lateral crown-stripes brown, streaked with dark brown; median crown-stripe whitish; supraloral spot yellow; eyeline dark brown; moustachial and malar stripes dark brown; submoustachial stripe whitish, ear-coverts brown to grayish-brown, darker on the back margin; *back:* dark (esp. in ne) to pale (esp. in w) brown, streaked, with scapulars and back feathers with dark centers and pale edges; *rump:* brown and streaked; *tail:* brown, slightly notched, with outer webs of feathers somewhat paler, but not white; *wing:* brown with indistinct beige wing-bars; *underparts:* whitish to buff, variably streaked with brown on flanks and breast (commonly coalescing into a central dot), flanks, and less extensively streaked on the chin, throat, and belly; *bill:* upper mandible brownish or horn-colored; lower mandible paler, yellowish-brown; *legs* and *feet:* pink; *iris:* dark brown.

Young in fall (July–Sept)—Resemble adults, but crown-stripes flecked with pale, buff feathers, making these stripes less distinct than in adults, the supercilium is thinner and yellower (in east) or very pale (in west), ear-coverts chestnut, breast and belly buffy with heavier streaking, wing feathers and coverts with broad beige edges, and throat and belly beige, and extensively streaked with dark brown.

Juveniles—Resemble adults, but crown with brown streaks, and narrow, indistinct yellowish or beige median stripe, wing-coverts with broad edges, and throat and belly beige, and extensively streaked with dark brown.

Ipswich Sparrow (North Atlantic Coast): Adults—Resemble typical Savannah Sparrows in pattern but are larger and noticeably paler in color, appearing grayish. The supercilium is pale yellow or whitish, and the ventral streaking is generally less extensive than other typical Savannahs. Breed on Sable I., NS (rarely on adjacent mainland), where they nest commonly in marram grass and beach peas. In winter, they are rarely found away from coastal dune areas.

Belding's Savannah Sparrow (California saltmarshes): Adults—Are more heavily streaked and darker brown than typical Savannah Sparrows, and have a brown (although sometimes pale) median crown-stripe; supercilium and, esp., supraloral spot yellow. The bill is more slender than that of other Savannah Sparrows. **Young** birds may lack the yellow in the supercilium.

Large-billed Savannah Sparrows (Salton Sea and coastal s California): Adults—Average larger than either Belding's or typical Savannah Sparrow, and have a large bill. They resemble other Savannah Sparrows in general plumage pattern, but are generally paler brown or brownish-gray (esp. in contrast with Belding's sparrows); supercilium pale beige or yellowish-beige; crown-stripe indistinct; back with indistinct streaking; underparts less heavily streaked than Belding's or most typical Savannah Sparrows; throat white with few indistinct brown flecks; legs horn-colored; bill horn-colored or grayish-brown, with lower mandible paler. **Young** resemble adults, but are generally paler in color, with no yellow in the supercilium; the crown lacks a distinct median stripe; the rump is usually unstreaked.

Hybrids There is a specimen of a hybrid Savannah Sparrow X Grasshopper Sparrow.

References Dickerman (1968), Swanson (1998), Wheelright and Rising (1993).

30.1 Adult 'Large-billed' Savannah Sparrow *P. s. rostratus*, Orange Co., California, USA, Nov 1999. The obviously large bill with strongly curved culmen differs from other Savannah Sparrows within range. The head pattern is quite diffused and lacks yellow on the supraloral. The underparts are white with even rows of brown streaking (Brian E. Small).

30.2 Adult 'Large-billed' Savannah Sparrow *P. s. rostratus*, Salton Sea, California, USA, Nov 1990. This individual appears quite plain grayish-brown on the upperparts with obscure streaking and no pale braces. Note also the diffused head pattern and evenly streaked whitish underparts. Large-billed 'Savannah Sparrows' are generally restricted to saltmarshes (Kevin T. Karlson).

30.3 Adult 'Belding's' Savannah Sparrow *P. s. beldingi*, Bolsa Chica, California, USA, Apr 1995. Restricted to coastal saltmarshes this small, heavily streaked 'Savannah Sparrow' is quite distinctive within range. Note the bold blackish streaking on the body and head and the strong yellow suffusion on the supercilium. The bill is moderate in size and somewhat spike-like in profile (Brian E. Small).

30.4 Adult Savannah Sparrow, Palo Alto, Baylands, California, USA, Jan 1998. This individual is quite boldly streaked and has a strong head pattern with bright yellow supercilium. If it is not a wintering migrant, it is, by range, *P. s. alaudinus*, which looks like *P. s. beldingi* but tends to be smaller billed (Brian E. Small).

30.5 Adult Savannah Sparrow *P. s. nevadensis*, North Dakota, USA, June 1994. A typical bird from the central portion of the range. Specific racial identification is generally not possible with much intergradation between the forms (Brian E. Small).

30.6 Adult Savannah Sparrow *P. s. anthinus*, Nome, Alaska, USA, June 1998. Western non-saltmarsh Savannah Sparrows, such as this bird, are pale with whitish underparts, and relatively sparse and well defined blackish streaking across breast and along flanks. The head pattern is well defined with narrow blackish lines on a pale ground color. This individual shows much yellow on the supraloral (Brian E. Small).

30.7 Adult Savannah Sparrow, Sulphur Springs Valley, Arizona, USA, Jan 1998. Specific racial identification is generally not safe when looking at wintering individuals. The pallid appearance of this bird, lacking any trace of yellow on the supraloral, suggests it is possibly of the form *P. s. nevadensis*. On all Savannah Sparrows note the very short primary projection and the shortish tail (Jim Burns/Natural Impacts).

30.8 Adult Savannah Sparrow, Carden Alvar, Ontario, Canada, June 1999. The plump, short-tailed appearance recalls some *Ammodramus* sparrows but the head pattern, usually with some yellow in the supercilium (rather bright here) is distinctive. Note the whitish outer webs to the outer tail feathers. This typical 'eastern' individual from southern Ontario is, on geographical grounds, *P. s. savanna* (Sam Barone).

30.9 Juvenile Savannah Sparrow *P. s. savanna*, South Walsingham, Ontario, Canada, July 1992. Differs from adult in appearing distinctly buffy with bold blackish streaking. The ear-coverts are tinged with warm brown and the buff supercilium is finely streaked blackish. The wing-coverts are broadly edged with pale buff (David Agro).

30.10 Juvenile Savannah Sparrow *P. s. savanna*, Carden Alvar, Ontario, Canada, July 1999. Another view of a typical juvenile showing the boldly streaked breast and finely streaked crown and neck (Sam Barone).

30.11 Adult 'Ipswich' Savannah Sparrow *P. s. princeps*, Long Island, New York, USA, Jan 2000. This large, pale form is distinctive within its restricted coastal range. Notice the pallid grayish ground color to the upperparts with fine brown streaking. The supraloral is pale lemon yellow, although the intensity of yellow is highly variable on all Savannah Sparrows. The whitish underparts are evenly streaked with brown (Michael D. Stubblefield).

30.12 Adult 'Ipswich' Savannah Sparrow *P. s. princeps*, Long Island, New York, USA, Jan 2000. Another view of a typical *P. s. princeps*, showing the grayish-brown color of the upperparts and the fine brown streaking on the underparts. Note the prominent rusty panel formed by broad edges to the tertials and secondaries (Michael D. Stubblefield).

30.13 Adult Savannah Sparrow, Ventura Co., California, USA, Dec 1999. This pale and grayish individual has a very small, slender bill and is possibly of the form *P. s. nevadensis*. Note the total lack of yellow on the supraloral area and overall pallid appearance (Don Des Jardin).

30.14 Adult Savannah Sparrow, Ventura Co., California, USA, Dec 1999. Another view of a possible *P. s. nevadensis*. The upperparts are grayish with blackish streaking, but lack contrasting pale braces noticeable on many other forms. Owing to the clinal nature of plumage features, subspecific identification is often difficult or impossible (Don Des Jardin).

30.15 Adult Savannah Sparrow, Gulf Coast, Texas, USA, Nov 1992. A dark 'eastern' bird with contrasty plumage, bold whitish mantle braces and strong yellow supraloral patch. Birds that breed in Labrador (*P. s. labradorius*) are generally dark, as this bird is (Don Des Jardin).

30.16 Adult Savannah Sparrow, Cape May, New Jersey, USA, Jan 1998. This back view captures the essence of a typical eastern Savannah Sparrow well. Note the well defined whitish braces on the mantle and the warm brown wing panel formed by the edges to the greater-coverts and tertials (Kevin T. Karlson).

30.17 Adult Savannah Sparrow, Jones Beach, New York, USA, Oct 1988. This dark individual is typical of birds that breed in Labrador and perhaps Newfoundland, and might be of the form *P. s. labradorius*. The upperparts are dark with pale braces and the wings are extensively rufous-brown. The whitish underparts are thickly streaked with black (Kevin T. Karlson).

30.18 Adult Savannah Sparrow *P. s. oblitus*, Churchill, Manitoba, Canada, June 1996. This individual is typical of birds found in the north-central portion of the range. The upperparts are quite dark with grayish feather edges and the underparts show bold black and brown streaking (Kevin T. Karlson).

30.19 Adult Savannah Sparrow, Jamaica Bay Wildlife Refuge, New York, USA, Apr 1999. The darkly colored individual probably comes from the Labrador Peninsula where *P. s. labradorius* breed (Michael D. Stubblefield).

31 **Grasshopper Sparrow**

(Ammodramus savannarum)

Measurements:
Length: 10.5–13.0 cm; 4.1–5.1 in.
  (males slightly larger).
Wing: 57–64 mm; 2.2–2.5 in.
Mass: Av = 17.8 g (16.9–18.5 g; males
  from Great Plains).

The Grasshopper Sparrow is a small- to
medium-sized grassland sparrow, with a
short tail. Adults are **unstreaked below**,
or at most faintly streaked, and brownish
and mottled above; the **crown has a distinct pale median crown-stripe**, with
wide, dark brown lateral crown-stripes.
Grasshopper Sparrows appear to be
rather flat-headed, with large bills.

Habitat
Grasshopper Sparrows breed in wet or dry grassy pastures of intermediate height,
often with clumped vegetation and sparse shrubs or weeds, interspersed with patches
of bare ground; in some parts of their range, they are found in alfalfa or clover, hayfields, and seasonally wet meadows. Where they are found together, Grasshopper,
Baird's, and Savannah sparrows can be found in the same fields, at times apparently
in the same habitat. However, Grasshopper Sparrows tend to favor more xeric habitats, and Baird's more mesic ones, than the others. In Florida, Grasshopper Sparrows
are resident in small, stunted saw palmetto and dwarf oaks, interspersed with sparse
grass and bare ground. In winter they are generally found in rather dense grass.

Behavior
Territorial males frequently sing from a conspicuous perch – the top of a tall weed or
bush, or from a fence wire – although sometimes from the ground. When not singing,
they can be inconspicuous, frequently running rather than flying when approached.
The flight is a weak zig-zag, low over the ground, after which the bird drops to the
ground. Females incubate closely, and when disturbed often run away from the nest
before taking off for a short flight.

Voice
The song is thin, high, and insect-like, and starts with 2–3 high notes followed by a
high trill, ***chip chip scheeeeeeeeee, tzick tzick tzrrrrr*** or ***c chit zhu zeeeeeeeeee***, with
the trill on a higher pitch; sometimes a more musical ***zeeee sic-a-zeedle sic-a-zeedle-
zeeee*** is given; the call is a weak ***tillic***. During the breeding season Grasshopper
Sparrows may sing at night.

Similar species

Adult **Le Conte's Sparrows** lack streaking on their breast, but have streaked flanks, a distinct, broad ochre superciliary stripe, and are smaller. **Baird's Sparrows** have a thin, but distinct necklace of dark brown spots on their breast; their heads are suffused with buffy or ochre, with rather indistinct markings; they are slightly larger. Juvenile Baird's are very similar (see Baird's Sparrow). Juvenile **Henslow's Sparrows** show ochre rather than buffy or whitish tones; the pale areas on the side of the face and nape of juvenile Grasshopper Sparrows are thinly streaked with dark brown, whereas on juvenile Henslow's these are olive and unstreaked or at least not obviously streaked.

Geographic variation

Four subspecies of Grasshopper Sparrows are found north of Mexico. *A. s. floridanus* breeds in central peninsular Florida; they have darker backs than other eastern Grasshopper Sparrows, with feathers dark brown or blackish, edged with grayish, and virtually no brown or rust; they are paler and less buffy below than other eastern Grasshopper Sparrows. *A. s. ammolegus*, which breeds in se Arizona and n Sonora, is paler and more rusty than other western Grasshopper Sparrows, with rust often appearing as faint streaking on the breast. *A. s. pratensis* breeds in the east, west to Wisconsin and e Oklahoma. *A. s. perpallidus* breeds in western North America, south to central Arizona. On average, *A. s. perpallidus* appears paler than *A. s. pratensis*, with less rusty on the crown, and a slightly smaller bill. With the exception of *A. s. floridanus*, these subspecies cannot be separated in the field.

Distribution

Breeds from s-central British Columbia, s Alberta, s Saskatchewan, s Manitoba, w Ontario, e Ontario, Michigan, sw Quebec, and s New Brunswick, south to central Georgia, central Alabama, Tennessee, Arkansas, Texas, se Colorado, ne New Mexico, e Wyoming, central and nw Montana, and in the west from s-central British Columbia, south to n Idaho, e Washington, Oregon, nw Utah, n Nevada, and south along the coast from n Oregon, to s California and nw Baja California, and locally in central California se Arizona, n Sonora and n Chihuahua; in most places in the west and northern Plains the status varies from year to year.

Winters from e North Carolina, Tennessee, Arkansas, Oklahoma, central Arizona, central California, south through Mexico to northern Central America and n-central Costa Rica, Belize, Quintana Roo, Cuba, the Isle of Pines, Caymen Is., Swan I., and the Bahamas.

Migrates throughout the 48 United States.

Conservation status

In the 19th Century, Audubon wrote that Grasshopper Sparrows were common from Maine to Maryland; they doubtless moved eastward following the clearing of land for agricultural purposes, and today are decreasing in most places in the east as marginal pastures are reverting to woodland. Burning, haying or heavily grazing fields during the nesting season (mid-Apr to late Aug) is deleterious to populations. In North Dakota they are commonest in fields 2–4 years following fires. In the Appalachians, they have colonized reclaimed strip mines, at least at lower elevations (Savannah Sparrows are found at higher elevations). There are only about 200 resident birds in the Florida populations.

Molt

The Prebasic I molt is complete, and begins in late June; birds from later broods may retain some of the juvenal plumage and may migrate in juvenal plumage. There is a partial Prealternate molt, Apr–June. The Definitive Basic molt is complete.

Description

Adults—Fairly small and short-tailed; sexes alike in color. *Head:* lateral crown-stripes dark brown, with edges of feathers lighter in unworn birds, and a pale buffy median crown-stripe; lores buffy yellowish; supercilium buffy yellowish in front of eye, grayish-white behind eye; side of face otherwise grayish-brown, with posterior edge of ear-coverts edged with dark brown; *back:* nape and side of neck grayish-buff, with centers of feathers rusty chestnut; mantle feathers with dark centers, edged with pale buff or rusty; *rump:* rump and uppertail-coverts mottled with rust; *tail:* brown, with feathers edged in pale grayish-brown, outermost feathers broadly edged and tipped in grayish-white; *wing:* brown, with feathers edged in pale brown; tertials and coverts with dark brown centers, tipped in rusty chestnut, and tipped in pale buff in unworn birds; *underparts:* throat pale buffy; breast and flanks buffy white and unmarked or faintly marked; belly whitish; undertail-coverts pale buffy; *bill:* pale horn-colored; lower mandible pinkish; *legs* and *feet:* pinkish, sometimes tinged with yellow; *iris:* brown.

First-winter (after July–Oct)—Like adults.

Juveniles (July–Oct)—Crown, nape, back, and rump dark brown, with edges of feathers pale buff or rusty brown; median crown-stripe indistinct and grayish-brown; breast and flanks whitish or buffy, streaked with brown spots; belly and undertail-coverts pale buffy or whitish and unmarked. Some individuals complete the first prebasic molt after migration; the upper bill is dark.

Hybrids

There is a specimen of a Grasshopper Sparrow X Savannah Sparrow hybrid and a Grasshopper Sparrow X Song Sparrow hybrid (probable).

References

Dechant *et al.* (1998c), Dickerman (1968), Jones *et al.* (MS) Petersen (1999), Rising (1996), Vickery (1996).

31.1 Adult Grasshopper Sparrow, Concan, Texas, USA, May 1997. Chunky and short-tailed with a stout bill. Note the complex quail-like markings on the upperparts with bold black streaking on mantle contrasting with whitish braces. Head with bright orange supraloral, black lateral crown-stripes and bold pale eye-ring. Underparts mostly uniform pale buff with limited streaking on breast sides (Brian E. Small).

31.2 Adult Grasshopper Sparrow, Concan, Texas, USA, May 1998. Concentrating on the head pattern note the narrow pale central crown-stripe contrasting with the black-streaked lateral stripes. The ear-coverts are brownish and contrast with the pale gray collar which is densely streaked with chestnut (Brian E. Small).

31.3 Adult Grasshopper Sparrow *A. s. pratensis*, Ontario, Canada, 19 June 1966. This breeding bird is in moderately worn plumage and has lost much of the pale edging to the back feathers and thus appears less contrasty. Note also the faded buffy supraloral spot (Dr. George K. Peck).

31.4 Adult Grasshopper Sparrow *A. s. pratensis*, near Clyde, Ohio, USA, May 1998. Another view of a fresh-plumaged adult, showing the distinctive pattern of black, chestnut and white on the back. Just visible here (though nearly always hidden by the scapulars) is a trace of the greenish lesser-coverts. The lemon-yellow edge to the bend of the wing is clearly visible (Larry Sansone).

31.5 Adult Grasshopper Sparrow *A. s. floridanus*, Highland Co., Florida, USA, 1996. This scarce, resident form differs from the widespread *pratensis* (which shares its range in winter) by being slightly larger-billed, darker on the back and decidedly more pallid on the underparts (Bill Pranty).

31.6 Juvenile Grasshopper Sparrow *A. s. floridanus*, Highland Co., Florida, USA, 1996. Very similar to juveniles of other subspecies but is perhaps whiter on the underparts with bolder streaking across the breast (Bill Pranty).

31.7 Juvenile Grasshopper Sparrow, June 1996. The head and underparts are paler than adult with a gorget of dusky streaks across breast. The supercilium and malar area show fine dusky streaking which extends onto the neck-sides. Note the neat buffy fringes to the back feathers and wing-coverts giving the upperparts a scaly-looking appearance (Mike Danzenbaker).

32 Baird's Sparrow

(Ammodramus bairdii)

Measurements
Length: 12.0–13.0 cm; 4.7–5.1 in.
  (males slightly larger).
Wing: 66–73 mm; 2.6–2.9 in.
Mass: 19.5 g (17.3–21.5 g) (North
  Dakota and Saskatchewan; males).

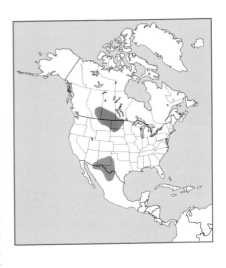

Baird's Sparrow is a medium-sized, rather short-tailed grassland sparrow with a **necklace of small, dark brown spots on the upper breast**, pale brown spots on the breast and upper flanks, pale ochre supercilium and ear-coverts, and **ochre in the crown**, and nape streaked with dark brown; head markings are generally indistinct. The feathers on the mantle and back are dark brown, broadly edged with pale ochre, giving them a **scaly appearance**. The pale lateral feathers are sometimes apparent in flight. In profile, Baird's Sparrows appear flat-headed, with no apparent crest. Territorial males sing from a conspicuous perch, and the song carries a long distance. However, females and wintering birds are difficult to see.

Habitat
Baird's Sparrow breeds in ungrazed or lightly grazed grassland, interspersed with scattered clumps of grass and low shrubs, with tangled matted grass on the ground, or in grasses in dry, shallow ponds or sloughs. In some areas it shows a strong preference for native grasses such as northern and western wheat grass, Junegrass, and needle grass, whereas in other regions it may also be common in introduced grasses, such as crested wheat grass, fescue, and Russian wild rye; also in alfalfa or planted clover. The wintering ecology is not well known, but they are found in dense reddish plains grassland in southeastern Arizona, and grasslands and overgrown fields in Texas.

Behavior
Territorial males sing from a conspicuous perch on a tussock of grass or small shrub, or from the ground; singing is most frequent in the morning and evening. Although aerial displays are not common, territorial males fly up with a series of upward flights to perhaps as high as 15 m, and flight-singing has been recorded. The female incubates closely, not flushing until immediately threatened. Breeding birds seem to be loosely colonial. In winter they may be solitary, and rarely sing. They often run mouse-like through the grass, and are among the most difficult sparrows to see well at that time of year.

Voice

The song is *zhe zhe she zurrrrrrrr, zhe zhe zheze chrrrrrrrrrr,* or *zee zee zee zee zee ze-lit,* with the last trill or note on a lower pitch. The song most commonly has a melodious trill at the end, which carries well. The song lasts only 2–3 s; actively singing birds will repeat it every 10–15 s. Although the song is variable, individuals tend to sing the same song repeatedly. They give a whining *meeer,* perhaps repeated two or three times if agitated, or a sharp *kee-keep*; the alarm note is a repeated *chip.*

Similar species

The **Savannah Sparrow** is similar in size, but more extensively streaked below, has more distinct facial markings, and usually has a yellow supercilium (which is less pronounced in the Great Plains than in the east); the buffy median crown-stripe and the yellowish cast to the head is characteristic of Baird's Sparrow. Except for singing males, Baird's Sparrows are difficult to see: if the bird is easy to observe, it is probably not a Baird's Sparrow – probably a Savannah. The **Grasshopper Sparrow** averages slightly smaller, and either lacks or has indistinct ventral streaking. Its mantle, back and rump feathers are rusty brown or brown, and edged with grayish-brown or pale brown, contrasting less distinctly than on Baird's Sparrow. The crown has a distinct beige – not ochre – median crown-stripe. Juvenile Grasshopper and Baird's sparrows are very similar, but the juvenile Baird's Sparrow, like the adult, has a yellow-ochre cast to its head and a scaly back. Some juveniles of both species migrate in juvenal plumage, but this is apparently commoner in Baird's and in Grasshopper sparrows. Le Conte's Sparrows are noticeably smaller than Baird's and Grasshopper sparrows, with distinctive facial and crown markings, streaked flanks, and no streaking on the breast. Juvenile Le Conte's Sparrows have a buffy head and could be confused with Baird's Sparrows, but Baird's has heavier breast streaks and dark moustachial and malar stripes.

Geographic variation

None described.

Distribution

Breeds from se Alberta, central Saskatchewan, south to sw Manitoba, nw Minnesota (formerly?), North Dakota, nw South Dakota, ne and n-central Montana, and perhaps e Wyoming.

Winters from se Arizona, New Mexico, and w Texas (rare; casual east of there), south to ne Sonora (few records), Durango, Chihuahua, and n Zacatecas.

Migrates east of the Rocky Mountains, east to w Nebraska, w Kansas, and w Oklahoma, and se Arizona and sw New Mexico (now rare). Migrates through central and western Kansas in mid- to late April, and in the fall in late Sept to mid-Oct (nw Texas).

Conservation status

In pre-settlement times, Baird's Sparrows were apparently abundant in suitable habitat in the Great Plains, but much of their habitat has been destroyed as grasslands have been converted to cultivated fields; also frequent burning of grassland and overgrazing are detrimental to their habitat. Generally, habitats with thick vegetation and dense litter are avoided; burns can enhance habitat, but numbers are depressed the first year after a burn.

Molt

The Prebasic I molt is partial and takes place July–Nov; many migrate in Juvenal plumage. It is started on the breeding grounds, but completed on the wintering grounds, and involves all of the median and greater-coverts, some tertials and central tail feathers. There is a partial Prealternate molt in Feb to Apr. The Definitive Prebasic molt is complete, and takes place Aug to Nov.

Description

Adults—Medium-sized and short-tailed; sexes similar. *Head:* ochraceous; crown heavily streaked with dark brown spots, with a more or less distinct buffy-ochre median crown-stripe that tends to become wider toward the nape; supercilium buff or ochre and indistinct; ear-coverts buffy or ochre, edged posteriorly with dark brown and a thin dark brown moustachial stripe; sub-moustachial stripe buffy or ochre; malar stripe thin and dark brown; throat pale buff; *back:* nape ochre or buffy, boldly streaked with thin black spots; mantle and back dark brown with feathers distinctly edged with pale buff; *wing:* brown with coverts and scapulars boldly edged with ochre, often rusty in color; *tail:* dark brown with pale edges, outermost rectrix pale, especially at the tip; *underparts:* breast and flanks pale to pale buffy ochre, thinly streaked with small dark brown spots; belly and undertail-coverts pale and unmarked; *bill:* brownish, with lower mandible pale flesh; *legs* and *feet:* pale flesh; *iris:* brown.

    First-winter (after Aug–Sept)—Resemble adults, but may be somewhat more buffy below.

    Juveniles (July–Sept)—Crown and nape buffy-ochre, heavily speckled with brown; mantle, back, and scapulars brown, broadly edged with buffy-ochre; breast and flanks more heavily spotted than adults.

Hybrids None reported.

References

Cartwright *et al.* (1937), Dechant *et al.* (1998b), Rising (1996).

32.1 Adult Baird's Sparrow, Lostwood NWR, North Dakota, USA, May 2000. A chunky *Ammodramus* with quite a stout, deep-based bill. Concentrating on the distinctive head markings, note the overall rich buff ground color and the crisp black lines. The lateral crown-stripes, post-ocular wedge, moustachial stripe and malar stripe are black. Note how the creamy submoustachial stripe curves around the rear edge and invades the ear-coverts below the bold post-ocular wedge (Jim Burns/Natural Impacts).

32.2 Adult Baird's Sparrow, Lostwood NWR, North Dakota, USA, May 2000. The ground color of the plumage is buff with bold black streaking on mantle and finer black streaking on lateral crown and nape. Note the whitish outer webs to the outer tail feathers (Jim Burns/Natural Impacts).

32.3 Adult Baird's Sparrow, Lostwood NWR, North Dakota, USA, May 2000. The central crown is bright ochraceous contrasting with finely streaked lateral areas. Note also the crisp black streaking across the buff-tinged breast (Jim Burns/Natural Impacts).

32.4 Adult Baird's Sparrow, Big Bend, Texas, USA, 8 May 1998. The upperparts on this fresh-plumaged bird are buffy-brown thickly streaked black and chestnut with obvious pale buff braces on the mantle (similar to some Savannah Sparrows). The white underparts are boldly streaked black on breast sides and along flanks (Greg W. Lasley).

32.5 Juvenile Baird's Sparrow, Pt. Loma, San Diego Co., California, USA, Oct 1981. Some fall individuals, as here, migrate in largely juvenile plumage. Overall quite similar to adult but note the scaly appearance of the upperparts created by neat buffy fringes to the back feathers. The wing-coverts and tertials are also edged and tipped pale buff (Herbert Clarke).

33 Henslow's Sparrow

(Ammodramus henslowii)

Measurements
Length: 12.1–13.3 cm; 4.8–5.2 in.
   (males slightly larger).
Wing: 49–57 mm; 1.9–2.2 in.
Mass: 11.4–14.8 g (breeding birds in
   Michigan).

Henslow's Sparrows are fairly small, **short-tailed** birds, with thin, dark **stripes** on the breast, and often with a slightly olive-green cast to the face; there is usually a **dark brown spot** on the posterior margin of the ear-coverts. The edges of the coverts, scapulars, and tertials are generally reddish, unlike those of other short-tailed grassland sparrows. They have a **large bill** and appear to be **flat-headed**.

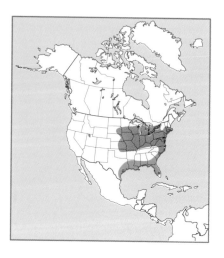

Habitat
They breed in native prairie with tall, dense grass with matted groundcover, and standing dead vegetation; they will also nest in infrequently mowed hayfields, or lightly grazed pastures. They are often found in fields that have not recently been burned, with scattered woody vegetation, but abandon fields as encroachment of woody plants progresses. They may be found in fairly moist fields, but are not restricted to these. Henslow's Sparrows may also nest in the upland portions of saltmarshes. They occur in extensive grasslands covering reclaimed strip mines. In winter, they are found in open prairies or open pine forests. They are most common in meadows in pine woods where broomsedge and wiregrass predominate.

Behavior
Territorial males sing persistently from the ground or from a perch in a bush or tall grass, commonly an exposed place on the top of a weed or in a small tree. They commonly start singing at dawn and may sing through the night. Henslow's Sparrows occasionally make short flights from weed to weed; their flight is low and jerky, and they twist their tails as they fly. Females rarely fly, and often run mouse-like off the nest. In winter, flushed Henslow's Sparrows fly short distances, then drop into the grass and run. Persistently flushed individuals may alight in an exposed place. Migrants are reluctant to flush, and may be approached closely.

Voice
The song is an unobtrusive but distinctive insect-like, short *tsi-lick*, or *flee-sic*. The song carries surprisingly far, perhaps up to 100 m on a calm day. Rarely, a longer

flight-song, *sis-r-r-rit-srit-srit*, is given. The call note is a *tsip*. The species is apparently silent in winter, but the males are singing when they arrive on their breeding grounds. They commonly sing at night.

Similar species

Henslow's Sparrow most closely resembles Baird's, Grasshopper, Le Conte's and Savannah sparrows. **Baird's Sparrow** is larger, has a rich yellow-ochre median crown-stripe, supercilium, and ear-coverts, and a scaly-looking back. Adult **Grasshopper Sparrow** lack breast streaks (these can be faint on Henslow's), has distinct crown-stripes, rusty stripes on the nape, and is paler in general appearance. The streaking on the undersides of **Le Conte's Sparrow** is restricted to the flanks, and Le Conte's has a dark lateral crown-stripe and eyeline stripe, accentuated by a bright yellow-ochre supercilium, a pale median crown-stripe, and a rusty, streaked nape; Le Conte's Sparrows appear paler and much more yellow than Henslow's Sparrows. **Savannah Sparrows** are larger, have a longer, notched tail, and a yellow supercilium, and a stronger, more direct flight.

Geographic variation

Two subspecies are generally recognized: *A. h. henslowii*, which breeds east to central West Virginia, and *A. h. susurrans* breeds (or bred – perhaps is extinct) from New England south to eastern North Carolina. The latter has, on average a slightly larger bill, and is said to be slightly darker in color, but differences are slight, and many do not recognize this subspecies. The population that bred in Houston, Texas was named *A. h. houstonensis*, but this race has generally been rejected, and that population has been extirpated.

Distribution

Breeds from e South Dakota (casual or extirpated), se Nebraska (local), w and se Minnesota (rare), central Wisconsin, central Michigan, s Ontario (rare), s Quebec (rare), New York (local), n and w Pennsylvania, central Vermont (declining), and se New Hampshire (no recent records), and Massachusetts (no recent records) south through e Kansas (increasing), ne Oklahoma (increasing), formerly to e Texas, e North Dakota, Iowa (expanding), central and w Missouri, s Illinois (expanding), Indiana (rare and local), central and w Kentucky, West Virginia (declining), Delaware (extirpated), Maryland (rare and local), Virginia (rare and declining), e North Carolina, and nw South Carolina.

Winters from coastal ne North Carolina, coastal South Carolina, central Georgia, central Alabama, south to central Florida, the Gulf Coast, and s Texas; in mild winters, found north to e-central Kansas. Most common in winter along the Atlantic Coast, from North Carolina to northern Florida, and along the Gulf Coast from western Florida to Corpus Christi, Texas.

Migrates east of the central plains; rare in the east. Spring migration begins in mid-Mar to early Apr; by mid-May they have reached the northern limit of their range. Fall migration begins my mid-Sept and continues into Dec.

Conservation status

Historically, clearing of the eastern forests created new habitat for Henslow's Sparrows as formerly forested areas were converted to grasslands and old-fields, and allowed them to extend their range in the east and northeast. Along the southeastern coast, the clearing of pocosins (wetlands dominated by evergreen shrubs) to plant pines has created some good habitat for them, at least in the early stages of succession, and the species may have increased in North Carolina since 1980. On the other hand, the conversion of tallgrass prairies to cropland and pastures destroyed much of their habitat in the plains. Today, as a consequence of habitat loss, their numbers have declined sharply throughout the east, and they apparently have virtually been extirpated in New England and along the coast north of North Carolina. They are now extremely uncommon in southern Ontario and Quebec. On the other hand, they readily colonize and breed in large patches of native prairie and reclaimed prairie; nesting may occur in small patches of good habitat, but these populations may not be large enough to sustain themselves. Burning grasslands every second or third year slows the incursion of woody plants, but allows for the necessary accumulation of dense groundcover; lightly grazed areas may be preferred to burnt ones. Although individual territories are small, they seem to prefer large grassland areas. As a consequence of habitat preservation and restoration of prairie habitats, the species appears to be increasing in southwestern Missouri, eastern Kansas, Iowa, Illinois, and western Pennsylvania, and has become established as a locally common nesting species in northeastern Oklahoma where historically they apparently did not breed.

Molt

Hatch year birds undergo a partial to complete Prebasic molt from July–Oct; a limited presupplemental molt of at least some back and scapular feathers may occur late Sept–Oct. Older birds complete Prebasic molt from July–Sept. A partial Prealternate molt occurs Feb–Apr.

Description

Adults—Fairly small; sexes similar. *Head:* lateral crown-stripes dark brown and streaked with buffy olive; median crown-stripe buffy olive; supercilium broad and buffy olive; lores and ear-coverts buffy olive; posterior margin of ear-coverts dark brown; side of neck buffy olive, sometimes with a greenish hue; eye, moustachial and malar stripes dark brown, and fairly thin; *back:* nape buffy olive, streaked with dark brown; mantle feathers dark brown, edged with buff; *rump:* buffy olive, feathers with dark brown centers; *tail:* middle rectrices dark brown with broad rusty-brown edges; lateral rectrices brown, with darker centers; rectrices pointed; *wing:* brown, with scapulars, tertials, and sometimes secondaries edged with rust; bend of wing yellow; *underparts:* throat pale buff and unstreaked; breast and flanks darker buff than throat and with thin, dark brown streaks; belly whitish buff; undertail-coverts buffy; *bill:* upper mandible brownish, or grayish, with paler tomium; lower mandible paler to flesh-colored; *legs* and *feet:* flesh-colored; *iris:* dark brown.

First fall and winter (after Sept)—Resemble adults, but are perhaps somewhat buffier on the head, breast, and flanks.

Juveniles (June through Sept)—Similar to adults, but buffier, and lacking moustachial and malar stripes, and with little or no streaking on the breast and flanks.

Hybrids

None reported.

References

Cully and Michaels (2000), Herkert (1998), Hyde (1939), Pruitt (1996), Rising (1996), Schulenberg *et al.* (1994), Sutton (1935), Walk *et al.* (2000), Zimmerman (1988).

33.1 Adult Henslow's Sparrow *A. h. henslowii*, Prairie State Park, Missouri, USA, May 1994. Typical chunky *Ammodramus* with a large, deep-based bill and flat-crowned profile. The combination of greenish-tinged head and extensively rufous wings are unique in the genus. The underparts are white with crisp black streaking across upper breast and along flanks (Rick and Nora Bowers).

33.2 Adult Henslow's Sparrow *A. h. henslowii*, Prairie State Park, Missouri, USA, May 1994. The back is boldly streaked with black and chestnut with whitish braces. The wing-coverts are extensively dull rufous with black blob-like centers which appear as a row of spots on the closed wing. Note the short, spike-tipped tail characteristic of the genus (Rick and Nora Bowers).

33.3 Adult Henslow's Sparrow *A. h. henslowii*, Prairie State Park, Missouri, USA, May 1994. Concentrating on the head pattern, notice the greenish tinge to the sides of the face. The blackish markings are not dissimilar to those of Baird's Sparrow although the lateral crown-stripes are more solid black and the creamy submoustachial stripe fades into the greenish neck sides thus isolating the buff spot in the upper rear corner of the ear-coverts (Rick and Nora Bowers).

33.4 Henslow's Sparrow, Brazoria NWR, Texas, USA, 16 Dec 1991. This bird is in fresh plumage, and the back feathers have neat pale buff fringes, creating a distinct scaly appearance. The green tint on the head and neck is somewhat variable, but is quite strong on this bird (Greg W. Lasley).

33.5 Henslow's Sparrow, Brazoria NWR, Texas, USA, 16 Dec 1991. Another view of a fresh-plumaged winter bird. The scaly-looking back is nicely depicted here. Note the prominence of the narrow whitish eye-ring against the greenish face (Greg W. Lasley).

34 **Le Conte's Sparrow**

(Ammodramus leconteii)

Measurements

Length: 10.5–12.5 cm; 4.1–4.9 in.
  (males slightly larger).
Wing: 49–54 mm; 1.9–2.1 in.
Mass: Av.=13.8 g (12.0–16.3 g) (northern
  Ontario).

Le Conte's is a very **small, sharp-tailed** sparrow, with a bright **ochre supercilium**, pale whitish median crown-stripe, broad, dark lateral crown-stripes, and **purplish-chestnut streaks on the nape.** The eye-stripe is dark brown, and becomes broader toward the neck, making it wedge-shaped. The **breast is usually ochre, unstreaked in adults**; the **flanks are ochre, distinctly streaked with dark brown.** Although territorial males may be conspicuous, migrating and wintering birds can be difficult to see as they often flush, fly a short distance, and drop into the grass, and run.

Habitat

Le Conte's Sparrow nests in wet freshwater grasslands, sometimes mixed with cattail, phragmites, and sourdock, or in sedge marshes, often interspersed with small alders, birches, and sweet gale; they also breed in large undisturbed pastures. In migration and in winter they are found in rank, tall grasses, damp weedy fields, stands of broomsedge, panicum, cattails or occasionally in overgrown shortgrass prairie.

Behavior

Territorial males often sing from near the top of a piece of grass. Otherwise, they can be difficult to see. When flushed, Le Conte's Sparrows usually fly a short distance in a light, jerky flight close to the grass, then drop into the vegetation out of sight. Occasionally, they will flush to a bush where they can be seen. In winter they are solitary.

Voice

The song of Le Conte's Sparrow is short (ca. 1 s), and insect-like: *reese-reese, z-z-z-buzz,* or *tzeek-tzzz tick*, sounding like the song began and ended with a click of a switch. In the breeding season, they often sing after dark, and occasionally while hovering. The flight-song is usually introduced by several *chips*, followed by an upslurred note, which is followed by a longer down-slurred one. The call note is a sharp *chip* or *tsip*, or a thin *ssisst*. They call infrequently in migration or winter.

Similar species

In size and behavior Le Conte's Sparrow most closely resembles **Henslow's Sparrow**, which, however, is darker (olive to greenish-olive), has a streaked breast, and a reddish cast to the wings. Le Conte's has a smaller bill, and does not appear to have a large, flat head, as Henslow's Sparrow does. The **Grasshopper Sparrow** is larger, and has a larger bill, and although the head patterning is similar, it does not show as much contrast as Le Conte's; the nape is not so rusty as in Le Conte's, and the flanks are unstreaked – or at most sparsely streaked (an important mark). **Baird's Sparrow** is larger, has distinct moustachial and malar stripes and breast streaking, and lacks the chestnut nape. **Nelson's Sharp-tailed Sparrows**, which often breed in the same marshes, are slightly larger, have a grayish median crown-stripe and side of neck, dark, white-streaked back, and little streaking on the flanks.

Geographic variation

None described.

Distribution

Breeds from e-central British Columbia, sw and s-central Mackenzie, Alberta, nw Montana, extreme ne Montana, central Saskatchewan, nw and central Manitoba, Ontario, and Quebec south through North Dakota to ne South Dakota, central Minnesota, central Wisconsin, n Michigan, and (formerly?) s Ontario.

    Winters from s Kansas, s Missouri, Illinois, and s Indiana, and along the Atlantic Coast from Virginia south to s Texas, Coahuila, the Gulf Coast, and n Florida; in mild winters occurs north to n Kansas, n Missouri, and central Indiana.

    Migrates throughout the east. Spring migration takes place in Apr and May; fall migration is in Aug through early Nov. In Kansas, most of the migration occurs in Apr and Oct. There is a late May record for northern California.

Conservation status

Destruction of suitable breeding habitat in the southern part of their range has depleted populations but they are still locally common in the northern prairies, and in the James Bay Lowlands. Le Conte's Sparrows use grazed areas in Minnesota and Wisconsin so long as adequate litter is present. Periodic burning, grazing, or mowing may be needed to maintain good breeding habitat in some areas.

Molt

The Prebasic I molt is partial and may occur on the breeding or wintering grounds; it involves median and greater-coverts, some tertials and occasionally some secondaries, but no rectrices. The Prealternate I molt, which occurs in Mar to May involves some greater-coverts and tertials, and occasionally some central rectrices. The Definitive Basic molt is complete and occurs primarily on the breeding grounds. The Definitive Prealternate molt is like the Prealternate I molt in extent and timing.

Description

Adults—Small and short-tailed; sexes alike. *Head:* median crown-stripe whitish, bordered by two dark brown or blackish lateral crown-stripes; supercilium broad and bright yellow ochre; lores ochre; eye-stripe blackish and wedge-shaped, being narrow at the eye, and broad toward the neck; ear-coverts grayish-ochre, thinly edged with brown; submoustachial stripe ochre; throat white; *back:* nape feathers rusty or chestnut, edged with ochre; mantle feathers dark brown or blackish, edged with pale buff, giving a scaly appearance; ***rump:*** blackish with light edges to feathers; ***tail:*** feathers narrow and pointed, and dark brown with broad beige edges; ***wing:*** brown, with coverts and tertials edged in light buff; ***underparts:*** throat white and unmarked; breast and flanks ochre with distinct, short black streaks on the flanks; belly white; undertail-coverts pale beige with dark centers; ***bill:*** upper mandible yellowish horn color; lower mandible paler; ***legs*** and ***feet:*** dull flesh color; ***iris:*** brown.

First-fall (after Aug–Sept)—Similar to adults.

Juveniles (June–Sept)—Resemble adults, but have a streaked breast, and less ochre, especially in the supercilium and breast, and have reduced or no chestnut in the nape.

Hybrids
A hybrid Le Conte's Sparrow X Nelson's Sharp-tailed Sparrow has been described.

References
Dechant *et al.* (1998e), Murray (1969), Pyle and Sibley (1992), Rising (1996).

34.1 Adult Le Conte's Sparrow, Churchill, Manitoba, Canada, June 1996. Typical spiky-tailed *Ammodramus* structure, but with a relatively slight bill and rounded head shape. Note the predominantly pale buff ground color to the head and body with clean black head stripes and streaking on mantle (Mike McEvoy).

34.2 Adult Le Conte's Sparrow, Lostwood NWR, North Dakota, USA, May 2000. Concentrating on the head pattern, note the rich buff supercilium (paler on the lores) which contrasts with the black lateral crown-stripes and flaring post-ocular stripe. The ear-coverts are pale gray and contrast with the deep buff submoustachial stripe which curves around the rear edge. The central crown-stripe, eye-ring and throat are whitish (Jim Burns/Natural Impacts).

34.3 Le Conte's Sparrow, Cape May, New Jersey, USA, Oct 1997. On this fresh-plumaged fall bird notice the broad pale buff edges to the back feathers and tertials giving a very streaky effect. The rich buff tones on the head are offset by the pale gray collar which is finely streaked with chestnut (similar to Grasshopper Sparrow). The pale underparts are suffused with buff on the breast and flanks with bold black and chestnut streaking on breast sides and flanks (Kevin T. Karlson).

34.4 Adult Le Conte's Sparrow, Thunder Cape, Ontario, Canada, Oct 1991. This fresh-plumaged adult (aged by skull ossification) shows the streaky upperpart pattern well. Note the grayish-brown flight feathers lacking any rufous tones and the notched black centers to the tertials and scapulars unique to this species (David D. Beadle).

34.5 Juvenile Le Conte's Sparrow, southeast Farallon Island, California, USA, Oct 1989. Many fall birds (as here) migrate in largely juvenal plumage. Overall more buffy than adult lacking gray collar and without chestnut suffusion within the black centers to the mantle feathers. The supercilium and malar area are lightly streaked and the breast displays more extensive, although narrower, streaking than on an adult (David D. Beadle).

34.6 Juvenile Le Conte's Sparrow, southeast Farallon Island, California, USA, Oct 1989. Another view of the same bird. Note the streaky buff and black appearance of this plumage. The central crown-stripe is buff contrasting with the mottled black lateral stripes. The short, spiky tail is characteristic of the genus (David D. Beadle).

35 Saltmarsh Sharp-tailed Sparrow

(Ammodramus caudacutus)

Measurements

Length: 11.5–13.0 cm; 4.5–5.1 in.
(males slightly larger).
Wing: 53–65 mm; 2.1–2.6 in.
Mass: 16.6–22.6 g (breeding birds).

The facial pattern of the Saltmarsh Sharp-tailed Sparrow is striking, and a bold **yellow-ochre supercilium, submoustachial stripe, and the posterior margin of the ear-coverts forming a triangle around the gray ear-coverts and lores**; this dark malar stripe separates the pale or whitish throat from the yellow-ochre submoustachial stripe. They are **streaked on both the back and breast**, have brown lateral crown-stripes, a gray median crown-stripe and side of neck, ochre breast, and **short, pointed tail feathers**.

Habitat

Saltmarsh Sharp-tailed Sparrows are found in coastal saltmarshes or wet meadows, where there is dense cordgrass, blackgrass, or saltmeadow grass, or along ditch margins or pool edges; they are usually found in tidal areas. Their winter status is unclear, but most probably winter along the coast in similar habitats.

Behavior

Males sing persistently from mid-May through early Aug, especially in the morning. When feeding, sharp-tailed sparrows walk or run, or hop slowly. When alarmed, they may climb to the top of vegetation; flight is direct and fairly rapid, and slightly undulating. Flying birds often drop into the vegetation, and on the ground they may run. They are not territorial, although males may supplant each other, and they often appear to be loosely territorial. In migration and winter, they are found in small, loose flocks, but usually are not in flocks of mixed species composition.

Voice

Males sing a continuous complex 'whisper song' that has a whispery, wheezy quality, and may last for over 1 min, a *ts-ts-sssss-tsik* or *tsi-lik tssss-s-s-s-s-s*; it contains phrases like the primary song of Nelson's Sharp-tailed Sparrow, abbreviated trills, and short accented syllables. Songs may be delivered from hidden or exposed perches, and may continue in horizontal flights. Calls are given by both sexes; females give a soft, toneless *chic* call, and a repeated series of *tsick, chuck*, or *chip* notes. A series of high-pitched *tic* calls is given by both sexes.

Similar species

Nelson's Sharp-tailed Sparrows lack conspicuous breast streaking, with the back more strikingly streaked, supercilium bright ochre, but ear-coverts, submoustachial, and post-auricular stripes more diffuse; they have a buffy throat, contrasting little in color with the submoustachial stripe. 'Acadian' (Nelson's) sparrows are duller and grayer in color, with back and breast not conspicuously streaked; yellowish supercilium dull. The **Seaside Sparrow** is larger, generally darker, with more extensive ventral streaking, and lacks the striking facial pattern. See **Le Conte's Sparrow**.

Geographic variation

Two subspecies have been named, *A. c. caudacutus*, and *A. c. diversus*. Variation is clinal, and these two do not seem to be separable.

Distribution

Breeds along the coast from s Maine south to the Delmarva Peninsula.

Winters in coastal marshes from Massachusetts (rare) and New York south to Florida, and reportedly along the eastern Gulf coast of Florida; they are uncommon in Levy Co., and rare west of there.

Migrates probably along the Atlantic Coast, although there is an inland record from Pennsylvania.

Conservation status

Saltmarsh Sharp-tailed Sparrows are dependent on coastal saltmarshes in all seasons, and the widespread destruction of these accounts for their decline in numbers.

Molt

The Prebasic I molt occurs late July to late Oct, and involves all of the body feathers (except for the greater primary-coverts) and sometimes some to all of the secondaries. There is an incomplete Prealternate molt in Mar to Apr that includes the inner greater-coverts, some tertials and occasionally the 6th secondary, and all of the rectrices; the Prealternate I and Definitive Prealternate molts are alike in extent and timing. The Definitive Basic molt is complete and occurs on the breeding grounds.

Description

Adults—Fairly small; sexes similar. *Head:* median crown-stripe gray; lateral crown-stripes, supercilium, submoustachial, and post-auricular stripes orange-buffy to yellow-orange, with the post-auricular stripe separated from the supercilium by a narrow, but distinct brown eye-stripe; malar stripe brown; edge of post-auricular narrowly edged with brown; nape grayish-brown; *back:* mantle and scapular feathers dark brown, narrowly edged in buffy white; *rump:* dark brown, with centers of feathers darker; *tail:* brown, unpatterned, with lateral feathers shorter than middle ones, and feathers narrow and pointed; *wing:* brown, coverts with dark centers, but no wing-bars, bend of wing edged with pale yellow; *underparts:* chin and throat pale yellow; breast and flanks dull whitish-yellow, distinctly marked with thin brown streaks; belly whitish; *bill:* upper mandible dusky; lower bluish-gray, paler toward base; *legs* and *feet:* pinkish-buff to dusky; *iris:* brown.

First-winter (Aug–Oct)—Resemble adults, but are more heavily streaked below; they retain some juvenal wing feathers through Mar.

Juveniles (July–Sept)—Have a blackish crown, sometimes streaked with light brownish, with a narrow median crown-stripe; the mantle and scapular feathers are dark brown, broadly edged with buff, producing streaks; the underparts are buffy, narrowly streaked on the breast and flanks; the belly is nearly white.

Hybrids Hybridizes regularly with Nelson's Sharp-tailed Sparrow in northern Massachusetts and southern Maine.

References Greenlaw and Rising (1994), Post (1998), Pyle (1997).

35.1 Saltmarsh Sharp-tailed Sparrow, Brigantine, New Jersey, USA, Sept 1999. Another typical, spiky-tailed *Ammodramus* with a relatively long and pointed bill. This fresh-plumaged fall bird shows the rich buff, gray and rufous plumage tones well. The whitish underparts show extensive streaking across breast and along the flanks (Larry Sansone).

35.2 Saltmarsh Sharp-tailed Sparrow, Brigantine, New Jersey, USA, Sept 1999. The underparts are white with a buff wash on the streaked breast and flanks. The crown is dark brown, streaked with black and with a narrow gray central stripe (Larry Sansone).

35.3 Saltmarsh Sharp-tailed Sparrow, Brigantine, New Jersey, USA, Sept 1999. Concentrating on the head pattern note the rich buff supercilium and submoustachial stripe contrasting with the slaty-gray ear-coverts. The brown lateral crown-stripes blend into the gray nape and neck sides. The back is mostly gray with blurry pale braces and contrasts with the largely dull chestnut wings (Larry Sansone).

35.4 Adult Saltmarsh Sharp-tailed Sparrow A. c. caudacutus, Long Island, New York, USA, July 2000. By mid-summer many adults, as here, show heavily worn and abraded plumage. Note the rather plain upperparts (whitish braces much reduced) and reduced blackish streaking on breast and flanks (Michael D. Stubblefield).

35.5 Juvenile Saltmarsh Sharp-tailed Sparrow *A. c. caudacutus*, Brigantine, New Jersey, USA, Aug 1988. Overall more buffy than adult with blurry, less distinct streaking on the breast and along flanks. The head pattern is subdued with some dusky streaking within the supercilium and on the neck sides (Kevin T. Karlson).

35.6 Juvenile Saltmarsh Sharp-tailed Sparrow *A. c. caudacutus*, near Port Mahon, Delaware, USA, 7 Aug 1993. Sharp-tails typically cock their tail, as this bird has, when walking on mud (Mike Danzenbaker).

36 Nelson's Sharp-tailed Sparrow

(Ammodramus nelsoni)

Measurements
Length: 11.0–13.0 cm; 4.3–5.1 in.
   (males slightly larger).
Wing: 52–65 mm; 2.0–2.6 in.
Mass: 13.7–16.6 g (prairies; males);
   15.5–20.0 g (maritimes; males).

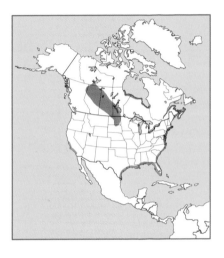

Nelson's Sharp-tailed Sparrow is a fairly small sparrow, with a **short, 'sharp' tail**. They have a **broad ochre supercilium, moustachial stripe, and edge to the ear-coverts**, that forms a triangle around the gray ear-coverts. The back is usually **conspicuously streaked with grayish or buffy white**; the yellowish-ochre breast is unstreaked (or faintly streaked). Maritime populations ('Acadian' sharp-tails) are much grayer in general appearance than those from the James Bay lowlands and prairies, and have indistinct stripes on the back, and faint gray streaks on the breast and flanks.

Habitat
In the prairies, Nelson's Sharp-tailed Sparrows breed in freshwater marshes where cordgrass, squirreltail, whitetop, and phragmites are common, in idle fields, and planted clover. Along the shore of James and Hudson bays, they are found in dense sedge bogs, generally with a few dwarf birch, willows, and sweet gale, and usually above the high tide line. Along the coast of the St. Lawrence River, they are found in freshwater marshes and bulrushes, cattail, and grasses. In the Maritime Provinces, they breed in rank grassland, saltmarshes, and in wet grasslands inland along the major rivers in freshwater habitats, and occasionally at the edge of fields and dunes adjacent to saltmarshes. In migration they may occur in wet fields and marshes (often cattail). In winter, they are found along the coast, in both freshwater and saltmarsh habitats, but principally in salt and brackish marshes.

Behavior
Males sing persistently after arrival on breeding grounds in early June, giving songs from perches, the ground, or in a complex aerial display; they commonly sing at night. In migration and winter, Nelson's Sharp-tailed Sparrows are found in small, loose feeding groups, and are not usually found in mixed flocks.

Voice

The song is variously described as a hissing buzz or a choking pop – like the sound of drops of water falling on a hot skillet, a *pschee-zipt* or *pshhh'pt* that lasts about 1 s. Only males sing, and tend to sing in song bouts that may last up to 30 min. They often sing from a conspicuous perch, and may fly from perch to perch while singing; however, they may sing from the ground. They also have an elaborate flight-song: they take flight, give a series of *tic* notes, fly up to 20 m, sing, then glide, then sing again, then drop to the vegetation, perhaps 100 m from where they started. This song can be given as *ticticticticticticticti taktektektek pshhh'ipt*. They often sing at night. Calls are like those of the Saltmarsh Sharp-tailed Sparrow.

Similar species

See **Saltmarsh Sharp-tailed Sparrow** and **Le Conte's Sparrow**.

Geographic variation

Three subspecies are recognized, *A. n. nelsoni*, which breeds in the prairies, *A. n. alterus*, which breeds in the James Bay lowlands, and *A. n. subvirgatus*. *A. n. nelsoni* and *A. n. alterus* are indistinguishable in the field and in the hand, although the latter average somewhat buffier, and have a grayer median crown-stripe. Differences between *A. n. subvirgatus* and the others are discussed in the descriptions of the plumages.

Distribution

Breeds locally in marshes from s Mackenzie, n Alberta, e-central British Columbia, south through sw Alberta, extreme ne Montana, central Saskatchewan, sw Manitoba, and se North Dakota, se South Dakota, n Minnesota, Wisconsin (Crex Meadows), w Ontario, and formerly south to ne Illinois; also around James and Hudson bays from Eastmain, Quebec to Churchill, Manitoba; also along the lower St. Lawrence estuary, locally on the North Shore, and on the South Shore from Montmagny to Point-au-Père, on the Gaspé Peninsula from Baie de Gaspé to the head of Chaleur Bay, and the Magdalen Is., Prince Edward I., New Brunswick, Nova Scotia, Maine (south to Sagadahoc Co.) and rarely to ne Massachusetts (Essex Co.).

Winters principally along the coast from Massachusetts, south to Florida, and along the Gulf Coast to s Texas and ne Tamaulipas; also regularly (but uncommonly) along the Pacific Coast from San Francisco to Newport Bay, California, and rarely to nw Baja California. Most of the James Bay and maritime birds apparently winter on the south Atlantic coast whereas most of the prairie birds winter on the Gulf coast.

Migrates through the interior and along the coast. Fall migration takes place Sept through Oct, with a peak in Kansas in mid-Oct; spring migration is late, May to early June.

Conservation status

Like other coastal birds, this species has experienced habitat destruction by draining of marshes. In the prairies, its numbers and range have been reduced by the draining of prairie marshes, although it is still locally common where suitable habitat occurs. It prefers areas with dense nesting cover.

Molt

The Prebasic I molt is incomplete, and includes coverts, some tertials, but no rectrices; it occurs on the breeding grounds. There is a partial Prealternate I molt that takes place primarily on the wintering grounds, but can be completed on the breeding grounds. The

Definitive Basic molt is complete, and takes place Aug to Oct. The extent and timing of the Definitive Prealternate molt is like the Prealternate I molt in extent and timing.

Description
(Prairie and James Bay populations): Adults—Fairly small and short-tailed; sexes alike. *Head:* with broad, but not sharply defined median crown-stripe, outlined by brown lateral crown-stipes; yellow-ochre supercilium and supraloral spot; brown eye-stripe; gray ear-coverts; yellowish-gray nape and post-auricular stripe; *back:* dark brown, usually with distinct grayish or buffy white stripes; *rump:* brown and unstreaked; *tail:* brown, unpatterned, with lateral feathers shorter than middle ones, and the feathers narrow and pointed; *wing:* brown to chestnut-brown; coverts with dark centers, but no wing-bars; bend of wing (alula) edged with pale yellow; *underparts:* chin and throat pale yellow; breast and flanks light yellow-ochre, with faint brown streaks on the side of the throat and flanks; belly whitish; *bill:* horn colored, with lower mandible paler than upper; *legs* and *feet:* pinkish-buff to dusky; *iris:* brown.
(Maritime populations): Adults—As above, but somewhat larger and larger billed, lores pale or yellowish, slightly contrasting with supercilium; crown and nape gray-ish; side of throat and flanks gray streaked, and back grayish brown without stripes.

First-fall and winter (Aug–Oct)—Resemble adults, but are buffier, and may retain some juvenal wing feathers through Mar.

Juveniles (July–Sept)—Crown blackish, with broad orange-buff (prairies) or olive-buff (maritimes) median stripe, and broad supercilium; nape chestnut (prairies) or rust-buff (maritimes); mantle and scapular feathers dark brown, broadly edged with buff, producing streaks; rump and uppertail-coverts slightly streaked (maritimes) or unstreaked; underparts variously streaked, males more so than females.

Hybrids
A hybrid Nelson's Sharp-tailed X Le Conte's sparrow has been reported. The species hybridizes regularly with Saltmarsh Sharp-tailed Sparrows in northern Massachusetts and southern Maine.

References Dechant *et al.* (1999c), Greenlaw (1993), Greenlaw and Rising (1994), Post (1998), Rising (1996).

36.1 Adult Nelson's Sharp-tailed Sparrow *A. n. nelsoni*, Lostwood NWR, North Dakota, USA, May 2000. Smaller-billed than Saltmarsh Sharp-tailed Sparrow with more rounded crown profile. Notice the sharp demarcation between the buffy breast and the white belly (Jim Burns/Natural Impacts).

36.2 Adult Nelson's Sharp-tailed Sparrow *A. n. nelsoni*, Lostwood NWR, North Dakota, USA, May 2000. Another view of the same bird (figure 36.1). Note the clean-cut, bright head pattern with contrasting gray ear-coverts. The flanks are densely streaked with brown and the crisply marked mantle shows well defined whitish braces (Jim Burns/Natural Impacts).

36.3 Nelson's Sharp-tailed Sparrow, Ventura Co., California, USA, Oct 1994. This fresh individual, probably *A. n. nelsoni*, shows distinct dusky streaking on the breast-sides and, especially, along the flanks. The head pattern is particularly striking with more contrast between the gray ear-coverts and the orange surrounding them than on the other two forms (Brian E. Small).

36.4 Nelson's Sharp-tailed Sparrow, Ventura Co., California, USA, Oct 1994. Another view of a probable *A. n. nelsoni*. The buffy breast-band contrasts with the paler throat and is sharply demarcated from the white belly. The distinct dusky streaking is heavier on the sides of the breast and flanks. First-winter birds and non-breeding adults are presumably duller, as here, than fresh spring individuals (Larry Sansone).

36.5 Adult Nelson's Sharp-tailed Sparrow, Anahuac NWR, Texas, USA, May 1997. This early spring individual shows rather indistinct, blurry streaking across the breast and is probably of the form *alturus*. Note also the somewhat dull head pattern compared with fresh *A. n. nelsoni* in Figs. 36.1 & 36.2 (Brian E. Small).

36.6 Nelson's Sharp-tailed Sparrow, Tuckerton, New Jersey, USA, Oct 1994. This fresh-plumaged fall individual (either *alturus* or *subvirgatus*) shows the indistinct breast streaking and dull head pattern typical of these forms (Mike Danzenbaker).

37 Seaside Sparrow

(Ammodramus maritimus)

Measurements
Length: 12.5–15.0 cm; 4.9–6.0 in.
(males slightly larger).
Wing: 54–65 cm; 2.1–2.6 in. (varies geographically).
Mass: 19.8–27.4 g.

The Seaside Sparrow is a geographically variable bird. It is **olive-gray** (especially along the Atlantic Coast) to **olive-brown** (Gulf Coast) in hue, and has a long bill, and a relatively short, sharp tail. The **back and breast are streaked**, but not always conspicuously; the facial pattern is distinctive: the **supraloral spot and supercilium are yellow** from above the eye to the bill, and the submoustachial stripe is pale; the malar stripe is dark, and the throat pale.

Habitat
In the north, Seaside Sparrows are invariably found in or at the edge of saltmarshes, and they nest in vegetation consisting chiefly of cordgrass, black grass, cattail, and marsh-elder. They often occupy the wettest, muddiest parts of marshes. In s Florida, 'Cape Sable' Seaside Sparrows breed in freshwater habitats, especially in sparse saw grass or *Muhlenbergia* grass prairies, in which they are commonest three years after a fire, and in cordgrass prairies; they avoid brushy prairie.

Behavior
When singing, males may perch conspicuously near the top of grass or a bush. When approached, Seaside Sparrows either descend into the grass or fly a short distance and drop into the vegetation. Their flight is low and direct. On the ground they often run.

Voice
The song is a buzzy *spitsh-sheer, tup tup zee reeeeee* (with the third syllable emphasized), *cut cut zhe-eeeeeee, chur-er eee, whi eegle eedle zhurr*, or *oka-che weeee* (sounds like a faint Red-winged Blackbird). The song generally lasts 1–2 s, and is extremely variable. An individual may sing one song repeatedly, then switch to another. During the height of the breeding season, males may give a flight song of 3–4 s duration. The song of the extinct Dusky Seaside Sparrow was distinctive, and more insect-like than most of the songs of the other Seaside Sparrows. The song of the Cape Sable Seaside Sparrow is also distinctive, and again very insect-like. Seaside Sparrows have a *chip-chip chip-chip* alarm note, as well as *tuck*, *chrit*, and *tsip* notes that are given during aggressive interactions.

Similar species

The **sharp-tailed sparrows** are conspicuously smaller; they often occur in the same marshes. Seaside Sparrows appear dark and dingy, whereas sharp-tails are paler, yellowish-ochre, with ochre or orangeish-ochre in their faces. Juvenile Saltmarsh Sharp-tailed Sparrows are yellowish in hue, with the edges of the ear-coverts, supercilium, supraloral spot, and breast yellow-ochre, and a distinctive wedge-shaped eye-stripe.

Geographic variation

Nine subspecies are generally recognized. Of these, two have at times been recognized as distinct species, the Dusky Seaside Sparrow (*A. m. nigrescens*), which is now extinct, and the Cape Sable Seaside Sparrow (*A. m. mirabilis*). Neither of these are known to have ever overlapped any of the other Seaside Sparrows in breeding range, and both are (or were) phenotypically distinct.

A. m. maritimus, which breeds from Massachusetts south to the Delmarva Peninsula, is grayish-olive above and grayish-white below, with indistinct grayish streaking. *A. m. macgillivraii*, which breeds from North Carolina south to the mouth of the St. John's River, is like *A. m. maritimus*, but darker on average, with perhaps more streaking. *A. m. pelonota*, which is very like *A. m. macgillivraii*, was resident from the St. John's River south to New Smyrna, in ne Florida, but is now extinct. *A. m. nigrescens*, once resident in the marshes in n Brevard and e Orange counties, had very dark dorsal striping, was white below, without any buffy wash, and had sharply defined black stripes. *A. m. mirabilis*, the only Seaside Sparrow breeding in s Florida, is pale whitish below, without any buffy wash, and sharply defined dark brown streaking, olive-brown on the back, with dark brown streaks on the crown and usually on the scapulars, and distinct yellow in front of the eye. The Seaside Sparrows breeding on the west coast of Florida have been divided into two subspecies, *A. m. peninsulae* and *A. m. juncicola*, but these are poorly differentiated, and grade into each other. They are dark, ash-brown below with diffuse streaking, and dark on the back, with dark cinnamon-brown centers to feathers. *A. m. fisheri*, which breeds from extreme w Florida west to San Antonio Bay in e Texas, is washed with bright ochre below, with distinct, thin dark brown stripes; the centers of the scapulars and greater-coverts are very dark, edged with pale or rusty in unworn birds. *A. m. sennetti*, which breeds in s Texas, is similar to *A. m. fisheri*, but paler and less ochre below, greenish-gray on the nape and supercilium (behind the eye), somewhat paler on the back, and with a brown-striped gray median crown-stripe.

Distribution

Breeds: from New Hampshire and ne Massachusetts south along the coast to ne Florida, s Florida (Everglades), along the coast of nw Florida, and from w Florida (Pensacola Bay) along the coast to extreme s Texas.

Winters: along the Atlantic Coast, usually south of Delaware, south to s Florida and s Texas.

Migrates: along the coast; in fall and winter wanders north to Maine, New Brunswick, and Nova Scotia.

Conservation status

Although still abundant in suitable habitat, habitat destruction has extirpated many populations, including the 'Dusky' Seaside Sparrow (which probably should be treated as a separate species): their habitat was destroyed by fire and development. In 1935, a hurricane was thought to have extirpated the 'Cape Sable' Seaside Sparrow, but it still occurs in brackish and freshwater marshes in southern Florida (Everglades Park).

Molt

The Basic I plumage is acquired by a partial or complete Prebasic I molt which starts in July (Florida) or Aug (New York), and may be completed as late as Dec, on the wintering grounds. There is no Alternate plumage. The Definitive Basic molt is complete and takes place July to Sept (Florida) or Aug to Oct (New York).

Description

Adults—Medium-sized; sexes alike. *Head:* lateral crown-stripes brown or dark brown; median crown-stripe gray, streaked with brown; supraloral spot and supercilium yellow to bright yellow from above the eye to the bill, and brown or grayish-brown behind the eye where it is usually indistinct; ear-coverts brown, olive-brown, or olive-gray; moustachial stripe sometimes the same color as the ear-coverts, sometimes somewhat darker; submoustachial stripe pale; malar stripe dark brown; throat pale and unspotted; *back:* olive-gray to brownish, with centers of feathers brown to dark brown, giving the back a streaked appearance in unworn individuals; *rump:* brown; uppertail-coverts brown with darker centers; *tail:* brown, sometimes faintly barred, with lateral edges of feathers darker than centers; relatively short, with pointed feathers; *wing:* brown to rusty brown; bend of wing (alula) yellow; greater-coverts and scapulars with dark centers; no conspicuous wing-bars; *underparts:* breast and flanks olive-gray, whitish, or pale ochre, striped with olive-gray, brown, or black; belly grayish to pale buff; undertail-coverts pale with dark centers; *bill:* dark horn-colored, paler below and near the head; *legs* and *feet:* yellowish-brown; *iris:* dark brown.

    First-winter (after Aug)—Resemble adults, but may be somewhat buffier below.

    Juveniles (June–Aug)—Crown and back olive-brown, streaked with dark brown; mantle feathers with pale edges; face patterned as adults, with supercilium and supraloral stripe pale rather than yellow, and post-auricular stripe sometimes pale; breast and flanks with thin brown streaks or without streaking (s coastal Texas).

Hybrids

A hybrid Saltmarsh Sharp-tailed X Seaside sparrow was collected in Connecticut.

References

Post and Greenlaw (1994), Rising, (1996), Quay *et al.* (1983), Walters, (1992), Woolfenden (1956).

37.1 Adult Seaside Sparrow *A. m. maritimus*, Stone Harbor, New Jersey, USA, June 1999. This chunky, spike-billed *Ammodramus* is distinct within its strictly coastal saltmarsh range. This individual is typical of the mid-Atlantic forms in being largely gray on the head and underparts with contrasting brown wings. The head shows a distinct whitish submoustachial stripe and throat patch and a yellow supraloral patch (Kevin T. Karlson).

37.2 Adult Seaside Sparrow *A. m. maritimus*, Port Mahon, Delaware, USA, Aug 1996. Although in partial molt this bird typically shows rather indistinct streaking on the grayish upperparts and relatively uniform-looking grayish underparts (Jim Burns/Natural Impacts).

37.3 Adult Seaside Sparrow *A. m. mirabilis*, Everglades Natonal Park, Florida, USA, May 1995. The olive tones on the head and back, bright yellow supraloral and boldly streaked whitish underparts are characteristic of this scarce, range-restricted subspecies (Stuart Pimm).

37.4 Adult Seaside Sparrow *A. m. fisheri,* Anahuac NWR, Texas, USA, May 1997. Birds from the Gulf coast of Texas are brighter and more densely streaked than Atlantic forms. Notice the bold blackish streaking on the breast of this bird. The upperparts are also crisply streaked blackish and the breast and flanks are tinged buffy-brown (Brian E. Small).

37.5 Adult Seaside Sparrow *A. m. fisheri,* Galveston, Texas, USA, Apr 1994. This individual shows a distinct buffy-orange wash to the submoustachial stripe which curves around the grayish ear-coverts. The mantle and underparts show well defined blackish streaking (Herbert Clark).

37.6 Juvenile Seaside Sparrow *A. m. maritimus,* Port Mahon, Delaware, USA, Aug 1996. Rather more pallid than the adult with buffy upperparts and whitish underparts. The mantle is boldly streaked with black and the breast and flanks show sparse dusky streaking. Note the greater-coverts and tertials are distinctly tipped whitish (Jim Burns/Natural Impacts).

38 **Sooty Fox Sparrow**

(Passerella unalaschensis)

Measurements

Length: 15.5–18.5 cm; 6.2–7.3 in.
(males slightly larger).
Wing: 73–86 mm; 2.9–3.4 in.
Mass: 25.3–42.1 g (wintering birds in California).

Sooty Fox Sparrows are large and very dark brown, with extensive dark brown streaking and spotting on the underparts. They often look rather large-headed and small-billed.

Habitat

Sooty Fox Sparrows are found in dense thickets, most commonly deciduous thickets, often along creeks or at the edge of bogs or ponds. In winter, in California, they are found in chaparral, often fairly dry chaparral, but especially in dense arborescent chaparral, or dense understory of oak woodlands. In s British Columbia, they like dense understory, often Himalayan blackberry.

Behavior

Territorial males sing from an exposed twig high in a bush, the top of a tree, or an exposed dead branch. When not singing, they are difficult to see. Sooty Fox Sparrows seldom fly long distances, but flit from bush to bush with a slow, jerky flight, often flicking their tail. They forage on the ground. In winter, they are found singly or in small groups, although they do not tend to form flocks. They respond vigorously to 'spishing'.

Voice

The song is a loud series of rather staccato notes rising and falling on different pitches, *she she shu tu-you tu-you*; many of the notes are slurred or buzzy. The common call is a loud *tik* or *thik*, or a sharp *zitt*; it is similar to, but perhaps lower in pitch and louder than the note of the Slate-colored Fox Sparrow.

Similar species

Other **fox sparrows** are similar in size, but are not so dark. Sooty Fox Sparrows have little if any gray in their plumage, although some may have gray on their face and upper back. Although variable, none show conspicuous rustiness, although the undertail-coverts, tertials, and coverts may be dark rusty brown. The side of the face is nearly uniformly brown in the lores and submoustachial area. The evenly dark-colored head allows the pale eye crescents (one above and one below the eye) to be quite noticeable.

Geographic variation

Several subspecies are named; they differ clinally in size and coloration, and are not clearly defined. *A. u. unalaschensis* breeds in the eastern Aleutians, Shumagin, and Semidi islands, and the Alaska Peninsula; they are relatively larger, larger billed, and lighter brown, with less ventral spotting than those from the Yakutat Bay south. *P. u. annectens* breeds in Yakutat Bay, Alaska, is smaller in size and bill size, the crown and back are medium brown, and the undersides are moderately heavily spotted. *P. u. ridgwayi*, which breeds on Kodiak I., is medium-sized and rather large-billed, but otherwise resembles *P. u. annectens. P. u. sinuosa*, which breeds on the coast of se Alaska, also resembles *A. u. annectens. P. u. townsendi*, from the Queen Charlotte Is., British Columbia, is small, with a small, relatively long bill, and is very dark, appearing nearly black, with heavy ventral spotting. *P. u. fuliginosa*, from coastal British Columbia and nw Washington, like the previous subspecies, is very dark.

Distribution

Breeds: from the Aleutian Is., west to Unalaska, Shumagin, Semidi, Kodiak, and Middleton Is., Alaska Peninsula, Iliamna Lake, and Cook Inlet, south along the coast to British Columbia (including the Queen Charlotte Islands) to nw Washington.

Winters from se Alaska (irregularly) and coastal British Columbia, south to nw Baja California, and very rarely in se Arizona (Chiricahua Mts.). There is a winter record for North Dakota.

Migrates mostly along the Pacific Coast, but regularly east to the western Great Basin. Spring migration starts in late Mar and early Apr in California with a peak in early May; they arrive in Alaska after late Apr. They appear in the fall in California after mid-Sept.

Conservation status

At present, the preferred breeding habitat of this species does not appear to be threatened by development. Widespread destruction of chaparral in southern California would reduce numbers; data on population trends are not clear.

Molt Not described. Presumably much like Red Fox Sparrow in pattern.

Description

Adults—Large; sexes similar. *Head:* crown uniformly dark brown to nearly black; side of face unpatterned with a few beige flecks sometimes evident in the submoustachial stripe and lores; *back:* nape and mantle dark brown to nearly black and unstreaked; *rump:* and uppertail-coverts dull rufous-brown and unpatterned; *wing:* brown or dark brown with some hint of rust in scapulars, tertials, and coverts; no wing-bars; *underparts:* chin and throat whitish, flecked – often extensively – with brown or dark brown; breast and flanks heavily streaked or spotted with triangular brown or dark brown spots, often showing a collar of spots, followed by a pale band, then a dark patch below that; belly whitish, often spotted; *bill:* upper mandible dusky to dark; lower mandible paler, usually orange-yellow at base; *legs* and *feet:* brownish; *iris:* dark brown.

Hybrids

It is not clear to what extent, if any, these hybridize with Slate-colored Fox Sparrows in British Columbia, but they apparently do not hybridize with Red Fox Sparrows.

References

Garrett *et al.* (2000), Pyle (1997), Rising (1996), Zink (1994), Zink and Kessen (1999).

38.1 Sooty Fox Sparrow, Los Angeles, California, USA, Jan 1996. The forms that now make up this species are all similar and not safely identified in the wintering range. The upperparts, as here, are generally brown with varying degrees of gray suffusion. The underparts are whitish, thickly spotted and streaked with dusky-brown. The pale eye-ring stands out on the plain brown face (Brian E. Small).

38.2 Sooty Fox Sparrow, Point Reyes, California, USA, Nov 1990. On this individual notice the extensive amount of dusky-brown on the sides of breast and along the flanks. The whitish eye-ring and mottling on the submoustachial area and throat contrast with the largely grayish-brown head. (Kevin T. Karlson).

38.3 Sooty Fox Sparrow, Dungeness National Wildlife Refuge, Washington, USA, Nov 1998. This very brown individual, perhaps *P. u. fuliginosa*, shows little gray suffusion on the upperparts and head. Notice again the extensive solid brown sides to the breast and flanks (Jim Burns/Natural Impacts).

38.4 Sooty Fox Sparrow, Charmlee Park, Los Angeles Co., California, USA, Nov 1990. The paler and grayer tone to the upperparts of this individual suggest it might be *P. u. unalaschensis*. Note the uniform appearance characteristic of the species (Larry Sansone).

38.5 Sooty Fox Sparrow, Riverside Co., California, USA, Oct 1993. The bright corn-colored lower mandible stands out on this particularly dusky individual. Note the lack of contrast between the tone of the upperparts and the wings and tail (Larry Sansone).

39 **Slate-colored Fox Sparrow**

(Passerella schistacea)

Measurements:
Length: 15.0–18.0 cm; 6.0–7.1 in.
  (males slightly larger).
Wing: 73–87 mm; 2.9–3.4 in.
Mass: no data available.

Slate-colored Fox Sparrows are **large**, with a **slate-colored head**, a back washed with brown, brown wings and rump, a **rusty brown tail**, pale lores, a yellowish lower mandible, and **breast and flanks heavily spotted with dark brown**.

Habitat
Slate-colored Fox Sparrows nest in deciduous thickets, and sometimes in thick, scrubby conifers, generally along streams. In winter, they are found in chaparral and streamside thickets.

Behavior
Breeding males sing persistently from bushy thickets, sometimes from an exposed perch but also from the ground or low vegetation. Slate-colored Fox Sparrows feed principally on the ground where they scratch for seeds and insects. In winter, they occur solitarily or in small flocks.

Voice
The song is clear and ringing, starting with 2 or 3 syllables on different pitches, ***too-wheet-whoo tweek-tsuck-tseeka tsew!***, with every other note emphasized, or ***shree-wee shu-shu-shu-shu-shu wit-wit-wit***; several of the elements may have a buzzy quality, and many may have bunting-like warbles. Individual males sing two to five different songs, not singing the same song twice in a row. The song may closely resemble that of the Green-tailed Towhee, and song mimicry may be involved. The call is a distinctive metallic ***tik***, or ***thick***, reminiscent of a sharp note from Lincoln's Sparrow; also they give a faint ***seet*** or ***psippt***.

Similar species
The **Red Fox Sparrow** is much more rufous, especially in the rump and tail, with rufous spotting ventrally. **Sooty Fox Sparrows** are variable, but all have browner backs, and are generally darker overall. **Thick-billed Fox Sparrows** are similar in coloration, but have a very large bill. With the exception of birds from the Aleutian Is., Song Sparrows are smaller, and have a dark, smaller bill.

Geographic variation

P. s. olivacea of s-central Washington and e Washington is medium-sized with the crown and back grayish-olive, with a reddish tinge. *P. s. shistacea* of se British Columbia south to central Colorado and e Oregon lacks the reddish tinge; *P. s. swarthi* of se Idaho south to se Utah are similar to *P. s. schistacea*; *P. s. canescens* of e California are small, with a stout bill and a grayer back than the other subspecies in this species. *P. s. altivagans*, of the interior of British Columbia and sw Alberta, is intermediate in appearance between the Red and Slate-colored Fox Sparrows.

Distribution

Breeds from sw and central interior of British Columbia, se British Columbia, and sw Alberta south to the mountains of s-central and sw British Columbia, central and e Washington, central and ne Oregon, se Idaho, w Montana, south to s-central Colorado, n-central Utah, central Nevada, and central Oregon.

Winters from n interior California, coastal s California, central Arizona, n New Mexico, south to n Baja California, s Arizona, n Sonora, and w Texas.

Migrates throughout the southwest, but rare east of nw Arizona; most of the Great Basin and Rocky Mountain birds migrate southwest to California. Spring migration is early, and birds start to arrive in Colorado in late Mar; fall migration starts in late Aug.

Conservation status

Slate-colored Sparrows are locally common and populations in Oregon may be increasing.

Molt

No information. Probably like Red Fox Sparrow in pattern. They molt before migrating.

Description

Adults—Large, sexes similar. **Head:** dusky grayish or brownish-gray; lores dark buff; ear-coverts brown, flecked with beige; malar stripe darker brown; **back:** nape and mantle brownish-gray and unpatterned; **rump:** and especially uppertail-coverts rusty brown; **tail:** rusty brown and unpatterned; **wing:** dull rusty brown; tertials and coverts rusty; median-coverts may be buff-tipped, forming one indistinct wing-bar; **underparts:** chin and throat whitish, generally lightly flecked with dark brown; breast and flanks brown spotted, generally with a brown central breast spot; belly white and usually unspotted; **bill:** upper mandible grayish-brown to grayish; lower mandible yellowish, often dusky at the tip; **legs** and **feet:** pale brownish; **iris:** dark brown.

First fall and winter (July–Sept)—Resemble adults, but upperparts more distinctly tinged with brown.

Juveniles (July–Aug)—Forehead, crown, and nape brownish-gray, and perhaps rusty-tinged; lower back, rump, and uppertail-coverts brown, faintly streaked, and becoming more rusty brown posteriorly; underparts light buffy, heavily spotted or streaked with brown; belly whitish; wing feathers gray-brown; coverts and tertials narrowly tipped with buff (no wing-bars).

Hybrids

There may be a narrow hybrid zone between Slate-colored and Thick-billed fox sparrows in central Oregon, and there may be hybridization between these near Mono Lake, California.

References Garrett *et al.* (2000), Martin (1977), Pyle (1997), Rising (1996), Zink (1986, 1994), Zink and Kessen (1999).

39.1 Slate-colored Fox Sparrow, Kern Co., California, USA, Nov 1994. This species is characterized by the neat contrast between the slate-gray head and mantle and the chestnut wings, rump and tail. The underparts are whitish thickly spotted and streaked with dull chestnut. The relatively small bill on this individual suggests it may be of the nominate form (Brian E. Small).

39.2 Slate-colored Fox Sparrow *P. s. canescens*, Wyman Creek, White Mountains., Inyo Co., California, USA, July 1989. This worn adult has a somewhat stouter bill than other forms and closely resembles some of the smaller billed forms of the Thick-billed Fox Sparrow (Larry Sansone).

39.3 Slate-colored Fox Sparrow, Galaleo Park, Kern Co., California, USA, Oct 1999. Bill size is often the only feature which will separate this species from Thick-billed and specific racial identification mostly is impossible during the winter months when several forms of both species might be present at a locality (Larry Sansone).

(Passerella megarhyncha)

Measurements
Length: 15.0–18.0 cm; 6.0–7.1 in.
   (males slightly larger).
Wing: 75–89 mm; 3.0–3.5 in.
Mass: no data available.

Thick-billed Fox Sparrows are **large** (though not for fox sparrows), with a **slate-colored head**, a back washed with brown, brown wings and rump, a **rusty brown tail**, pale lores, a yellowish lower mandible (bluish in some populations), and **breast and flanks heavily spotted with dark brown.**

Habitat
Slate-colored Fox Sparrows nest in deciduous thickets, and sometimes in thick, scrubby conifers, generally along streams. In winter, they are found in chaparral and streamside thickets.

Behavior
On the breeding grounds, males sing persistently from bushy thickets, sometimes from an exposed perch but also from the ground or from low vegetation. Thick-billed Fox Sparrows feed principally on the ground where they scratch for seeds and insects. In winter, they occur solitarily or in small flocks.

Voice
The song is clear and ringing, starting with 2 or 3 syllables on different pitches, *too-wheet-whoo tweek-tsuck-tseeka tsew!*, with every other note emphasized, or *shree-wee shu-shu-shu-shu-shu wit-wit-wit*; several of the elements may have a buzzy quality, and many may have bunting-like warbles. Individual males may sing more than a single song. The song may closely resemble that of the Green-tailed Towhee, and song mimicry may be involved. The call is a distinctive metallic *chink*, *chek*, or *klink*, reminiscent of the call of the California Towhee, or a faint *seet* or *psippt*.

Molt
No information. Probably like Red Fox Sparrow in pattern. They molt before migrating.

Similar species
The **Red Fox Sparrow** is much more rufous, especially in the rump and tail, with rufous spotting ventrally. **Sooty Fox Sparrows** are variable, but all have browner backs, and are generally darker overall. **Slate-colored Fox Sparrows** are similar in appearance, but are usually a little more brightly colored, and the lower bill is often a brighter yellow; the

very large bill is the best distinguishing feature. With the exception of birds from the Aleutian Is., Song Sparrows are smaller, and have a dark, smaller bill.

Geographic variation

P. m. megarhyncha breeds from s-central Oregon south to central California; *P. m. brevicauda* breeds in coastal nw California; *P. m. fulva* breeds in central and se Oregon; *P. m. monoensis* breeds in e-central California; and *P. m. stephensi* breeds in the coastal mountains of s California, perhaps south to San Diego Co. Variation among these is clinal, and generally slight; many authors do not recognize either *P. m. fulva* or *P. m. monoensis*.

Distribution

Breeds from central and se Oregon south to ne California, and in the Sierra Nevada to Tulare Co. and east to Lake Tahoe, and in the west to Humboldt, Trinity, Mendocino, Glenn, and Lake cos., and locally in the mountains in Santa Barbara, Ventura, Kern, Los Angeles, Riverside and San Bernardino cos.

Winters from at lower elevations in central California and s California, south to n Baja California; smaller numbers winter north to n California along the flanks of mountains.

Migrates through California. Fall migration occurs from late Aug through late Sept; spring migration begins as early as mid-Feb, but is mostly from late Mar through late Apr.

Conservation status

Little is known about numbers, but they are locally common.

Description

Adults—Large, sexes similar. *Head:* dusky grayish or brownish-gray; lores dark buff; ear-coverts brown, flecked with beige; malar stripe darker brown; *back:* nape and mantle brownish-gray and unpatterned; *rump:* and especially uppertail-coverts rusty brown; *tail:* rusty brown and unpatterned; *wing:* dull rusty brown; tertials and coverts rusty; median-coverts may be buff-tipped, forming one indistinct wing-bar; *underparts:* chin and throat whitish, generally lightly flecked with dark brown; breast and flanks brown spotted, generally with a brown central breast spot; belly white and usually unspotted; *bill:* upper mandible grayish-brown to grayish; lower mandible dull yellowish or blue-gray large-billed group, often dusky at the tip; *legs* and *feet:* pale brownish; *iris:* dark brown.

First fall and winter (July–Sept)—Resemble adults, but upperparts more distinctly tinged with brown.

Juveniles (July–Aug)—Forehead, crown, and nape brownish-gray, and perhaps rusty-tinged; lower back, rump, and uppertail-coverts brown, faintly streaked, and becoming more rusty brown posteriorly; underparts light buffy, heavily spotted or streaked with brown; belly whitish; wing feathers gray-brown; coverts and tertials narrowly tipped with buff (no wing-bars).

Hybrids

There is a narrow hybrid zone between Slate-colored and Thick-billed fox sparrows in central Oregon; there may be hybridization between these near Mono Lake, California.

References Garrett *et al.* (2000), Pyle (1997), Rising (1996), Zink (1986, 1994), Zink and Kessen (1999).

40.1 Thick-billed Fox Sparrow, Ventura Co., California, USA, Oct 1994. This species is very similar to Slate-colored in general plumage pattern and color although the bill generally is much deeper based. There is much individual variation and some individuals cannot be safely identified. This particularly large-billed individual presents no problem and is probably of the form *P. m. stephensi*. Note the extensively corn-colored lower mandible on this bird (Brian E. Small).

40.2 Thick-billed Fox Sparrow *P. m. monoensis*, Aspendell, Inyo Co., California, USA, May 1993. This individual shows the typical contrast between the slate-gray head and mantle and the dull chestnut wings and tail. The whitish underparts are neatly streaked blackish. The bill is moderately deep based. The color of the lower mandible seems to be highly variable and is distinctly grayish on this bird (Larry Sansone).

40.3 Thick-billed Fox Sparrow, Charmlee Pk., Los Angeles Co., California, USA, Nov 1990. On this profile notice the deep base to the bill and the gray and dull chestnut plumage. The underparts show extensive gray suffusion on the side of the breast and along the flanks. This wintering individual cannot be safely identified to subspecies (Larry Sansone).

41 Red Fox Sparrow

(Passerella iliaca)

Measurements
Length: 15.0–17.0 cm; 6.0–6.7 in.
    (males slightly larger).
Wing: 79–92 mm; 3.1–3.6 in.
Mass: 29.6–49.0 g (Pennsylvania).

Red Fox Sparrows are **large** and **rusty red**, especially on the ear-coverts, back, rump, and tail (which is conspicuous in flight), and have **extensive rusty to almost blackish streaking on the breast and flanks**, and gray and rusty streaking on the back.

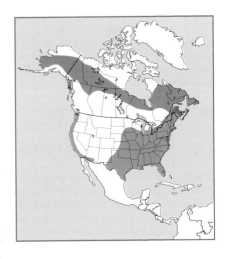

Habitat
Red Fox Sparrows breed in dense decidu-ous thickets (commonly alders or wil-lows), in bogs, and dwarf spruce or fir. In migration and winter, they are generally found in low, moist areas with rank, tall brush, and brush piles, often at woodland edge, or in wet woods; in the southwest they are found in chaparral and streamside thickets.

Behavior
On the breeding grounds, males sing persistently at least until mid-July, usually from a perch 1–3 m high; they occasionally sing in winter. They are generally difficult to see, but respond vigorously to play-back and to 'spishing'. In winter, the birds are usually found in small, loose flocks. Their flight is strong and direct, but when flushed they may fly from bush to bush with a nervous jerking of the tail. They feed on the ground, often using a towhee-like double-scratch; often they can be heard scratching among the leaves.

Voice
The song is a series of more than 6 loud, clear, slurred ringing whistles on different pitches, usually ending with a buzzy whistle, often sounding rather like '*aujourd-hui*.' The alarm note is a loud *smack*, *tchek*, or *chick*.

Similar species
Other **fox sparrows** are similar in size, but lack the rust on the head and back, streaks on the back, and have less or no rust in the rump and tail. Red Fox Sparrows have a pale triangular patch above the end of the pale submalar stripe that is not obvious on other fox sparrows.

    With the exception of the Aleutian subspecies, **Song Sparrows** are smaller; east-ern Song Sparrows are brown or sometimes rusty brown, but never so rufous as Red Fox Sparrows. The malar stripe of Song Sparrow is much darker. **Swamp Sparrows** may have extensive rust in the crown, coverts, and tertials, but are substantially smaller. **Hermit Thrushes** show a conspicuous rusty rump and tail in flight, and in the east they and Red Fox Sparrows are migrating at the same time.

Geographic variation

P. i. iliaca breeds from the northeast west to Manitoba, where it grades into *P. i. zaboria*, which breeds west to the interior Alaska, and south to central Alberta. These two subspecies are similar, and cannot be separated in the field.

P. i. altivagans breeds in the interior of British Columbia and sw Alberta. It is somewhat smaller than the other two, and the crown and back are less rusty; the breast spots are a dull rusty brown. This subspecies is intermediate between the Red Fox Sparrow and the Slate-colored Fox Sparrow.

Distribution

Breeds from w Alaska, n Yukon, nw and e-central Mackenzie, sw Keewatin, n Manitoba, n Ontario, n Quebec, and n Labrador south to n British Columbia, n and central Alberta, central Saskatchewan, central Manitoba, n Ontario, se and s-central Quebec, Newfoundland, nw New Brunswick, Prince Edward I., Nova Scotia, and extreme n Maine.

Winters from e and s Minnesota, s Wisconsin, s Michigan, s Ontario, sw Quebec, Nova Scotia, and s Newfoundland south to Florida, the Gulf Coast, and s Texas. Rare but regular on the west coast from Washington south to California; most winter east of the Great Plains, from central Missouri south to central Texas, and New Jersey south to Georgia.

Migrates throughout the east. Red Fox Sparrow is an early spring and late fall migrant: most move through Kansas from late Feb and s Ontario in early Mar to mid-Apr, and in Oct and early Nov. One record for England (June).

Conservation status

Much of the breeding range of Red Fox Sparrows is north of regions greatly affected by human activities, and their preferred nesting habitat to date has been little changed. Clear-cutting in some areas would create rank brush suitable for fox sparrows, so they may have benefited from recent habitat changes in the north. Changes in numbers are little known.

Molt

There is a partial Prebasic I molt in July to Sept that involves the median and greater-coverts, but no tertials or rectrices. The Prealternate molt, when present, is limited to a few head feathers. The Definitive Prebasic molt is complete, and takes place July to Sept.

Description

Adults—Large; sexes similar. *Head:* almost always with a mixture of gray and rust in the crown; lores buffy; supercilium dull gray; ear-coverts mixed with buff, rufous, and gray; moustachial stripe bold rusty or brownish-rusty; submoustachial stripe thin and buffy; malar stripe rusty or brownish-rusty; *back:* nape and mantle gray or brownish-gray with centers of feathers rusty brown, forming streaks; *rump:* brown to rusty brown; uppertail-coverts bright rusty and unpatterned; *tail:* rusty brown and unpatterned; *wing:* rusty brown with extensive rust in scapulars, tertials, and coverts; median and greater-coverts narrowly tipped with buff, forming two indistinct wing-bars; *underparts:* chin, throat, and upper breast whitish, speckled with rust; breast with a bold necklace of rusty spots and a darker rusty brown central spot; flanks extensively rusty, spotted with triangular spots; belly white and unspotted; undertail-coverts whitish and usually unspotted; *bill:* upper mandible grayish-brown; lower mandible paler, yellowish; *legs* and *feet:* pale brownish or pinkish-brown; *iris:* dark brown.

First-fall and winter (July–Sept)—Resemble adults, but average duller in coloration.

Juveniles (June–July)—Crown and back brown, with centers of feathers dark brown or rusty brown, rump and tail bright rusty; underparts light buffy, heavily streaked with brown, paler and lightly streaked on belly; coverts and tertials broadly edged with rust. Molt before migrating.

Hybrids
Red Fox Sparrows probably hybridize with Slate-colored Fox Sparrows where their ranges overlap in Alberta and British Columbia.

References Pyle (1997), Rising (1996), Zink (1994), Zink and Kessen (1999).

41.1 Red Fox Sparrow, Rio Grande, New Jersey, USA, Jan 1998. This hefty, brightly colored sparrow is unmistakable. The gray and rusty upperparts and whitish underparts thickly spotted with rust are distinctive. Note the solidly rufous tail and the stout bicolored bill (Kevin T. Karlson).

41.2 Red Fox Sparrow, Irma, New Jersey, USA, Feb 1998. Another view showing the extent of gray on the head (largely confined to the supercilium and nape) and the distinctly triangular spotting on the underparts. The whitish eye-ring stands out on the rufous and gray face sides (Kevin T. Karlson).

41.3 Red Fox Sparrow *P. i. zaboria*, Irvine, Orange Co., California, USA, Jan 2000. This western form is similar to *P. i. iliaca* (which Figs. 41.1 and 41.2 probably illustrate), and some individuals cannot be safely subspecifically identified. Note the distinct grayish cast to the upperparts with more extensive, darker gray on the crown than *P. i. iliaca*. The spotting on the underparts is darker brown with less rufescent tones (Larry Sansone).

41.4 Red Fox Sparrow *P.i. altvagans*, Mackenzie, B.C., Canada, Aug 1998. This form is much duller and more uniformly grayish-brown than *P. i. iliaca* or *P. i. zaboria*. Note the dull chestnut wings and tail contrast with the grayish-brown upperparts and head. The whitish underparts are streaked and spotted with dusky-gray rather than rust or brown (Paul N. Prior).

42 Song Sparrow

(Melospiza melodia)

Measurements

Length: 12.0–17.0 cm; 4.7–6.7 in.
(males slightly larger; geographically variable).
Wing: 56–87 mm; 2.3–3.4 in.
Mass: 11.9–29.8 g (Pennsylvania);
40.2–53.0 g (Aleutian Is., Alaska);
av.=18.8 g (San Francisco Bay).

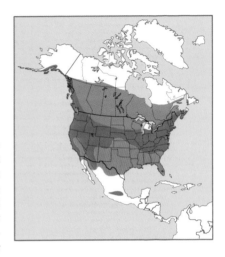

The Song Sparrow is extremely geographically variable. It is **rusty brown to dark brown** in general coloration, with **streaked back, flanks, and breast**, the streaks often concentrated into a central **breast spot**. The throat is whitish or white, often somewhat spotted, and outlined by **conspicuous, dark malar stripes**. The **long, round tail** is characteristically flopped to one side, or pumped up and down, in flight.

Habitat

Except for the Aleutian Is. and coastal Alaskan populations, the habitat used by Song Sparrows is remarkably similar throughout their range. They are generally found in open, bushy habitats, often near water (invariably so in the southwest), saltwater (California) and freshwater marshes, thickets, and woodland edge, sometimes in urban areas. In winter, they are also found in tall weedy fields, marshes, moist ravines, and brush piles.

In the Aleutians, they are found in beach grass just above the high tide line, in grassy areas near the beach amongst boulders and driftwood, and in winter they feed on tidal mudflats. Around San Francisco Bay they are resident in or at the edge of salt and brackish marshes with cordgrass and pickleweed. Along both coasts they are found in brackish marshes; they often forage on mudflats.

Behavior

On the breeding grounds, males sing persistently from an exposed perch or wire; flight-singing is rare. Individuals sing throughout the year, but infrequently in the winter. Territorial birds sometimes sing at night. Although they tend to stay in dense vegetation, usually they are not difficult to see, and respond readily to spishing. In winter they are found in small, loose flocks, and often associate with other sparrows. Their flight is jerky, not strong, and their rather long tail is characteristically flipped to one side and pumped during flight. In spring, territorial defense is vigorous, and fights and chases are frequent. Song Sparrows generally forage on the ground.

Voice

The song, though variable, is distinctive. It characteristically starts with a series of 2 to 4 loud, clear whistles on the same pitch, followed by a trill, often a buzzy trill, then several short notes, ***chrup chrup chee chee tceeeeee tzcu***, the ***chee chee*** higher and the ***tzcu*** lower in pitch. Sometimes they give a Swamp Sparrow-like trill, followed by a buzzy trill, ***chril-chril-chril-chril-chril churzzzzzzzzzzzz tik-zp***. In central California, we have heard Song Sparrows that sound very like Cassin's Sparrows. An individual generally sings several different songs, commonly singing one several times, then switching to another. The call note is a distinctive ***txhenk***, ***tchip***, or ***chimp***, and often is a useful aid to identification. They also give an indistinctive ***tseep***, and a note that is a stuttering trill.

Similar species

Lincoln's Sparrows are somewhat smaller, shorter-tailed, and more gracile, with thinly striped flanks and breast, usually without a conspicuous central spot, and a buffy cast to the flanks, breast, and submoustachial stripe, grayish side of neck and supercilium, and gray central crown-stripe. Adult **Swamp Sparrows** generally have a conspicuously rusty cap, rusty cast to the wings, especially in the coverts, reddish-buff flanks, and inconspicuous ventral streaking. In juvenal plumage, the three *Melospiza* are very similar. In the east, Song Sparrows are larger than the others (tail 60 mm or longer) with a whitish submoustachial stripe, and a relatively unstreaked crown, often with a paler median crown-stripe (see Lincoln's Sparrow). **Savannah Sparrows** often have a central breast spot (this is not a good field mark), but are slimmer, have sharper striping, and a slimmer, often paler bill. They usually have a pale yellow supercilium and obviously pink legs. Their flight is direct and stronger than that of the Song Sparrow, and their tail is distinctly shorter (and notched, rather than round). **Fox Sparrows** are larger (large Alaskan I. Song Sparrows do not migrate); Red Fox Sparrows are much more rufous, and have gray in the crown; Sooty Fox Sparrow have very dark, apparently unstreaked backs, and large bills, with the lower mandible yellowish.

Geographic variation

Twenty-nine subspecies from north of Mexico are commonly recognized. Although there is indeed much geographic variation in the species, much of the variation is clinal, and many of the subspecies are poorly defined; these populations seem to be little different at the molecular level. We will discuss them by regions:

Eastern Song Sparrows: Song sparrows are generally absent in the Great Plains. East of the Plains there are four subspecies; these are medium-sized and brownish. *M. m. atlantica* (along the coast from New York to North Carolina), *M. m. melodia* (e Ontario to Newfoundland, south to Virginia), *M. m. euphonia* (s Ontario west to Wisconsin, and south to Missouri), and *M. m. juddi* (ne British Columbia, east to w Ontario and Michigan). *A. m. atlantica* have reddish streaking on the upper back; the browns of *M. m. melodia* average more reddish than *M. m. euphonia* or *M. m. juddi*, with reddish streaking on the lower back; *M. m. juddi* and *M. m. euphonia* are very similar. None of these is clearly differentiated, and they cannot safely be separated in the field.

Southern Rocky Mountains and southwest: In the montane west there are five subspecies, found from the interior of s British Columbia south to Baja California. These are pale brownish to pale reddish-brownish. *M. m. merrilli* (interior of s British Columbia and sw Alberta and nw Montana) has a grayish-brown back, with indistinct dusky streaking; the underparts have dark rusty streaks. *M. m. fisherella* (e Oregon, to sw Idaho and w Nevada), is similar, but less rusty; *M. m. montana* (ne Oregon and central Montana south through Wyoming to n New Mexico) has pale reddish-brown markings; *M. m. fallax* (resident in se Nevada and sw Utah, to Arizona) is paler yet, and somewhat smaller than *M. m. montana*; *M. m. saltonis* (deserts of s California, s Nevada, sw Arizona, and Baja California) are very like *M. m. fallax*, but slightly smaller. *M. m. fallax* and *M. m. saltonis* cannot be separated in the field.

San Fransisco Bay Saltmarshes: In the saltmarshes in the San Francisco Bay region there are three relatively distinct subspecies: *M. m. samuelis* (resident in northern San Francisco Bay), *A. m. pusillula* (resident in southern San Francisco Bay), and *M. m. maxillaris* (resident in Suisun Bay). *M. m. samuelis* is small and has a small bill, and the upper back has blackish streaking, underparts are pale with distinct streaks; *M. m. pusillula*, is paler with darker streaking below; *M. m. maxillaris* has a relatively large bill, with back with blackish streaking, underparts pale with distinct streaking. These are all dusky sparrows.

Non-saltmarsh California Populations: At least four subspecies of Song Sparrows that are not characteristically found in saltmarshes are generally recognized. Differences among them are clinal, and not great. These are small, and brownish-olive in color. *M. m. cleonensis* is resident in coastal sw Oregon and nw California. It is small-billed and has chestnut streaking on the upper back, and blackish streaking on the lower back, and rusty streaks on the undersides. *M. m. gouldii*, which is resident on the coast of central-w California, is similar; its ventral streaking is less rusty. *M. m. heermanni*, resident in the interior of central California is medium-sized, with a medium-sized bill. In general coloration it is like eastern Song Sparrows but with warmer colors, with buffy edges to the back feathers, buffy flanks, and blackish streaks on the underparts. *M. m. cooperi*, resident in coastal central and sw California, is similar.

California island Populations: Three subspecies of Song Sparrows are, or were, resident on the Channel islands; these are small, and pale grayish to brownish. *M. m. micronyx*, resident on San Miguel I., has a grayish back with dark brown streaking, and rusty edges to the tertials and coverts; underparts are white with narrow blackish streaking. *M. m. clementae*, which is resident on Santa Rosa to San Clemente I. is similar, but has a longer claw (not a good field mark!) and less ventral streaking. *M. m. graminea* was formerly resident on Santa Barbara I., but is now extinct. It was small and small-billed, and like *M. m. clementae* in general coloration.

Northwest Coastal Populations: Five subspecies of Song Sparrows from the coast of s-central Alaska south to central-w Oregon are generally recognized. These are large and very dark in color; differences among them are clinal. The southernmost, *M. m. morphna* breeds from coastal sw British Columbia south to w-central Oregon. It has a long and relatively slender bill; it is dark rusty brown and has dark rusty breast streaking, and a buffy throat, submoustachial stripe, lores, and belly. *M. m. rufina* breeds in se Alaska and the Queen Charlotte Is., British Columbia. It is less rusty than *M. m. morphna*, and has a somewhat shorter bill, and indistinct black streaking on the lower back. *M. m. inexpectata* breeds on coastal se Alaska and s Yukon to the interior of central British Columbia and sw Alberta. These are somewhat smaller than the above two subspecies in size, smaller billed, with the mantle dark rufous with gray streaking, and the back with indistinct black streaking; the underparts are grayish with brownish-rufous streaking. *M. m. caurina*, which breeds from coastal s-central and se Alaska, is large and long-billed; the mantle is dark grayish-brown with reddish-brown streaking, and underparts grayish with thin indistinct reddish-brown streaks. *M. m. kenaiensis,* which breeds on coastal central Alaska, is much like *M. m. caurina,* but larger billed.

Alaskan island Populations: Four subspecies have been named from Alaskan islands. As a group, these are quite distinctive; all are resident. They are very large and grayish with rusty markings. *M. m. insignis* is resident on coastal s-central Alaska and Kodiak I. It is large, with a long, but relatively slender bill. Its mantle is dark grayish-brown; there are no, or indistinct, streaks on the back; the underparts are grayish with indistinct rusty stripes. *M. m. amaka,* resident in western Alaska and Amak I., is similar, but has broad rufous streaks on the underparts. *M. m. sanaka,* on average the largest Song Sparrow, has a large bill. The mantle and back are dark grayish-brown with indistinct rusty streaks; the belly is dull grayish with diffuse rusty stripes. The submoustachial stripe and lores are whitish. *M. m. maxima* is resident from Attu to Atka Is., in the Aleutians. It is large with a very large bill. The back is grayish-brown with rusty brown streaking; underparts are grayish-white with rusty streaks.

Note on Field Identification

Although there are great differences among these groups of subspecies, within a group, identification in the field to subspecies – and in many cases in the hand – is problematic. We urge conservatism. Remember that much of the variation within the groups is clinal, and that there is a great deal of overlap among subspecies in these groups. Also, remember that subspecies are defined by (1) breeding range, and (2) morphology. Thus, if you see a Song Sparrow on Amak I., it is **by definition** *M. m. amaka* (or a very unusual record), because that is the only Song Sparrow found on that island. If you see a salt-marsh Song Sparrow in the northern marshes of San Francisco Bay it is *M. m. samuelis.* If you see a very dark, northwest coast Song Sparrow in winter along the coast of Oregon you may attempt to determine to which subspecies it belongs, but unless it was banded on its breeding ground, you can never be certain. This is the reason that we have emphasized differences among birds from breeding grounds in these descriptions, and not emphasized their supposed wintering ranges.

Distribution

Breeds from Aleutian Is. (west to Attu), Shumagin Is., Semidi Is., Amak and Middleton is., Kodiak I. group, s Alaska, s-central Yukon, s Mackenzie, n Manitoba, Akimiski I., Ontario, s Quebec and sw Newfoundland, south through Maritime Provinces to coastal and nw South Carolina, n Georgia, ne Alabama, Tennessee, Missouri (north of Missouri River), ne Kansas, rarely in s-central Kansas, South Dakota, Nebraska, Colorado, n New Mexico, Arizona, and central Baja California, central Baja California Sur, and locally through the Mexican highlands from Durango to Michoacán, and Puebla.

Winters from s Alaska, central and s British Columbia, central Minnesota, s Ontario, sw Quebec, s New Brunswick, Prince Edward I., Nova Scotia, and s Newfoundland, south to Florida, the Gulf Coast, and south to n Nuevo León, central Coahuila, central Chihuahua, and n Sonora.

Resident in the Aleutian Is., Kodiak I., Alaska Peninsula, most of California, south to central Baja California, central Baja California Sur, and in the southern parts of its breeding range elsewhere.

Migrates from high elevations to lower ones. Seven records for the British Isles (Apr, May, Oct).

Conservation status

Song Sparrows are doubtless more common in many places in the east than they were in pre-Columbian times, as the clearing of forests created suitable habitat for them. More recently, they have benefited from the abandonment of marginal farm land, and their range has spread southward into central North Carolina, southern Kentucky, and western Tennessee. In Arizona, Song Sparrows were locally common along waterways in the 1800s, but their numbers declined greatly there in the late 19th Century as a consequence of drainage and destruction of grasslands. Today, their numbers appear to be relatively stable throughout their range.

Molt

The Basic I plumage is acquired by a partial Prebasic I molt in July to Nov (geographically variable); this molt is variable and includes all greater and median-coverts, the innermost secondaries, and none to all of the rectrices. There is no Prealternate plumage. The Definitive Basic molt is complete and occurs July to Oct.

Description

Adults—Medium-sized; sexes alike. *Head:* brown to light rusty (southwest), streaked, with paler brown or gray-brown median crown-stripe; supercilium pale in front of eye; gray to gray-brown behind the eye; eye-stripe brown; ear-coverts gray to gray-brown, edged with dark brown moustachial stripe; submoustachial stripe pale; malar stripe dark brown; throat white or whitish, with or without (southwest; Rocky Mountains) brown spotting; head markings on birds from coastal British Columbia and Alaska are indistinct, with birds appearing to have nearly uniformly dark brown heads, somewhat paler in the supercilium, submoustachial stripe, and throat; *back:* brown to rusty brown (southwest) with centers of feathers dark brown or rusty brown; brown streaking on back indistinct on north Pacific Coast, where birds appear to have nearly uniformly colored dark backs; *rump:* brown to rusty brown and streaked; *tail:* rusty brown (southwest) to brown or dark brown, relatively long and rounded or double rounded; *wing:* rust-brown to dark brown, often with rust-brown in greater-coverts; *underparts:* chin and throat whitish, spotted or unspotted (southwest; Rocky Mountains) with brown; breast and flanks usually boldly streaked or spotted, with spots concentrated into a usually conspicuous central spot; belly whitish and unspotted (except on the Pacific Coast); undertail-coverts whitish with darker centers; *bill:* dark brown to horn-colored, lower mandible paler than upper, especially toward the base; *legs* and *feet:* pale yellowish-brown; *iris:* dark brown.

First fall and winter (July–Nov)—Resemble adults, but are buffier on breast and flanks.

Juveniles (June–Aug)—Have a brown crown, with paler median stripe in most populations; back brown, with centers of feathers dark brown and appearing rather streaked; rump and tail brown to rusty brown; underparts like adults, but buffier and streaking somewhat thinner; birds from coastal British Columbia and Alaska have nearly uniform dark backs. Usually but not always molt before migrating.

Hybrids

A hybrid Song Sparrow X White-crowned Sparrow was collected in Washington, and there is a probable Song Sparrow X Grasshopper Sparrow from Massachusetts.

References Aldrich (1984), Dickerman (1961), Marshall (1948), Jones *et al.* (MS), Petersen (1999), Pyle (1997), Rising (1996), Zink and Dittmann (1993).

42.1 Song Sparrow, Irma, New Jersey, USA, Jan 1998. This familiar, widespread species shows more geographical variation than any other sparrow. This typical eastern bird (possibly *M. m. atlantica*) is mostly grayish with brown and black head-stripes and body streaking and whitish underparts. Note the wide blackish malar and dense streaking on breast, forming a smudge on the center (Kevin T. Karlson).

42.2 Song Sparrow, Cape May, New Jersey, USA, Oct 1997. This fresh fall bird shows the short-winged, long-tailed profile of the species. Notice the dense black and brown streaking on the breast and flanks and the warm brown tone to the wings and tail (Kevin T. Karlson).

42.3 Song Sparrow *M. m. melodia*, Orono, Ontario, Canada, 28 July 1984. Mid-summer birds, as here, are often quite dull and worn with much gray and buff edging abraded. The wings and tail can appear quite ragged and lack the warm brown tones characteristic of fresh birds. The head pattern still remains quite bold, note especially the white submoustachial stripe contrasting with the wide blackish malar (James M. Richards).

42.4 Juvenile Song Sparrow *M. m. melodia*, Walsingham, Ontario, Canada, July 1992. Differs from adult in being much buffier overall with weaker head pattern and much dusky streaking within the supercilium and on the neck and breast. The wing-coverts have buff tips broken by black centers forming spotted wing-bars (David Agro).

42.5 Song Sparrow, Ventura Co., California, USA, Feb 1997. This west coast individual, is similar to eastern birds in basic plumage pattern but is brighter rufous on the wings and tail and has bolder black streaking on the head and underparts; the whitish supraloral and submoustachial stripe are typical of western non-saltmarsh Song Sparrows. Identification to subspecies level is often not possible out of breeding season (Don Des Jardin).

42.6 Song Sparrow, Ventura Co., California, USA, Mar 1998. Another western Song Sparrow. Notice the sharply defined black streaking on the otherwise white underparts. The whitish supraloral and submoustachial stripe stand out on the head. This individual is possibly of the form *M. m. cooperi* (Don Des Jardin).

42.7 Song Sparrow *M. m. pusillula*, Palo Alto Baylands, Santa Clara Co., California, USA, Jan 1992. Relatively small and short-tailed, this heavily-streaked individual is quite distinct within its restricted range (Mike Danzenbaker).

42.8 Song Sparrow *M. m. pusillula*, Palo Alto, San Mateo Co., California, USA, Jan 1998. This shortish-tailed, densely streaked individual is typical of the San Francisco Bay saltmarsh forms. Note the bold black streaking on the back and underparts and the grayish tone to the upperparts (Larry Sansone).

42.9 Song Sparrow, Bolsa Chica Reserve, California, USA, Mar 1999. Compared with the above figures (42.7 and 42.8) this non-saltmarsh "California" Song Sparrow appears more rufescent on the mantle and wings. Note also the more sullied underparts, with spottier, blackish streaking (Brian E. Small).

42.10 Song Sparrow, Santa Monica Mountains, California, USA, Oct 1994. A typical western bird. The wings and tail are quite dark rufous and contrast with the boldly streaked grayish upperparts. The white underparts are suffused with buff on the flanks and boldly streaked with black. Subspecific identification is often not possible (Brian E. Small).

42.11 Song Sparrow, Pima Co., Arizona, USA, Sept 1994. This strikingly pale individual is typical of the form *M. m. fallax*. The head and underparts are ashy-gray with bold pale rufous streaking relieved only by the blackish centers to the wing-coverts and tertials (Rick and Nora Bowers).

42.12 Song Sparrow, Patagonia, Arizona, USA, Feb 2000. Another view of a typical *M. m. fallax*. The supraloral, submoustachial and underparts are white with bold pale rufous streaking across breast and on flanks. Note the breast smudge (Jim Burns/Natural Impacts).

42.13 Song Sparrow, Homer, Alaska, USA, Aug 1995. Northwestern birds average darker than other forms. This striking individual, possibly *M. m. kenaiensis,* is quite dark sooty-gray with dark brown head stripes and wings with bold blackish streaking. The underparts are strongly suffused with gray on the flanks and evenly streaked blackish. The bill is quite long and spike-like (Jim Burns/Natural Impacts).

42.14 Song Sparrow, southeast Farallon Island, California, USA, Sept 1989. This very dark bird is probably *M. m. morphna.* The upperparts and head are strikingly dark chocolate-brown with obscure darker streaking. The underparts are heavily streaked and mottled with chocolate-brown (David D. Beadle).

42.15 Juvenile Song Sparrow, Mackenzie, B.C., Canada, Aug 1998. Northwestern juveniles are decidedly darker than eastern birds and are more richly colored. Note the dense dusky streaking on the underparts and the spotted buff wing-bars (Paul N. Prior).

42.16 Juvenile Song Sparrow molting into first basic plumage, Jones Beach State Park, New York, New York, Oct 2000 (Michael D. Stubblefield).

42.17 Adult Song Sparrow *M. m. maxima*, Attu, Alaska, USA, May 1988. This is the largest subspecies. It has a large, spike-like bill and, like other forms in the Alaska region, has largely gray and rusty-brown plumage (Erik Breden).

42.18 Adult Song Sparrow *M. m. maxima*, Attu, Alaska, USA, May 1984. The head and underparts are largely gray with dense rusty-brown streaking. The throat, submoustachial stripe and supraloral are contrastingly white (Erik Breden).

43 Lincoln's Sparrow

(Melospiza lincolnii)

Measurements
Length: 11.5–14.5 cm; 4.5–5.8 in.
 (males slightly larger).
Wing: 54–69 mm; 2.1–2.7 in.
Mass: 14.8–24.0 g (Pennsylvania;
 spring migrants).

Lincoln's Sparrow is a medium-sized
sparrow with a rather short tail, a broad
gray supercilium and **median crown-
stripe**, and a **thinly streaked, buffy
breast and flanks**.

Habitat
Lincoln's Sparrows breed in boggy areas
with stunted tamarack, black spruce, and
low willows and alders, willow thickets,

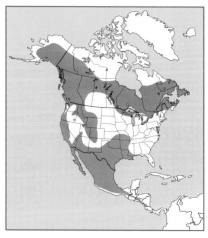

and cut-over areas where there is dense vegetation. In winter, they are often found in
moist areas, tangles, brushy edges of ponds, and dense weedy fields.

Behavior
On the breeding grounds, singing males are inconspicuous as they sing from dense
thickets. The adults around the nest are nervous, flitting in and out of sight, uttering
rapid *chits*, and will run away from the nest; they may give a broken-wing distraction
display. In migration and winter, they occur in dense, low cover, and are rarely far
from cover. They are not generally found in flocks, and are skulkers, but respond well
to 'spishing' and usually are not hard to see.

Voice
The song of Lincoln's Sparrow is sweet and gurgling, and has the quality of Purple
Finch and House Wren songs: ***churr-churr-churr-wee-wee-wee-wee-wah-wah***, or ***ootle
ootle ootle weetle weetle eeteeteetyaytoo***. Occasionally, a flight-song is given. The call
note is a variable sharp ***tep*** or ***chip***, or a faint ***tsick***, ***tschuk***, or ***tit***, or a buzzy ***zzeet***.

Similar species
The **Song Sparrow** is generally larger with a longer tail; the breast spotting of the
Song Sparrow is bolder, and although Lincoln's Sparrow may have a central breast
spot, it is generally more pronounced on Song Sparrows. Song Sparrows have a conspicuous brown malar stripe, whereas the malar stripe of Lincoln's Sparrow is thin.
The buffy, thinly streaked breast and flanks, and grayish face of Lincoln's Sparrow are
distinctive. In fact, the two are easy to distinguish, but they (especially Lincoln's
Sparrow) are often poorly illustrated in guides (but see Beadle's pictures in Rising
1996). Lincoln's Sparrow appears to be a more 'delicate' bird, and is usually shyer –

although both respond well to 'spishing'. **Savannah Sparrows**, which generally occur in open fields, not tangles or thickets where Lincoln's Sparrows are likely to lurk, lack the buffy breast, have a yellowish supercilium, and a shorter, notched tail.

Juvenile *Melospiza* are very similar, and the real identification challenges are here. Happily, for those not interested in these challenges, they usually molt before migrating. (Eastern) Song Sparrows are larger then the other two, and have a white or whitish malar stripe; Lincoln's and Swamp Sparrows have a buffy or buffy white malar stripe. Swamp Sparrows often appear to have unstreaked, black crowns Lincoln's Sparrows have some streaking in the chin and throat, but Swamp Sparrows may not have this. Swamp Sparrows consistently have more rusty edges to their coverts and tertials, but this too is variable. In the hand, Lincoln's Sparrows often have a gray mouth lining, and Swamp Sparrows a yellow lining, but this is variable.

Geographic variation
Three subspecies are commonly recognized; these are only slightly (if at all) different, and variation is clinal. *M. l. lincolnii* breeds in the east; *M. l. alticola* breeds in the mountains of Montana and Oregon, southward; and *M. l. gracilis* breeds along coastal Alaska and central British Columbia. *M. l. gracilis* is said to be somewhat darker on the back than *M. l. lincolnii*; many workers do not recognize this subspecies. *M. l. gracilis* is somewhat smaller than the others, and similar in coloration to *M. l. alticola*.

Distribution
Breeds from w and central Alaska, central Yukon, w-central and se Mackenzie, n Saskatchewan, n Manitoba, n Ontario, Quebec, south in mountains to s California, w-central Nevada, central Idaho, Utah, e-central Arizona, n New Mexico, w Colorado, Wyoming, w Montana, se and central Alberta, central Saskatchewan, Manitoba (except sw), se Minnesota, n Wisconsin, n Michigan, s Ontario, New York, s Vermont, w Massachusetts, n New Hampshire, central Maine, New Brunswick, Prince Edward I., central Nova Scotia, and Newfoundland.

Winters uncommonly from sw British Columbia, w Washington and Oregon, and from n California, s Nevada, sw Utah, Arizona, central New Mexico, Oklahoma, s Missouri, s Kentucky, and n Georgia south to Florida, the Gulf Coast, and Texas to Costa Rica, and rarely in the Caribbean.

Migrates throughout North America in the east; spring migration mostly in May; fall migration is mid-Sept through late Oct.

Molt
The Prebasic I molt is partial and includes all feathers except remiges and rectrices and occurs on the breeding grounds (Aug in Canada). The Definitive Basic plumage is acquired by a complete molt that occurs on the breeding grounds in Aug. Some birds may molt some body feathers in early spring, but this is not confirmed.

Description
Adults—Medium-sized; sexes alike. **Head:** crown brown or rusty brown, with a gray median crown-stripe; supercilium and side of neck gray; ear-coverts brownish, outlined with darker brown; moustachial and malar stripes brown; submoustachial stripe buffy ochre; chin and throat buffy white, thinly streaked with dark brown; **back:** nape, mantle, and scapulars buffy olive, sharply streaked with black; **rump:** olive and brown streaked; **tail:** grayish-brown, middle rectrices with brown centers; **wing:** brown, sometimes with slightly rusty edges to the greater-coverts and tertials; **under-**

parts: throat whitish or ochre, thinly streaked with dark brown, and sometimes with a median breast spot; belly whitish; undertail-coverts buffy with brown centers; ***bill:*** horn-colored, lower mandible slightly yellowish; ***legs*** and ***feet:*** brownish; ***iris:*** brown.

First fall and winter (July–May)—Resemble adults, but are more buffy, with marking less sharply defined.

Juveniles (July–mid-Sept)—Resemble adults, but crown brown or grayish-brown streaked, and supercilium brownish; edges of coverts and tertials may be somewhat rusty.

Hybrids None reported.

References Ammon (1995), Rimmer (1986), Rising (1996).

43.1 Lincoln's Sparrow *Melospiza l. lincolnii*, Jones Beach State Park, Long Island, NY, USA, Oct 2000. The finely-streaked buffy breast and buffy sub-moustachial stripe are distinctive. This individual has a distinct dark breast spot, often cited as a field mark for the Song Sparrow, but commonly found on other species (Michael D. Stubblefield).

43.2 Lincoln's Sparrow, Kern Co., California, USA, Oct 1994. This retiring and shortish-tailed *Melospiza* has a very distinctive head pattern, note the rich buff submoustachial stripe, and shows fine streaking across the breast and along the flanks (Brian E. Small).

43.3 Lincoln's Sparrow, Riverside Co., California, USA, May 1999. When agitated or excited Lincoln's Sparrows often raise the crown feathers to form a short crest. This, together with the eye-ring create a curious 'wide-awake' look. Note the gray central crown-stripe contrasting with the chestnut lateral stripes (Larry Sansone).

43.4 Lincoln's Sparrow, s Texas, USA. A classic Lincoln's pose with the crown feathers raised and tail slightly cocked. Notice how streaky this bird looks with very fine blackish streaking on throat, breast and along flanks (Laura Elaine Moore).

43.5 Lincoln's Sparrow, Ventura Co., California, USA, Feb 1999. The wings are warm brown with obscure buff tips to the coverts, forming ill-defined wing-bars (Don Des Jardin).

43.6 Lincoln's Sparrow, Mission, Texas, USA, Feb 1995. This front view shows the extent of rich buff on the submoustachial stripe and breast. Notice the prominent pale buffy eye-ring. The throat and breast are evenly streaked with black which can sometimes, as here, form a slight smudge on the center of the breast (Kevin T. Karlson).

43.7 Juvenile Lincoln's Sparrow *M. l. gracilis*, Mackenzie, B.C., Canada, Aug 1998. Differs from adult in being distinctly more buffy on the head and upperparts. The pale eye-ring stands out from the rest of the face. Note the fine streaking within the supercilium and malar area. The wing-coverts are tipped with buff forming spotted wing-bars (Paul N. Prior).

44 Swamp Sparrow

(Melospiza georgiana)

Measurements
Length: 12.0–15.0 cm; 4.7–6.0 in.
   (males slightly larger).
Wing: 52–66 mm; 2.0–2.6 in.
Mass: 14.8–24.0 g (Pennsylvania, May).

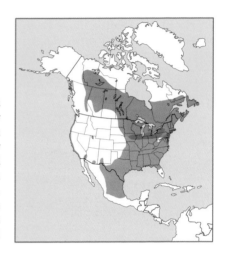

The Swamp Sparrow is a medium-sized Sparrow with a **rusty crown**, **rusty wings**, **black streaks on back**, grayish supercilium and ear-coverts separated by a brown eye-stripe, grayish **unstreaked** or faintly streaked **breast**, whitish throat, and slightly rusty-buff flanks. The rusty crown is variable, and often brownish, with a brownish or grayish median crown-stripe, especially in fall and winter.

Habitat
Swamp Sparrows nest in marshes, open bogs, and pond margins with emergent vegetation such as cattail, bulrushes, willows, alders, or leather-leaf. In both the breeding and winter seasons they may be found in saltmarshes, but are more generally found in freshwater marshes.

Behavior
Territorial Swamp Sparrows sing persistently, usually from an exposed perch, in a cattail or small bush. They usually fly only short distances, but territorial chases are common in breeding season. In winter, they are found in dense vegetation, often in low, open and wet areas, commonly at the edge of ponds or flooded fields. They are not difficult to flush, and respond readily to 'spishing'.

Voice
The song of the Swamp Sparrow is a musical trill on a single pitch, ***weet-weet-weet-weet-weet-weet***, resembling that of the Chipping Sparrow, but not so dry, and slower and louder, and somewhat more variable. They alternate trills of different tempos. During the nesting season, Swamp Sparrows may start to sing before dawn, and continue into the night, and occasionally give a flight-song. Some sing in the autumn, and occasionally in the winter. The call note is a distinctive metallic ***chink*** or ***chip***.

Molt
The Prebasic I molt is partial, and includes the body feathers, coverts, but usually not the remiges or rectrices; it occurs in July to Oct. There is a partial Prealternate I molt in Feb to Apr that involves head feathers. The Definitive Basic plumage is acquired by

a Definitive Basic molt in Aug to Sept. The Definitive Prealternate molt is similar to the first prealternate molt in extent and timing.

Similar species

Swamp Sparrows are more likely to be confused with **Lincoln's Sparrows** than any of the other 'rusty crowned' sparrows. Juvenile *Melospiza* sparrows are very difficult to separate in the field (see Lincoln's Sparrow account).

Geographic variation

M. g. ericrypta, which is found in the north and west, and *M. g. georgiana,* in the east, are similar and vary clinally; they cannot be separated in the field, although the former is said to be somewhat paler on the back, and less rusty in the wings. *M. g. nigrescens,* which apparently is resident along the Atlantic Coast from New Jersey south to Maryland, has a much broader black band on the forehead than the others (at least in breeding plumage), and the black streaking on the back, especially on the nape and mantle, is distinctly heavier; it is grayer, and its bill is larger than other Swamp Sparrows.

Distribution

Breeds from s Alaska, w-central and s Mackenzie, n Saskatchewan, n Manitoba, n Ontario, central Quebec, s Labrador, and Newfoundland, south through Yukon and e British Columbia, Alberta, central Saskatchewan, e North and South Dakota, and Nebraska, Minnesota, n and central Illinois, central Indiana, central Ohio, central West Virginia, and Maryland.

    Winters from s Alberta, e Nebraska, Kansas, Iowa, Illinois, s Great Lakes region, east to Massachusetts, south to Florida, the Gulf Coast, Texas, and irregularly south to Tamaulipas, San Luis Potosí, and Jalisco.

    Migrates throughout eastern North America, east of the Rocky Mountains, and rarely (especially in the fall) along the Pacific Coast. Spring migration mainly in late Apr, early May; fall migration principally in late Aug through early Oct.

Conservation status

Swamp Sparrows probably benefited, at least locally, by clearing of the eastern forests. However, draining of marshes has destroyed much suitable habitat for them, and their numbers have declined in many areas in the east. Recently, their numbers in the Great Lakes Region have increased, presumably as a consequence of a rise in the lake levels.

Description

Adults—Medium-sized; sexes alike. ***Head:*** forehead black; crown rusty, sometimes streaked with blackish, divided by more less distinct grayish or buffy brown median stripe; supercilium, lores, and ear-coverts grayish, the supercilium often being paler above and in front of the eye; eye and moustachial stripes dark brown or black, outlining the gray ear-coverts; submoustachial stripe thin and pale; malar stripe thin and dark; throat whitish and unstreaked or lightly streaked; ***back:*** nape grayish, or grayish-brown; mantle and scapulars light brown, broadly streaked with black, some broadly edged with buff; ***rump:*** rusty brown, streaked with dark brown, with median rectrices with dark brown centers; ***tail:*** rusty brown; ***wing:*** brown with the exposed edges of the coverts rusty, the inner edges black; ***underparts:*** chin and throat whitish or white, sometimes flecked with brown; breast grayish or grayish-brown, sometimes with slight streaking; flanks rusty beige, and thinly streaked; belly white; undertail-coverts whitish with brown centers; *bill:* upper mandible dark brown; lower mandible yellowish with a brownish tip; brown in young birds; *legs* and *feet:* brown; *iris:* brown.

First winter (Aug–Mar)—Resemble adults, but the nape, supercilium, and ear-coverts are buffy brown rather than grayish, and the crown is dark brown, heavily streaked, with little or no rusty.

Juveniles (July–Sept)—Resemble adults, but underparts streaked; crown blackish or darkly streaked; facial markings pale brown rather than gray; usually some rusty in coverts.

Hybrids None reported.

References Bond and Stewart (1951), Mowbray (1997), Rising (1996).

44.1 Adult Swamp Sparrow *M. g. georgiana*, New York City, New York, USA, Apr 1997. This primarily marsh-dwelling *Melospiza* is distinctive in having largely rufous wings and crown in breeding plumage. The face and underparts are pale gray, whiter on throat, submoustachial stripe and belly with a buffy wash on ear-coverts and flanks (Michael D. Stubblefield).

44.2 Adult Swamp Sparrow *M. g. georgiana*, New York City, New York, USA, Apr 1997. The amount of rufous on the crown is variable. This breeding individual shows an obscure gray central stripe and some black streaking, and is possibly a female. Concentrating on the head, note the blackish post-ocular stripe and ill-defined dusky moustachial and malar stripes (Michael D. Stubblefield).

44.3 Swamp Sparrow, Patagonia Lake State Park, Arizona, USA, Jan 1999. The back pattern is quite bold on fresh-plumaged birds. Note the thick black streaking contrasting with the pale buff feather edges on the mantle. The wings are largely rufous with contrasting pale buff edges to the tertials (Jim Burns/Natural Impacts).

44.4 Swamp Sparrow *M. g. georgiana*, Bombay Hook NWR, Delaware, USA, Oct 1999. This fresh individual, perhaps a first-winter bird, is like a spring adult, but is duller with extensive brown suffusion on head and underparts and blurry streaking on breast sides. The crown is evenly streaked with black with a grayish central stripe. Note the rufous wings relieved only by the black centers to the greater-coverts and tertials (Michael D. Stubblefield).

44.5 Swamp Sparrow *M. g. georgiana*, New York City, New York, USA, Oct 1998. Fall and winter birds tend to be duller than breeding-plumaged individuals. Notice the strong brownish suffusion on the flanks and ear-coverts. This bird shows some fine dusky streaking on the sides of the breast and lower flanks. The clear gray supercilium and neck suggest this bird is an adult (Michael D. Stubblefield).

44.6 Juvenile Swamp Sparrow *M. g. georgiana*, Great Swamp NWR, New Jersey, USA, July 2000. Differs from adult in having buff wash on head and underparts and fine streaking on breast. Can be very difficult to separate from juvenile Song Sparrow (often found in same habitat) but note the largely blackish lateral crown-stripes (brown on Song) and the more slender bill (Michael D. Stubblefield).

44.7 Swamp Sparrow *M. g. georgiana*, Jones Beach State Park, New York City, New York, Oct 2000. The breast and facial markings are clearly shown on this bird (Michael D. Stubblefield).

45 White-throated Sparrow

(Zonotrichia albicollis)

Measurements
Length: 15.0–17.0 cm; 5.9–6.7 in.
  (males slightly larger).
Wing: 60–77 mm; 2.4–3.0 in.
Mass: 19.0–35.4 g (migrants,
  Pennsylvania).

The White-throated Sparrow is a fairly large sparrow, with a pale or white super-cilium, which is **yellow in front of the eye,** pale or white median crown-stripe, **pale or white throat abruptly delimited against the unmarked or slightly streaked gray breast,** and brown or rusty brown wings.

Habitat
The White-throated Sparrow is a brushland bird at all seasons. It most commonly breeds in semi-open, mixed woods, often where spruce, balsam fir, birch, and aspen predominate, but may also breed in hemlocks, northern white-cedar, and tamarack-alder and white pine swamps, and conifer plantations. In winter it is often found in dense deciduous thickets or brush piles, often at woodland edge or in woodland clearings.

Behavior
On the breeding grounds, males sing persistently, commonly from a perch, but often not an exposed one. They start singing early in the morning, but sing only occasionally during the mid-day. Members of both sexes may sing. The white-morph individuals are both more aggressive and sing more often. In winter White-throated Sparrows are usually found in small, loose flocks, and sometimes in flocks of mixed species composition. When flushed, they usually fly up into low branches or a bush. They respond readily to 'spishing'.

Voice
The song is a clear, loud whistle, characteristically starting with a lower note followed by 3 or 4 higher, wavering notes; less frequently, the first note is the highest, followed by a lower one, then by 2 or 3 yet lower ones. The song almost always has at least one change in pitch, and may have up to three. It is a characteristic bird song of the 'north woods.' The most common call note is a distinctive *tseet*; they also may give a quiet *tip* note or a louder *pink* alarm call.

Similar species
The **White-crowned Sparrow** is generally grayer, especially on the nape, and the back is not so brown as that of the White-throated Sparrow; the White-crowned has a

yellow or pinkish bill, not a horn-colored one, as does the White-throat. Although the throat is pale on the White-crown, is it not white, nor sharply delimited with the gray on the breast. Except in juvenal plumage, White-crowns never have streaking on the breast, which some White-throats have. First winter White-crowns have rusty-beige crown-stripes. Eastern White-crowns are 'longer, slimmer birds' than White-throats.

Geographic variation None described.

Distribution
Breeds mainly east of the Rocky Mountains, from se Yukon, w-central and s Mackenzie, central and n Saskatchewan, n Manitoba, n Ontario, and central Quebec, south to s-central Alberta, s Saskatchewan, n-central North Dakota, n and e Minnesota, central Wisconsin, central Michigan, s Ontario, New York, Vermont, New Hampshire, Maine, Massachusetts, and n Pennsylvania.

Winters from s Maritimes, sw Quebec, s Ontario (rare), s Michigan, s Wisconsin, and e South Dakota, south to s Florida and the Gulf Coast, n Tamaulipas, Nuevo León, s Texas, New Mexico, and s Arizona, and uncommonly along the Pacific Coast from s British Columbia to n Baja California.

Migrates throughout the east and Great Plains. Spring migration especially late Apr through mid-May; fall migration especially mid- to late Aug through Sept. Eighteen records for the British Isles (Apr–June; Oct–Dec).

Conservation status
White-throated Sparrows were abundant in colonial times, and remain so today. They prefer forest-edge habitats, and forestry practices have probably created good breeding habitat for them.

Molt
The Prejuvenal molt occurs June–Aug. The Prebasic I plumage is acquired by a partial Prebasic I molt that includes all body plumage and greater coverts, but not rectrices and remiges. This molt takes place late July–Aug and occurs on the breeding grounds. The Definitive Alternate plumage is acquired by a partial Prealternate molt that takes place from late Feb–early May. This molt is variable, but generally involves head, throat, breast, and flank feather, the middle two rectrices, and three inner secondaries. The Definitive Basic plumage is acquired by a complete Prebasic molt, occurring from late June–early Oct.

Description
Adults—Fairly large; sexes similar, but females generally duller than males; polymorphic in color. *Head:* polymorphic with median crown-stripe and supercilium either both white or both pale brownish tan (a few birds seem intermediate); lateral crown and eye-stripes dark chocolate-brown to black, generally darker in white morph birds; ear-coverts and lores gray; submoustachial stripe faint or absent; *back:* mantle and scapulars brown or rusty brown, streaked with dark brown or black, the feathers edged with beige; *rump:* gray-brown with faint streaks; *tail:* long, brown, and slightly notched; *wing:* brown, with median and greater-coverts tipped with whitish, forming two narrow wing-bars, the anterior one more distinct than the posterior one; innermost greater-coverts and tertials edged with rusty brown; *underparts:* throat white or dull white, sharply delimited against the gray breast, which may be faintly streaked; flanks light brown and faintly streaked; belly dull white and unmarked; *bill:* upper

mandible horn-colored; lower mandible paler; *legs* and *feet:* pale pinkish-brown; *iris:* brown to reddish-brown.

First fall and winter (July–Feb)—Similar to more dull-colored females, but even duller, with beige instead of white on head and throat, and throat patch not so sharply delimited; gray of chest with indistinct streaking.

Juveniles (late June–early Aug)—Median crown-stripe indistinct, yellow in super-cilium reduced or absent; forehead, crown, and nape chestnut-brown, streaked with black; chin and throat whitish, flaked with dusky, with dark moustachial stripe; breast and flanks heavily streaked with dark brown; belly and undertail-coverts white and generally unmarked.

Hybrids

There are several records of 'Slate-colored' Junco X White-throated Sparrow hybrids. There is a record of a White-throated X Golden-crowned sparrow hybrid as well as of a White-throated X White-crowned sparrow hybrid (see photo).

References Banks (1970), Falls and Kopachena (1994), Payne (1979), Rising (1996).

45.1 White-throated Sparrow, Rondeau Provincial Park, Ontario, Canada, May 1996. The striking head pattern of this 'white-stripe' adult is distinctive. Note especially the broadness of the white supercilium and the contrasting bright yellow supraloral patch. The snowy-white throat is surrounded by the gray face and breast (Sam Barone).

45.2 White-throated Sparrow *Zonotrichia albicollis,* Pelham Bay Park, New York City, NY, USA, Feb 2001. Compared to the individual above, this tan-striped individual has a more subdued head pattern. As is commonly the case with with tan-striped individuals, the pale throat is crossed by thin, dark malar stripe; notice also the thin dusky striping on the breast and along the flanks, not uncommon for this species (Michael D. Stubblefield).

45.3 White-throated Sparrow, Cape May, New Jersey, USA, Oct 1996. Another 'white-stripe' bird showing the bold head pattern. The back feathers are broadly edged with rich buff and the wings show much chestnut on the coverts and tertials (Kevin T. Karlson).

45.4 White-throated Sparrow, Athens, Georgia, USA, Nov 1992. Non-breeding 'white-stripe' birds are duller than spring individuals and show some buffy-brown suffusion to white head stripes and brown fringes to lateral crown-stripes (Rick and Nora Bowers).

45.5 White-throated Sparrow, High Island, Texas, USA, May 1996. This 'tan-stripe' individual is notably duller and browner overall with reduced dusky-yellow supraloral patch. The crown-stripe and supercilium are buffy-gray and the throat is dirty-white and invaded by a thin dark malar stripe. The dusky streaking on the underparts is highly variable and tends to be more pronounced on 'tan-stripes' (Brian E. Small).

45.6 Second-year White-throated Sparrow, High Island, Texas, USA, Apr 1999. This interesting individual, perhaps a 'white-stripe' molting into Alternate I plumage, still shows some retained juvenile streaking on the underparts (Rick and Nora Bowers).

45.7 White-throated Sparrow, Cape May, New Jersey, USA, Oct 1995. Ageing 'tan-stripe' birds in the fall can be problematic owing to the variability of the extent of dusky streaking on the underparts. Eye-color can be useful but is not always apparent in the field. The extent of the streaking on the underparts of this bird suggests it may be in its first winter (Kevin T. Karlson).

45.8 First-winter White-throated Sparrow, Kern Co., California, USA, Oct 1997. This drab individual shows extensive and sharply defined blackish retained juvenile streaking on the breast and flanks. Note also the dark fringes to the pale feathers on the throat and submoustachial stripe (Brian E. Small).

46 Harris's Sparrow

(Zonotrichia querula)

Measurements:
Length: 16.0–19.0 cm; 6.3–7.5 in.
 (males somewhat larger).
Wing: 76–91 mm; 3.0–3.6 in.
Mass: 31.4–41.7 g.

Harris's Sparrow is a large sparrow. In breeding plumage the **black face** and **cap**, and **large pink bill** are diagnostic. In first winter plumage, the white chin and throat are flecked with a **necklace of dark brown feathers across the breast**; the crown is brown and streaked, with light brown lores and eyeline.

Habitat
On the breeding grounds, males sing persistently, often from the top of a spruce tree or an exposed rock, in open spruce woods often near the spruce tundra border, or in woodland edge, or burns. Nests may be some distance from the nearest woods. In winter, they are found in weedy fields, hedgerows, low brush, or the edge of deciduous woods.

Behavior
On the breeding grounds, males sing persistently, often from the top of a spruce tree or an exposed rock. In winter, Harris's Sparrows are generally found in loose flocks or small groups, and often in flocks of mixed species composition. They rarely sing in winter. When flushed, they often fly into a small tree or bush where they are easily seen. They readily respond to 'spishing'.

Voice
The song is one to several clear whistled notes on the same minor key, often followed by other notes that may be higher or lower, sometimes ending with a slow trill. Call a distinctive series of musical tinkling notes. Note a loud *chip* or *wink*.

Similar species
This is a distinctive sparrow. The black on the throat and breast separates Harris's Sparrow from the other *Zonotrichia*; first winter Harris's Sparrows may lack black on the throat, but the ochre on the side of the face is distinctive. Harris's Sparrows are obviously larger than most other sparrows.

Geographic variation
None described.

Distribution

Breeds from Mackenzie, s Keewatin, n Manitoba, and nw Ontario south to eastern Great Slave Lake, nw Saskatchewan and n-central Manitoba.

Winters from se Alaska, s British Columbia, n Utah, n Colorado, Iowa, sw Minnesota (occasionally n Minnesota) south to w Tennessee, Arkansas, Texas, s New Mexico, and on the Pacific Coast rarely through Washington and Oregon to s California mostly east of the Sierra Nevada. Commonest in winter in central Kansas, central Oklahoma, and n-central Texas.

Migrates principally through the central Great Plains, but rarely throughout the United States and eastern Canada north to Alaska and Newfoundland, and south to Florida. Spring migration mostly in Apr; fall migration in Oct (peak in Kansas late Oct).

Conservation status

Because Harris's Sparrow breeds only in isolated areas of northern Canada, it is unlikely that there have been any significant disturbances to their breeding habitat. There seems to have been some expansion of their wintering range in the last 60 years, but this may reflect better information rather than any change in status.

Molt

The Basic I plumage is acquired by a partial Prebasic I molt that involves body feathers and wing-coverts, but not the rectrices or remiges; this molt takes place on the breeding grounds, July to Sept. There is a Prealternate molt in Mar and Apr that involves many of the body feathers, the secondary-coverts, and some of the greater- and underwing-coverts. The Definitive Prebasic molt is complete, and takes place July to Sept.

Description

Adults—Large; males average brighter in coloration. *Head:* crown, face, chin, and throat black, extending back to eye; eye-stripe behind eye and ear-coverts brownish-buffy, becoming grayish on ear-coverts and side of neck and pale next to the black throat patch; black spot or patch at back of ear-coverts; *back:* hindneck and nape brownish; back and scapulars brown, broadly streaked with brownish black; *rump:* brownish; *wing:* brown; median and greater-coverts edged with white or buffy white, forming two wingbars; *tail:* brown, slightly notched; *underparts:* breast and flanks white, flecked with dark brown; belly white; *bill:* pink; *legs* and *feet:* light brown; *iris:* brown.

First winter (Aug–Apr)—Like adults, but crown mostly brown, flecked with dark brown or black feathers; brown around the bill and side of face; chin and throat white; malar stripe dark brown connecting to a dark brown necklace on upper breast; most dull-plumaged winter birds are probably first-winter individuals.

Juveniles (July–Aug)—Forehead and crown heavily streaked with black; side of head creamy buff, with some black streaking; back and nape dull chestnut and mottled with dark; back streaked and mottled; rump grayer and mottled with black; wings blackish, with feathers narrowly edged with buff; median and greater-coverts narrowly edged in white, making two narrow wing-bars; chin and throat white, spotted with black; center of breast with a conspicuous black spot; chest and flanks buffy white and heavily streaked; belly white.

Hybrids There is one record of a hybrid Harris's X White-crowned sparrow collected in southern Ontario.

Reference Norment and Shackleton (1993).

46.1 Adult Harris's Sparrow, Durham Region, Ontario, Canada, May 1994. This large and handsome *Zonotrichia* should not be confused with any other sparrow. The silvery-gray sides to the head, black crown, lores and throat and stout pinkish-orange bill are unique. Note the white underparts with thick black streaking on sides of breast (James M. Richards).

46.2 Adult Harris's Sparrow, Hagerman National Wildlife Refuge, Texas, USA, Nov. In non-breeding plumage the sides of the head are grayish-buff and the black crown appears scaly due to pale fringes to the feathers. The white underparts are washed with buffy-brown on the flanks and there is some chestnut within the black streaking on the sides of the breast (Rick and Nora Bowers).

46.3 Adult Harris's Sparrow, Iron Mountains, San Bernadino Co., California, USA, Nov 1998. The head pattern is less well defined in non-breeding plumage. Note the whitish fringes to the black feathers on the crown, lores and throat. The ear-covert wedge is chestnut rather than black (Larry Sansone).

46.4 First-winter Harris's Sparrow, Thunder Cape, Ontario, Canada, Oct 1991. Similar to non-breeding adult except the throat is white, bordered by narrow black malar stripes and thick black streaking below the lower edge, usually appearing as a black smudge on the center of the upper breast. The crown appears scaly due to bold buff fringes to the feathers (David D. Beadle).

46.5 First-winter (second calendar year) Harris's Sparrow, Durham Co., Ontario, Canada, Feb 1999. Another view showing the obviously scaled crown and white throat. Note also the chestnut post-ocular wedge and streaking on sides of breast (Sam Barone).

47 White-crowned Sparrow

(Zonotrichia leucophrys)

Measurements

Length: 14.0–17.0 cm; 5.5–6.7 in. (males slightly larger).

Wing: 62–84 mm; 2.4–3.4 in. (geographically variable; resident west coast birds relatively small (62–74 mm)).

Mass: 21.4–38.5 g (geographically and seasonally variable).

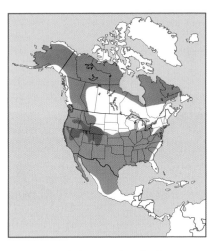

The White-crowned Sparrow is a fairly large sparrow. Adults are distinguished from other sparrows by the **black and white striped head**, grayish breast, and by **bill color** (yellowish to reddish-pink; geographically variable). First-winter birds (before Feb) resemble adults in color pattern, but are warm, rusty beige where the adults are black, and pale buffy where the adults are whitish. Some west coast birds retain some of the rusty crown feathers into the first summer.

Habitat

In northern and montane habitats, White-crowned Sparrows are birds of open stunted trees (conifers, willows, or birch), where they are often a common and conspicuous species. On the Pacific Coast, from central California north to British Columbia, they breed commonly in deciduous thickets along the coast and in urban gardens. In winter, White-crowns occur in brushy areas, hedgerows, woodland edges, multiflora rose, and gardens. They tend to occur in more open areas than either White-throated or Golden-crowned sparrows.

Behavior

On the breeding grounds, males sing persistently throughout the day from an exposed perch in a small tree, or from a rock. They also commonly sing at night, and occasionally in winter. In winter, White-crowned Sparrows occur in small, loose flocks, sometimes in flocks of mixed species composition, often with other *Zonotrichia*. They forage on the ground, usually in fairly open areas. When flushed, they commonly fly up into a small tree or hedge where they are easily seen. They respond vigorously to 'spishing'.

Voice

The song is variable with many regional dialects, but distinctive. In the east and north it is characteristically 2 (1 to 4) clearly whistled notes, the second slightly lower than the first, followed by 3 descending buzzy or husky notes, ***dear-dear buzz buzz buzz***. Along the Pacific Coast, the song usually starts with a long, clearly whistled note that is higher pitched than the rest of the song, and is followed by 2 to 4 notes that may be clear, buzzy, or warbled; the song may be the best way to distinguish west coast breeding birds from northern migrants. There are geographical dialects. The commonest call note is a hard ***pink***, ***tsit***, or ***zink*** (geographically variable), or a thin ***seep***; around the nest adults use a warning ***tip*** or ***tsit*** note.

Similar species

First-winter birds (before Feb) resemble first-winter **Golden-crowned Sparrows**, but are more pallid in color, with a distinct buffy median crown-stripe and rusty brown lateral crown-stripes. White-crown's bill is pinkish or yellowish; Golden-crown's is darker. White-crowned Sparrows resemble **American Tree** and **Rufous-crowned sparrows** in general coloration, but are easily separable.

Geographic variation

Five subspecies are generally recognized; these are fairly distinct, and their ranges fairly clearly defined. *Z. l. leucophrys* breeds in the northeast, west to n-central Manitoba; from there westward, it is replaced in the north by *Z. l. gambelii* (which has been reported east to the Atlantic Coast; one bird which was banded in California as a juvenile was recaptured in Apr in Maryland); in n Manitoba these occur sympatrically, and some individuals from there are intermediate. *Z. l. leucophrys* and *Z. l. gambelii* are similar in size; the white supercilium of *Z. l. leucophrys* stops at the eye, and the lores are black, whereas in *Z. l. gambelii* the white goes to the bill, and the lores are pale gray; the bill of *Z. l. leucophrys* is pinkish, whereas the bill of *Z. l. gambelii* tends to be orange-yellow or orange-pink. *Z. l. oriantha*, which breeds in mountains from s Alberta south to e California, central Arizona, and nw New Mexico, moves to lower elevations in the winter, and south into northern Mexico and Baja California Sur, is very like *Z. l. leucophrys*, although perhaps on average slightly paler; their ranges, however, do not overlap. Most dark-lored birds wintering in the east are probably *Z. l. leucophrys*, whereas those wintering in the west are probably *Z. l. oriantha*. *Z. l. pugetensis* breeds from coastal sw British Columbia south to nw California, and winters south to coastal sw California; some pass through e Oregon in migration; *Z. l. nuttalli* is resident on the coast from central California south to Santa Barbara Co. These both have pale lores, but are smaller and browner than the other subspecies, and generally have yellow bills. *Z. l. nuttalli* is relatively large-billed and short-winged; *Z. l. pugetensis* has a somewhat smaller bill.

Distribution

Breeds from w and n Alaska, n Yukon, n Mackenzie, central Keewatin, n Manitoba, n Quebec, Labrador, and nw Newfoundland, south to s Alaska, the Alaska Peninsula, Kodiak I., south in mountains and coastal areas (but absent along the n and central coast of British Columbia and the Queen Charlotte Is.) to s California, n Nevada, n and e-central Arizona, n New Mexico, se Alberta, and sw Saskatchewan, n Saskatchewan, n Manitoba, n Ontario, s-central Quebec, southeast to the outer north shore of the St. Lawrence River, and nw Newfoundland.

Winters from s British Columbia, Washington, Idaho, Wyoming, s Ontario (uncommon), and Nova Scotia, south to s Baja California Sur, Michoacán, Querétaro, San Luis Potosí, Tamaulipas, s Texas, Gulf Coast east to Florida, and Georgia.

Migrates throughout North America (uncommon in the southeast; very rare in Cuba), south to central Mexico. Spring migration mostly in mid-Apr through early May;

fall migration from late Aug through Oct; peak migration in mid-Sept. There are two records for the British Isles (May). *Z. l. nuttalli* are resident on the coast of California.

Conservation status

Eastern and northern populations of White-crowned Sparrows nest in habitats that have been little disturbed by humans, and there is no reason to suspect that their numbers have been significantly affected by human activities. In the 1980s they declined in numbers in Utah, the southern Rocky Mountains, and Sierra Nevada, but increased in Nevada, the northern Rocky Mountains, and Newfoundland.

Molt

There is a partial Prebasic I molt that involves body plumage and coverts, but not remiges and rectrices; this occurs on the breeding grounds except in *Z. l. gambelii*. There is a partial Prealternate I molt that involves head feathers, wing-coverts and some body feathers; in *Z. l. nuttalli* the Prealternate molt is limited to some of the crown and throat feathers. The Definitive Basic plumage is acquired by a complete Definitive Prebasic Molt that takes place on the breeding grounds. The Definitive Prealternate molt is partial. The timing of the molts varies geographically.

Description

Adults—Fairly large and rather slender; sexes alike. *Head:* a broad, white median crown-stripe extends from the back of the head to just behind the bill; black lateral crown-stripes join over the top of the bill; supercilium white, extending to the eye (eastern and western mountain populations) or to the base of the bill (western and west coast populations); eye-stripe and lores black (eastern or western mountain populations) or white (western and west coast birds); chin, throat, ear-coverts, and nape gray, with some brown in the nape; may have a faint dark malar stripe (west coast); *back:* mantle feathers with dark rusty brown or brown (west coast) centers and beige edges, making back appear streaked; scapulars grayish-brown, broadly edged in pale brown in fresh plumage; tertials dark brown, broadly edged with pale brown; *rump:* grayish-brown, lightly streaked; *wing:* brown, with tips of median and greater-coverts white, forming two conspicuous wing-bars; *underparts:* unstreaked and grayish, paler on the chin and belly than on the breast and flanks; *tail:* long, slightly notched; *bill:* pinkish, reddish-pink, yellow-orange to pinkish-orange (northwest) or yellowish (Pacific Coast); *legs* and *feet:* yellowish; *iris:* dark brown.

   First winter (July–Feb, Mar)—Like adults, but median crown-stripe, supercilium, and chin pale buff, lateral crown-stripes and eye-stripe light rusty brown, and belly suffused with buff. Head markings become black and white by Apr in most populations, but brown feathers are retained through the first year in Pacific Coast birds.

   Juveniles (June–Aug)—Like young in first fall, but forehead and crown pale and streaked with black; back and rump streaked; primaries edged with buff; secondaries and tertials edged with dull rust; chin, throat, breast, and flanks pale and heavily streaked with black; belly and undertail-coverts unstreaked. Some west coast individuals retain this plumage into Nov.

Hybrids

Hybrids with Golden-crowned, Harris's, White throated, and Song sparrows are reported.

References

Banks (1964), Chilton *et al.* (1995), Dunn *et al.* (1995), Pyle (1997), Rising (1996).

47.1 Adult White-crowned Sparrow *Z. l. leucophrys*, Point Pelee, Ontario, Canada. This 'eastern' bird shows the characteristic black lores with the white supercilium stopping just in front of the eye. The mantle is pale gray with sharply defined dark chestnut streaks. Note the mostly reddish-pink bill and comparatively long primary extension (Mike McEvoy).

47.2 Immature White-crowned Sparrow *Z. l. leucophrys*, Falcon Dam, Texas, USA, Mar 1996. Overall pattern that of adult but head stripes are chestnut and creamy-white instead of black and white. This individual, although dark-lored, shows some whitish mottling within the area – a variable feature. Note the ground color of the mantle is buffy-brown rather than pale gray (Kevin T. Karlson).

47.3 Adult White-crowned Sparrow *Z. l. oriantha*, Riverside Co., California, USA, May 1990. This form is very similar to *Z. l. leucophrys* and cannot be identified except by range. The head pattern is similar to *Z. l. leucophrys* with extensive solid black on the lores. The bill is slightly darker and redder, but this is variable (Brian E. Small).

47.4 Adult White-crowned Sparrow *Z. l. oriantha*, Aspendell, Inyo Co., California, USA, May 1993. A nice view of the head pattern, note especially the solid black lores. The bill is deep reddish-pink with a blackish tip and culmen. The paleness of the underparts is quite apparent here (Larry Sansone).

47.5 Adult White-crowned Sparrow *Z. l. gambelii*, Churchill, Manitoba, Canada, June 1994. This excited adult shows the striking head pattern well, note the pale gray supraloral area (although with some dusky mottling perhaps indicating an intergrade with *leucophrys*). The bill on this bird is pinkish-orange and is generally paler than is usual for *Z. l. leucophrys* or *Z. l. oriantha* (James M. Richards).

47.6 Adult White-crowned Sparrow *Z. l. gambelii*, Riverside Co., California, USA, May 1997. The orangish bill and whitish supraloral can clearly be seen here, but note some dark feathering on the lores. Otherwise this form is very similar to both *Z. l. leucophrys* and *Z. l. oriantha* and shares a longish primary extension (compare with *Z. l. nuttalli* and *Z. l. pugetensis*) (Brian E. Small).

47.7 Adult White-crowned Sparrow *Z. l. gambelii*, Los Angeles, California, USA, Feb 2000. A classic *Z. l. gambelii* with pale supraloral area and yellow-orange bill. Note the 'clean-cut' appearance of this bird with pale gray ground color to the mantle (Rick and Nora Bowers).

47.8 Immature White-crowned Sparrow *Z. l. gambelii*, Charmlee Park, California, USA. Obviously pale-lored, this bird can be separated from *Z. l. nuttalli* and *Z. l. pugetensis* by the orange bill and comparatively long primary extension. The ground color to the mantle is pale buff and the streaking perhaps more well defined than would be expected on the two coastal forms (Brian E. Small).

47.9 Immature White-crowned Sparrow *Z. l. gambelii*, Los Angeles, California, USA, Feb 2000. This front-on shot displays the pale lores well. Note also no trace of any darker malar stripe, usually evident on *Z. l. nuttalli* and *Z. l. pugetensis*. The bill is orange with a limited dusky tip (Rick and Nora Bowers).

47.10 Adult White-crowned Sparrow *Z. l. nuttalli*, Santa Barbara Co., California, USA, Aug 1997. This resident form is similar to *Z. l. pugetensis* and most cannot be safely identified to race in the field. This adult *Z. l. nuttalli* shows the generally sullied plumage and very short primary projection characteristic of the form. Note also the yellow bill (Larry Sansone).

47.11 Adult White-crowned Sparrow *Z. l. nuttalli*, Santa Barbara Co., California, USA, Aug 1997. On this view note the buffy-brown ground color to the mantle and extensive brown wash on the underparts forming a streaked effect on the breast sides. The yellow bill and short primary extension are also obvious (Larry Sansone).

47.12 First-winter White-crowned Sparrow *Z. l. nuttalli*, central coastal California, USA, Aug 1997. Note the sullied appearance of this immature bird with extensive brown suffusion on head and underparts (Herbert Clarke).

47.13 Adult White-crowned Sparrow *Z. l. pugetensis*, Ventura Co., California, USA, Jan 1995. This form is virtually identical to *Z. l. nuttalli*, and not safely identifiable in the field. This adult shows pale lores, dark malar stripe and yellow bill characteristic of the pair. On the whole this *Z. l. pugetensis* appears somewhat cleaner-looking with less brown suffusion on the underparts and sharper black and white head stripes (Larry Sansone).

47.14 Adult White-crowned Sparrow *Z. l. pugetensis*, Ventura Co., California, USA, Jan 1997. Another view of an adult. Compared to *Z .l. gambelii* note the buffy-brown ground color to the mantle, more extensive brown wash on the underparts and the obviously yellow bill. This bird shows a slightly longer primary extension than would be normal for *Z. l. nuttalli*, but this is variable (Don Des Jardin).

47.15 Immature White-crowned Sparrow *Z. l. pugetensis*, Ventura Co., California, USA, Feb 1999. Very similar to immature *Z. l. nuttalli* and probably not safely identified except by range. Tends to appear somewhat cleaner-looking with slightly longer primary projection. Told from immature *Z. l. gambelii* by yellowish bill and shortish primary extension (Don Des Jardin).

47.16 Juvenile White-crowned Sparrow *Z. l gambelii*, Inglutalik, Agulik River Delta, Alaska, 6 Aug 1977. The underparts of this juvenile are heavily streaked. Note that the head markings reflect those of the adult (Declan Troy).

48 **Golden-crowned Sparrow**

(Zonotrichia atricapilla)

Measurements
Length: 15.0–18.0 cm; 6.0–7.1 in.
  (males slightly larger).
Wing: 74–83 mm; 2.9–3.3 in.
Mass: 21.2–36.5 g (California; Mar).

The Golden-crowned Sparrow is a fairly large sparrow with a **yellow crown, bordered by a heavy black line** in summer; crown-stripes are indistinct in winter.

Habitat
On the breeding grounds, Golden-crowned Sparrows are found in rank deciduous thickets, commonly alders and willows, or dwarf conifers, near timberline, often along hillsides or along ravines, and in similar habitats near sea level. In winter, they occur in thickets and weed patches along rivers, fence rows, or in dense brushy margins of cultivated fields.

Behavior
On the breeding grounds, males sing persistently from an exposed perch, often a dwarf willow or alder, or tall weed (cow parsnip). They sing throughout the day. In winter, Golden-crowned Sparrows are generally found in small loose flocks, commonly with White-crowned Sparrows. They do not fly far when flushed, but move from bush to bush. The juveniles can be difficult to see. Golden-crowned Sparrows respond vigorously to 'spishing'.

Voice
The song characteristically consists of 3 clearly whistled descending notes, in a minor key, sometimes followed by a quiet trill; the song is sometimes transcribed as 'three blind mice,' or 'oh dear me.' They sing year round, although infrequently in winter. Rarely, there are variations (such as the reversal of the second and third notes, or the addition of a fourth note). They also give a hard, loud slurred *chink* or *chip* note and a sharp *tizeet* note.

Similar species
The crown color separates the Golden-crowned Sparrow from the other *Zonotrichia*, which it otherwise resembles. Some, perhaps mostly first-year birds, resemble first-year **White-crowned Sparrows**, but the lateral crown-stripes are brown with a yellow spot in the center of the crown above the bill, the supercilium is light gray-brown (not buffy), and the ear-coverts are gray (not buffy); the bill is dusky (not yellowish or pinkish) and most have yellowish lores. White-crowned Sparrows are, in general,

warm buffy in color, whereas Golden-crowned Sparrows are brown. Golden-crowned Sparrow has a rather dull, unmarked face, and lacks a strong eyeline, making the dark eye stand out; White-crowned Sparrow has a strong eyeline stripe. Golden-crowned Sparrow's head looks round in profile, whereas White-crowned Sparrow often shows a peak behind the eye. The dull, brown winter or immature may be mistaken for a female **House Sparrow** if seen from behind.

Geographic variation
None described.

Distribution
Breeds in w and n-central Alaska and central Yukon, and probably sw Mackenzie, the Alaska Peninsula and Aleutian Is. (to Unimak I.) and Shumagin Is., south to s British Columbia, and extreme nw Washington and sw Alberta.

Winters from s Alaska and s British Columbia, south (mainly west of the Cascades and Sierra Nevada, but fairly commonly in the western Great Basin) to central Baja California ('norte'), and rarely east to Colorado and Kansas, and south to Sonora and w Texas. Rare east to the east coast (Nova Scotia, Massachusetts, south to Florida).

Migrates throughout the west, east to the western Great Basin (where fairly common in fall).

Conservation status
There is little information on changes in the status of the Golden-crowned Sparrow, but clearing of forests in its breeding range may have created suitable breeding habitat in some places where it would otherwise not be available.

Molt
The Prebasic I molt is partial, and includes body feathers and coverts but not the primaries and rectrices; it occurs before migration. There is perhaps a supplemental molt in Oct to Nov that includes only upper contour feathers. There is a partial Prealternate I molt in Mar and Apr that involves most of the contour feathers. The Definitive Basic plumage is acquired by a complete Definitive Basic molt in July and Aug, and a partial Definitive Alternate molt that occurs from late Feb through late Apr; this involves contour feathers, tertials, and the two central rectrices.

Description
Adults—Fairly large; sexes similar. *Head:* blackish-brown sides of crown become brown behind the head; median crown-stripe is broad and yellow; it becomes light gray rather abruptly toward the back of the head; lores yellow or gray; ear-coverts gray; nape brownish-gray, with or without faint streaking; *back:* grayish olive-brown, with back and scapulars broadly streaked with brownish-black, suffused with rusty brown; *rump:* grayish-brown; *tail:* long, brown, slightly notched; *wing:* brown with chestnut-brown or brown greater and median-coverts tipped with white, forming two wing-bars; outer webs of greater-coverts and tertials more or less chestnut-brown; *underparts:* throat, side of neck and breast gray, becoming paler on belly, and buffy on flanks; *bill:* dark, with upper mandible darker than lower mandible; *legs* and *feet:* pale brownish; *iris:* brown.

Adults in winter—Have a duller head pattern than in summer, with lateral crown-stripes brown. This plumage is quite variable.

First winter (Aug–Mar)—Variable, and not separable from all adults. Median crown-stripe indistinct, but with some yellow or yellow-brown between the lores; the head markings become more distinct with age.

Juveniles (June–July)—Forehead and lateral crown-stripes brown, median crown-stripe buff, extending posteriorly; entire crown streaked with black; nape with tinge of rusty brown; ***back:*** streaked with black and buffy brown; ***rump:*** and uppertail-coverts brown; ***wing:*** dark gray, edged with buffy white, tertials and greater-coverts edged with rust and tipped with buffy white; chin and throat whitish, flecked in dark brown; sides of throat, breast and flanks cream colored and heavily streaked with black; belly paler and spotted with black.

Hybrids

Golden-crowned X White-crowned sparrow hybrids are scarce, and Golden-crowned X White-throated sparrow hybrids are even rarer.

References

Linsdale and Sumner (1934), Norment *et al.* (1998), Rising (1996).

48.1 Adult Golden-crowned Sparrow, Riverside Co., California, USA, May 1992. A typical, chunky *Zonotrichia* with quite dull grayish-brown plumage, but note the striking head pattern. This alternate plumaged adult has very broad black sides to the head contrasting with a dull yellow central crown patch which becomes gray on the back of the crown and nape. Note the pale lower eye-crescent, the long tail, and the short primary projection (Brian E. Small).

48.2 Adult Golden-crowned Sparrow, Los Angeles Co., California, USA, Dec 1990. Non-breeding adults are duller overall with head pattern obscured with grayish and brown mottling and often, as here, with duller yellow crown patch. Note the uniform appearance of the grayish face and underparts with a slight brownish suffusion to the flanks (Larry Sansone).

48.3 Golden-crowned Sparrow, Ventura Co., California, USA, Oct 1994. Some individuals can be difficult to age. This bird shows quite extensive mottled black on the lateral crown and has rather a lot of yellow on the crown and above the eye. These features are intermediate and the bird cannot be aged in the field (Brian E. Small).

48.4 First-winter Golden-crowned Sparrow, Ventura Co., California, USA, Nov 1994. The dull head pattern with only a hint of black above the grayish supraloral identify this bird as an immature. The crown and area above the eye show some greenish-yellow which is finely streaked dusky. Otherwise, note the pale lower eye-crescent and the grayish-pink bill with darker culmen (Brian E. Small).

48.5 First-winter Golden-crowned Sparrow, Ventura Co., California, USA, Nov 1994. Another view of a typical immature bird. The plumage is overall gray-brown, suffused with buff on face and flanks. There is a trace of yellow on the crown and above the eye and the bill appears bicolored with pinkish lower mandible (Brian E. Small).

48.6 First-winter Golden-crowned Sparrow, Irma, New Jersey, USA, Jan 1998. This relatively dull immature still shows a hint of the distinctive adult head pattern with a dusky suffusion on the lateral crown and some greenish-yellow on the crown. Note that the crown is finely streaked dusky. Otherwise note the bland face with the whitish lower eye-crescent (Kevin T. Karlson).

Hybrid zonotrichia

1. Presumed White-throated Sparrow X Dark-eyed Junco *Z. albicollis* X *Junco hyemalis*, Long Point, Ontario, Canada, 1994. The overall pattern on this bird is that of a White-throated Sparrow but the extensive gray suffusion on the head and upper breast are suggestive of hybridization with Dark-eyed Junco (Paul N. Prior).

2. Presumed White-crowned Sparrow X Golden-crowned Sparrow *Z. leucophrys* X *Z. atricapilla*, Half Moon Bay, San Mateo Co., California, USA, Apr 1998. This remarkable individual is superficially like a White-crowned Sparrow but note the grayish suffusion to the pale head stripes and the obvious yellow forward portion of the central crown-stripe and patch above eye (Alvaro Jaramillo).

3. Presumed adult White-throated X White-crowned sparrow, *Zonotrichia albicollis* X *Z. leucophrys*, Long Point, Ontario, Canada, April 1994. This interesting individual is like a typical White-throated Sparrow, but the head, with the pale gray ground color and black-and-white crown stripes, is more suggestive of a White-crowned Sparrow. Note the faint ghost-like White-throated pattern on the malar and throat. Notice also the pale lores, partial post-ocular stripe (lacking the wedge typical of both species) and lack of yellow on the supraloral (pale buff here) (Felix Jachmann).

49 Dark-eyed Junco

(Junco hyemalis)

Measurements

Length: 13.0–17.0 cm; 5.1–6.7 in.
(males slightly larger; geographically variable).

Wing: Geographically variable; see separate accounts below.

Mass: Geographically variable; see accounts below.

Note: There are five major types (subspecies or groups of subspecies); we treat these separately. Additional studies may indicate that some of these should be recognized as specifically distinct.

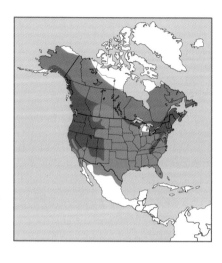

'Slate-colored' Junco
(*Junco h. hyemalis* group)

Measurements

Wing: 69–84 mm; 2.7–3.3 in.
Mass: 14.3–25.4 g (Pennsylvania, various seasons).

The 'Slate-colored' Junco is a **slate-gray** sparrow with a **white, unmarked belly** and **white outer tail feathers**. The **bill is pink**. Females and first-year birds are paler and often have considerable brown in their plumage, especially in the back and flanks.

Habitat

'Slate-colored' juncos breed in a variety of woods, but especially in open woods, cut-over areas, plantations, commonly but not necessarily in coniferous or mixed woods; in the north, they may occur in urban parklands and gardens. In the Allegheny Mountains, they are found at 700–900 m, and are most common in brushy edge habitats; farther south, in the Appalachians, they nest up to 1350 m. In ne Ohio, they nest in cool hemlock ravines and mature beech-maple forest. In the north, they are more strictly birds of coniferous woods, and are especially common in young jack pines. In winter, they are found in brushy woodland edge, and open woodlands with brushy understory.

Behavior

On the breeding grounds, males sing persistently, especially early in the season, from an exposed perch, often from near the top of a conifer, a snag, or tall dead tree. In winter, they are generally found in loose flocks or small groups, and may be in flocks with other sparrows. They are often found in open woods, or in weedy areas at the edge of woods, hedgerows, or fields. They do not tend to fly far when flushed, and are easy to see. They respond vigorously to 'spishing'.

Similar species

'Oregon' juncos have a dark gray or gray head, with contrasting brown or brownish-gray back and pinkish-brown on the flanks; the gray on the throat and flanks of the slate-colored junco is concave – forms an inverted 'U' on the breast – whereas that on the Oregon junco has a convex hood. These forms intergrade with each other in the northwest, and intermediate individuals occur. The **'white-winged' junco** is larger, usually has two white wing-bars and always has more white in the tail (a few individuals of all of the subspecies of Dark-eyed Juncos have white wing-bars). The hood and face of 'white-winged' juncos is a uniform gray, and generally a lighter gray than that of the 'slate-colored' junco.

Geographic variation

Three subspecies of *J. h. hyemalis* are generally put in the 'slate-colored' group, *J. h. hyemalis, J. h. carolinensis,* and *J.h. cismontanus. J. h. hyemalis* breeds in the northeast and north, *J. h. carolinensis* in the Appalachian Mountains; and *J. h. cismontanus* breeds east of the coastal ranges from central Yukon southeast to n-central and e British Columbia and w-central Alberta. These birds represent a stable population of apparent hybrids between 'Oregon' and 'slate-colored' juncos, and are intermediate in color between the two. The hood of *J. h. carolinensis* is a uniform light gray, whereas that of *J. h. hyemalis* is darker; *J. h. carolinensis* also may have a dark spot on the base of the upper bill which may be bluish in color. Male *J. h. cismontanus* are browner than others in this group, and the edge of the gray is convex rather than concave; females (especially) have flanks washed with pink or brown rather than gray. Most of the 'slate-colored' juncos that winter in coastal British Columbia appear to be this subspecies.

Distribution

Breeds from w and nw Alaska, n Yukon, nw and central Mackenzie, s Keewatin, n Manitoba, and Ontario, Quebec and Labrador (north to the limit of trees) and Newfoundland south to s-central Alaska, ne British Columbia, sw Alberta, central Saskatchewan, s Manitoba, central Minnesota, se Wisconsin, central Michigan, s Ontario, ne Ohio, n Pennsylvania, south in mountains to se New York, w and central Massachusetts, w Connecticut, ne West Virginia, w Maryland, w Virginia, w North Carolina, e Kentucky, e Tennessee, sw South Carolina, and n Georgia.

Winters from s Canada and Newfoundland south to Florida, Alabama, Louisiana, Texas, Tamaulipas, central Chihuahua, n Sonora and n Baja California. They are uncommon along the west coast and south and west of New Mexico, and in s Florida.

Migrates throughout the east; spring migration mostly Mar to mid-Apr and fall migration mid-Sept, and mid-Oct through Nov. There are 16 records for the British Isles (mostly Apr and May, and Nov to Jan).

Conservation status

Always a common sparrow, the 'slate-colored' junco remains one today, although recently numbers in New Brunswick and New Hampshire have declined, probably reflecting habitat loss.

Molt

The Prebasic I molt is partial, and involves body feathers and some of the coverts, and occasionally the central rectrices; it occurs mostly on the breeding grounds, from July to Oct (timing varies geographically). There is a limited Prealternate molt in Feb to Apr that involves primarily feathers around the head, but not coverts, remiges or rectrices. The Definitive Prebasic molt is complete, and takes place July to Oct.

Description

Medium-sized sparrow; sexes slightly different in color. **Adult males—*Head:*** neck, chest, upper breast, sides, flanks, and upperparts plain slate-color, darker on the head, paler on the rump and sides; ***tail:*** outer rectrix (6th) white; extensive white on the 5th; some white on the 4th; ***wing:*** slate-gray; ***underparts:*** belly, lower breast, and undertail-coverts white; ***bill:*** pink, sometimes dusky at tip; ***legs:*** dark pinkish-brown; ***feet:*** darker; ***iris:*** dark brown.

Adult females—Like adult male, but slate-color lighter, sometimes decidedly so, and less white in the tail.

First-winter (Aug–Mar)—Like adult, but grays dull, and head, and especially breast, flanks, back, and rump washed with brown, often pinkish-brown; eye grayish-brown, becoming darker with age; females browner than males, with wide brown edging on tertials.

Juveniles (June–Aug)—Crown, back, and rump brown, sometimes slightly rufescent on back, streaked or mottled with dark brown; throat, breast, and flanks buffy or buffy gray, streaked with dark brown; belly and undertail-coverts unmarked white; legs pinkish.

Hybrids

There are several records of 'slate-colored' junco X White-throated Sparrow hybrids. Individuals of this group intergrade with 'Oregon' juncos in the northwest where hybridization is frequent but restricted to zones where the ranges of these two are in contact.

49.1 'Slate-colored' Junco, Orono, Ontario, Canada, Jan 1990. The slate-gray upperparts, hood, and flanks contrasting with the white belly are distinctive. The bill is pale pink. Note the white outer tail feathers (James M. Richards).

49.2 Adult male 'Slate-colored' Junco *J. h. hyemalis*, Orono, Ontario, Canada, Mar 1989. A nice front view showing the concave lower edge to the hood as it extends onto the flanks. The pale pink bill stands out from the slate-gray face (James M. Richards).

49.3 Adult male 'Slate-colored' Junco *J. h. hyemalis*, Sudbury District, Ontario, Canada, June 1989. This worn mid-summer individual still appears uniform slate-gray on the upperparts and hood although the flight feathers and tail are browner with wear and sun-bleaching (Mark K. Peck).

49.4 First-winter male 'Slate-colored' Junco *J. h. hyemalis*, Hamilton, Ontario, Canada, Dec 1995. Similar to adult male but with brownish wash on mantle and crown and obvious contrast between gray-edged (fresh) inner greater-coverts and brown-edged (retained juvenile) tertials. The outer greater-coverts are also retained juvenal feathers and are narrowly tipped whitish (Sam Barone).

49.5 Adult 'Slate-colored' Junco *J. h. hyemalis*, St. Williams, Ontario, Canada, Jan 1992. Rarely, as here, some individuals will show pale or whitish wing-bars suggesting 'White-winged' Junco. However, the darker tone of the upperparts and hood, smaller size and less extensive white in the tail should reduce confusion (David Agro).

49.6 Male Dark-eyed Junco *J. hyemalis*, Kern Co., California, USA, Oct 1997. Although out of range, this individual appears to be of the eastern form *hyemalis* although a *hyemalis/cismontanus* intergrade or even pure *cismontanus* cannot be eliminated (Brian E. Small).

49.7 Female 'Slate-colored' Junco *J. h. hyemalis*, New York City, New York, USA, Jan 2000. This rather drab female shows a distinct brownish cast to the head and mantle and appears to show some contrast between the outer greater-coverts (with pale tips) and the somewhat more uniform inner feathers and is possibly in its first winter, although accurate ageing is not always possible in the field (Michael D. Stubblefield).

49.8 Female 'Slate-colored' Junco *J. h. hyemalis*, Hamilton, Ontario, Canada, Jan 1997. Another female with even browner plumage than Fig. 49.7. The pale tips to the outer greater-coverts are quite obvious here, indicating this bird is almost certainly in its first winter (Sam Barone).

49.9 Juvenile 'Slate-colored' Junco, Alaska, USA, June 2000. Obvious dusky streaking on head and breast. The upperparts are washed brownish and moderately streaked darker. Note the buffy tips to the greater-coverts forming a noticeable wing-bar. Differs from other streaky juvenile sparrows in having outer tail feathers extensively white (Alaska Bird Observatory).

'White-winged' Junco

(Junco hyemalis aikeni)

Measurements
Wing: 78–92 mm; 3.1–3.6 in. (males slightly larger).
Mass: no information.

'White-winged' junco is a large junco with a **large bill**, which may be an important diagnostic feature in the hand, but not in the field. They are like 'slate-colored' juncos, but the **slate is lighter**. The greater and median secondary coverts are usually white-tipped, forming **two distinct white wing-bars**, and the **outer 3 (6th, 5th, 4th) rectrices are white** (or largely white), **with white usually on the 3rd.**

Habitat
'White-winged' juncos are most common in pine forests, but may also be found in spruce or aspen. In winter, they are found in brushy habitats, around feeders, but avoid open grassland.

Behavior
On the breeding grounds, males sing from an exposed perch, typically a pine tree. In fall and winter, the birds form small flocks that frequently forage on the ground; other species, especially other juncos, may join them.

Voice
The song is like 'slate-colored' junco; the *chip* calls are said to be more musical.

Similar 'species'
'Slate-colored' juncos are smaller, and rarely have white on the 3rd rectrix or white wing-bars. Although all of the juncos may have white wing-bars, they are unusual, and other **western juncos** have pink or reddish in their plumage.

Geographic variation None.

Distribution
Breeds in se Montana, ne Wyoming, w-central South Dakota (Black Hills), and nw Nebraska.

Winters in the Black Hills (lower elevations) south through Colorado (mostly in foothills) to n-central New Mexico, n Arizona, and east to central South Dakota and e Kansas (uncommon), and w and central Oklahoma. Casual west of the Rocky mountains (Arizona, California and Oregon), and n Texas.

Conservation status
No information. They are not uncommon in their limited range.

Molt
Presumably like 'slate-colored' junco in pattern.

Description

See above. 'White-winged juncos' are less sexually dimorphic in both size and color than other juncos.

First-winter (Aug–Mar)—Like adults, but more or less tinged with light grayish-brown, especially on the back.

Juveniles (July–Aug)—Like 'slate-colored' juncos, but with white wing-bars, and three white outer tail feathers.

Hybrids

Rarely hybridizes with 'pink-sided' junco in southeastern Montana (Powder River Co.), and a hybrid individual has been collected in Colorado in winter. As a consequence of habitat destruction the breeding ranges of these two probably no longer overlap.

49.10 Adult male 'White-winged' Junco *J. h. aikeni*, Black Hills near Keystone, South Dakota, USA, May 2000. Overall quite similar to 'slate-colored' group but distinctly paler with obvious white wing-bars and tertial edges (John W. Herbst).

49.11 Adult male 'White-winged' Junco *J. h. aikeni*, Black Hills near Keystone, South Dakota, USA, May 2000. The mid-gray tone of the upperparts, breast and flanks is well shown on this profile. The extensive white in the outer tail feathers is distinctive but rarely (as here) visible on a perched bird. Note the contrasting blackish lores on this bird (John W. Herbst).

'Gray-headed' junco

(J. hyemalis caniceps)

Measurements
Wing: 72–87 mm; 2.8–3.4 in. (males slightly larger).
Mass: 18.0–26.0 g (Arizona).

'Gray-headed' juncos are medium-sized, dark-eyed and gray-headed sparrows. The head, wings, rump, and tail are gray, with **black around the eye and lores; lower mandible yellow;** upper mandible yellow or gray (varies geographically); **back a bright rusty red**, red usually confined to the interscapular region; their throat, breast and flanks are pale gray, **without a line of demarcation between the breast and flanks**; outer three tail feathers partly or completely white. Females are slightly duller in color than males, sometimes with less white in the tail.

Habitat
'Gray-headed' juncos breed in mountains, generally above 1800 m, and are often found in conifers (spruce, Douglas-fir, ponderosa and lodgepole pines, and fir), but also in aspen, oak, and mountain mahogany. They are more likely to be found in rather arid woodlands than other Dark-eyed Juncos. In winter, they are found along the lower edges of coniferous forests, brushy ravines with scrub oak, mountain mahogany, and hawthorn, sagebrush, and woods, but not generally in open fields.

Behavior
As do other juncos, during the nesting season males sing persistently from an exposed perch near the top of a tall tree, often the top of a conifer. Singing occurs Feb through July, and is most intense during nesting, after mid-Mar. In winter, in the southern part of their range, some males apparently stay on or near their breeding territories, but most form flocks, often with other juncos. They feed almost exclusively on the ground.

Voice
The song is like other Dark-eyed Juncos, but perhaps more varied than that of the 'slate-colored' junco.

Similar 'species'
Yellow-eyed Juncos are similar in general coloration, but have a bright yellow iris; Yellow-eyed Juncos also have rust-edged greater-coverts and tertials. **'Oregon'** and **'pink-sided' juncos** have a throat that contrasts with the flank color, and usually have darker gray heads.

Geographic variation

There are two named subspecies, the northern *J. h. caniceps*, which breeds south to n-central Arizona and e-central New Mexico, there they intergrade into the southern *J. h. dorsalis*. *J. h. caniceps* has a pale-colored upper bill whereas *J. h. dorsalis* has a dark one. *J. h. dorsalis* are sometimes called 'Red-backed' Juncos.

Distribution

Breeds: from s Idaho, se Oregon (probable), n Nevada, central Nevada, sw Nevada, n Utah, n-central Colorado, south through central and w New Mexico to Catron Co., and w Texas, central Arizona, and west to se California.

   Winters at lower elevations in breeding range, south through w Texas, Arizona, and s California, north to Santa Barbara Co., and south to n Sinaloa, Chihuahua, and n Durango. Rare in W. Nebraska, Kansas and Oklahoma, and e Montana. Accidental in British Columbia and Manitoba (Dec; Jan to Mar) and nw Louisiana (Mar).

Conservation status

Little information, but generally common where found.

Molt

Presumably similar to 'slate-colored' junco in pattern, but most or all of the greater-coverts and 1–3 tertials may be replaced in the Prebasic I molt.

Description

Adults—See above.

   First-winter (Aug–Mar)—Like adults, but the grays are paler, and less strongly contrasting with the white of the belly; flanks more or less tinged with buff; reddish-brown or black duller; bill somewhat darker, and dusky at tip.

   Juveniles (July–Sept)—Head buffy brown, streaked with brown; back and rump bright rusty red, streaked with dark brown; rump buffy, streaked with black; rectrices dark gray, with outer two white; underparts buffy, streaked with dark brown on throat, breast, and flanks; belly whitish; legs yellowish.

Hybrids

'Gray-headed' juncos hybridize with 'pink-sided' juncos in n Utah, and s Wyoming, n Nevada, and s Idaho, and with 'Oregon' juncos in sw Nevada and e California.

49.12 Adult ' Gray-headed Junco *J. h. caniceps*, Portal, Arizona, USA. Overall gray with contrasting bright reddish-brown mantle, the scapulars are contrastingly gray. The pinkish-yellow upper mandible separates this individual from *J. h. dorsalis*. There is no obvious hooded effect and the pale gray throat and breast blends into the whitish belly. Sexes similar (Brian E. Small).

49.13 Adult 'Gray-headed' Junco *J. h. caniceps*, Portal, Arizona, USA, Feb 2000. On this form the bill is wholly pinkish-yellow, sometimes, as here, with a dusky tip to the culmen. The blackish lores contrast with the gray head. The wing-coverts and tertials are edged with pale gray, lacking any brown tones. Note the sharp contrast between the reddish mantle and the gray scapulars (Larry Sansone).

49.14 Juvenile 'Gray-headed' Junco, North Rim Grand Canyon, Arizona, USA, Aug 1994. Overall ground colors as adult but, as in other forms, note the extensive fine streaking on head, mantle and breast. The flanks appear to show less streaking than other forms. Note the spotted buffy wing-bars (Jim Burns/Natural Impacts).

49.15 Juvenile 'Gray-headed' Junco *J. h. dorsalis*, Great Basin National Park, California, USA, Sept 1991. A somewhat duller individual than Fig. 49.14. Note again the restricted dusky streaking on the underparts (Larry Sansone).

49.16 Adult 'Gray-headed' Junco, Madera Canyon, Arizona, USA, Jan 1994. This *J. h. dorsalis* is similar to *J. h. caniceps*, although it has much paler underparts, especially noticeable on throat and breast. The bill is a little larger with a completely dark upper mandible. Notice the plain gray wings (Rick and Nora Bowers).

49.17 Second-year 'Gray-headed' Junco *J. h. dorsalis*, Madera Canyon, Arizona, USA, Feb 1990. A duller individual showing brownish edges to the tertials and buffy suffusion on the lower flanks. In particular, note the contrast between the gray-edged inner tertial and greater-coverts and the worn, brown-edged outer tertials and inner secondaries (Rick and Nora Bowers).

'Pink-sided' junco

(J. hyemalis mearnsi)

Measurements
Wing: 73–86 mm; 2.9–3.4 in. (males slightly larger).
Mass: 15.5–26.0 g (Arizona).

The 'pink-sided' junco is like the 'slate-colored' junco, but the **head and breast are gray** (lighter than in 'slate-colored'), the **lores dark slate**, the back dull brown, and the **flanks pinkish cinnamon-brown.**

Habitat
'Pink-sided'juncos most commonly breed at the edge of pine woods, but also will nest in other edge habitats, in spruce, aspen, or mountain mahogany. In winter, they are often in thickets and shrublands at lower elevations, and are common around feeders.

Behavior
Like other juncos, on the breeding grounds males sing from an exposed perch, most commonly from a pine. In fall and winter they are found in loose flocks, commonly with other juncos and sparrows.

Voice
The song is like that of other Dark-eyed Juncos.

Similar 'species'
'White-winged' juncos are gray-backed, and have white wing-bars and more white in the tail, and no pink in the flanks. The head is not so dark as that of **'Oregon' juncos,** which also tend to have a pinkish (not dull brown) back, and browner flanks. 'Pink-sided' juncos have lores that contrast with the paler, grayer head; this contrast is not so noticeable in 'Oregon' juncos. **'Slate-colored' juncos** have a darker head and chest, with the lores not contrasting in color.

Geographic variation
None described.

Distribution
Breeds from se Alberta and sw Saskatchewan (Cypress Hills), and n-central Montana, e Idaho, nw Wyoming, and south to se Idaho.
   Winters from Utah, Wyoming, w and central Nebraska south to n Sonora, central Chihuahua, and w Texas, and rarely to California; has been reported east to Nova Scotia.

Conservation status
Little information. They are common in suitable habitat.

Molt
Presumably like 'slate-colored' juncos in pattern.

Description

Adults—Medium-sized; sexes similar; see above.

First-winter (Aug–Mar)—Like adult.

Juveniles (July–Aug)—Like 'slate-colored' junco, but back browner, or cinnamon-brown.

Hybrids

'Pink-sided' juncos hybridize with 'gray-headed' juncos in n Utah, s Wyoming, and s Idaho; rarely hybridize with 'white-winged' juncos in se Wyoming.

49.18 Adult 'Pink-sided' Junco *J. h. mearnsi*, Portal, Arizona, USA, Feb 2000. Overall pattern similar to the 'Oregon' group but note the mid-gray hood (with darker lores), dull brown back and extensively pinkish-brown flanks. Sexes similar (Larry Sansone).

49.19 Adult 'Pink-sided' Junco *J. h. mearnsi*, Portal, Arizona, USA, Feb 2000. Another view showing the extent of pinkish-brown on the flanks. The wings are mostly gray with brown edges to the greater-coverts and tertials. The blackish lores are quite obvious and should prevent any confusion with females in the 'Oregon' group (Larry Sansone).

'Oregon' junco

(J. hyemalis oreganus)

Measurements
Wing: 67–84 mm; 2.6–3.3 in. (males slightly larger).
Mass: No data available.

Adult male 'Oregon' juncos have a **dark gray to black hood, with a convex bib on their breast, dark chestnut back and scapulars**, and rusty brown flanks. Females are slightly duller, with grayer hoods, often brown on the nape. The white on the tail is generally restricted to the outer two rectrices – slightly more on males than females.

Habitat
'Oregon' juncos usually breed in open coniferous forests, moist red-wood canyons, dry pine forests in the California interior, aspens, compact low conifers at timberline, heavy but arid live oak, oak-madroño associations, digger and Coulter pine forests, Monterey cypress, eucalyptus, and along the coast in city parks and gardens. Migrating and wintering juncos may be found in a variety of habitats, including chaparral, fence rows, piñon-juniper woods, sagebrush, brush, and urban gardens.

Behavior
Like other Dark-eyed Juncos, males sing persistently from an exposed perch. In winter 'Oregon' juncos are found in small flocks, often with other juncos and sparrows.

Voice
Vocalizations are similar to those of other Dark-eyed Juncos.

Similar 'species'
'Oregon' juncos can generally be separated from **'pink-sided' juncos** by their darker hoods and browner flanks, although female 'Oregon' juncos are confused with 'pink-sided' juncos (see that account). **'Gray-headed' juncos** have gray heads with grayish-white underparts, redder backs, and grayish flanks.

Geographic variation
Five subspecies of 'Oregon' juncos from north of Mexico are commonly recognized. *J. h. oreganus* breeds from se Alaska south to central coastal British Columbia; *J. h. montanus* breeds from the interior of British Columbia, Washington, w Idaho and Montana, and Oregon; *J. h. shufeldti* breeds from sw British Columbia south along the coast to central California; *J. h. thurberi* breeds from the s interior of Oregon south to n Baja California; and *J. h. pinosus* is resident in the coastal hills of central California. Variation in size and color among these is clinal, and they are poorly delimited; each is within itself quite variable. *J. h. oreganus* generally have more reddish backs than *J. h. montanus*. which resemble *J. h. shufeldti* in color, but are generally brighter and on average smaller. *J. h. thurberi* has a lighter and more pinkish-red back than *J. h. shufeldti*, and *J. h. pinosus* has a ruddier back and sides than *J. h. thurberi*. Individual birds probably cannot be identified to subspecies.

Distribution

Breeds from se Alaska, south along the coast from the central interior of British Columbia, and extreme w Alberta south through the interior of British Columbia, n and central-w Idaho, nw Montana, Washington, Oregon, extreme w Nevada, and in the mountains through California to n Baja California.

Winters from s Alaska, s British Columbia, n Idaho, w Montana, Wyoming, and South Dakota south to n Baja California, n Sonora, central Chihuahua, and central Texas.

Migrates throughout the west; resident or partly resident throughout much of the range, but many move to lower elevations in winter. Reported rarely but regularly east of the Great Plains, to Nova Scotia, Massachusetts, and Tennessee.

Conservation status

Little information. They are generally common where found.

Molt

Probably like the 'slate-colored' junco in pattern.

Description

Adults—Medium-sized; slightly dimorphic in plumage. See above.

First-winter (July–Apr)—Like adults, but males show less color contrast.

Juveniles (June–Aug)—Forehead and crown brown, profusely streaked with dark brown; back, rump, and uppertail-coverts rusty, streaked with darker brown; tail dark brown with two lateral rectrices white; wings blackish, with coverts tipped with whitish or buffy white, forming two whitish wing-bars; throat and breast heavily streaked; flanks strongly tinged with buffy pink; belly white or buffy white.

Hybrids

'Oregon' juncos hybridize with 'slate-colored' juncos in s-central Yukon and nw British Columbia, e British Columbia, and w Alberta, and with 'gray-headed' juncos in s Nevada and se California.

References Browning (1990), Miller (1941), Patten *et al.* (1998), Pyle (1997), Rising (1996).

49.20 Male 'Oregon' Junco, Pine Mountain, California, USA, Oct 1996. The blackish hood contrasting with the rufous-brown back is distinctive. The underparts are whitish with buffy-pink sides to the breast and flanks. Several forms in the 'Oregon' group are all quite similar and are difficult to identify to subspecies, especially in the winter (Don Des Jardin).

49.21 Female 'Oregon' Junco, Pine Mountain, California, USA, Oct 1996. Like a dull version of the male with gray hood and browner back. Compare with female 'slate-colored' and note the convex lower edge to the hood, which does not extend onto the pinkish breast sides (Don Des Jardin).

49.22 Female 'Oregon' Junco, Ventura Co., California, USA, Nov 1995. The gray hood is well defined and contrasts with the brown back. The wings are mostly gray with broad brown edges to the inner greater-coverts and tertials (Brian E. Small).

49.23 Juvenile 'Oregon' Junco J. h. pinosus, near Mount Abel, California, USA, July 1996. Overall colors similar to a female but with extensive dusky streaking on head, back, breast and along flanks. The wing-coverts show thick black shaft-streaks and are tipped with buff, forming spotted wing-bars (Don Des Jardin).

50 Yellow-eyed Junco

(Junco phaeonotus)

Measurements
Length: 14.0–16.0 cm; 5.5–6.3 in.
(males slightly larger than females).
Wing: 72–85 mm; 2.8–3.3 in. (males slightly larger).
Mass: 18.3–22.0 g (Arizona).

Yellow-eyed Juncos have a **gray head, with black lores and around the eyes, a yellow iris** (as adults), black upper mandible, yellowish lower mandible, rusty red back, rusty outer webs of the greater-coverts and tertials, a light gray throat, flanks, and rump, and a gray tail with white outer feathers.

Habitat
Yellow-eyed Juncos are found in montane conifer and pine-oak forests, from 1850 to 2500 m. They generally feed in understory, in brush or thickets, scratching in litter for insects and seeds; they are common around picnic sites.

Behavior
Territorial males sing from an exposed perch, as high as 20 m, often from a pine tree. They feed on the ground, often scratching for food among pine needles; they 'shuffle' rather than hop. They do not tend to flock with other juncos or sparrows, but are generally found in family-sized groups. Chases can occur at any time of the year, but most commonly in winter and early spring, when territories are being established.

Voice
The song characteristically consists of three parts of contrasting rhythm and pitch, *chip chip chip wheedle wheedle kee kee kee kee kee*. It has also been described as being Chipping Sparrow like, but lower in pitch. The notes are a sharp *chip* or a softer *tssspt*, softer and less blunt than those of the Dark-eyed Junco.

Similar species
Southern 'gray-headed' juncos have similar bill color, but have a dark iris, and no rusty in coverts or tertials; Yellow-eyed Juncos are paler on the rump, throat, and belly.

Geographic variation
None described north of Mexico. *J. p. palliatus* breeds in the US and n Mexico.

Distribution
Resident from sw New Mexico and se Arizona south to Chihuahua, n-central Coahuila, Nuevo León, sw Tamaulipas, Oaxaca, w Veracruz, Chiapas, and w Guatemala; also in

the cape district of Baja California Sur. Has been recorded out of the breeding range in Arizona where it may wander, and move to lower elevations in winter.

Conservation status

Yellow-eyed Juncos are common in suitable habitat in range.

Molt

The partial Prebasic I molt, which occurs July to Sept, includes body feathers and usually all median and greater wing-coverts, and often 1–3 tertials; central rectrices are replaced in some individuals. There is a partial Prealternate I molt in Feb to Apr that is limited to body feathers. The complete Definitive Basic molt occurs July to Sept, and the Definitive Prealternate molt is like the Prealternate I molt.

Description

Adults—Medium-sized; sexes similar. *Head:* and nape gray; black lores and around the eye; *back:* mantle rusty red; *rump:* pale gray; *tail:* rectrices gray, with two (rarely three) lateral rectrices white; *wing:* gray; greater-coverts and tertials edged with cinnamon-rufous; *underparts:* chin, throat, breast, flanks, and belly pale gray to white; *bill:* upper mandible blackish; lower mandible yellow; *legs:* yellowish, *feet:* darker; *iris:* bright yellow.

First winter (Sept–Dec)—Like adults, but paler in color, throat almost white, with iris olive-gray to grayish-yellow; iris brown to gray or pale yellow.

Juveniles (June–Oct)—Forehead, crown, and nape gray, streaked with black; lores and area around eye black; ear-coverts gray; back rusty red, streaked with black; scapulars gray, streaked with black; rump and uppertail-coverts gray, and faintly streaked; rectrices black, with extensive white in outer two; wings dark, with tertials and greater-coverts edged with chestnut; no wing-bars; breast and flanks grayish, streaked with black; belly and undertail-coverts dull white. Iris dark brown.

Hybrids None reported.

References Miller (1941), Pyle (1997), Rising (1996), Sullivan (1999).

50.1 Adult Yellow-eyed Junco *J. p. palliatus*, Santa Catalina Mountains, Arizona, USA, June 1994. The bright yellow eye is distinctive amongst juncos. Overall pattern similar to the 'Gray-headed' Junco group, but notice the reddish-brown mantle color extends onto the upper scapulars and the inner greater-coverts show extensive chestnut bases. The bicolored bill resembles that of *J. h. dorsalis* (Brian E. Small).

50.2 Adult Yellow-eyed Junco *J. p. palliatus,* Santa Catalina Mountains, Arizona, USA, June 1994. The underparts are mostly pale gray, whiter on belly and undertail-coverts. The face is mid-gray with contrasting blackish lores highlighting the yellow eye. The chestnut in the greater-coverts is just visible here (Brian E. Small).

50.3 Adult Yellow-eyed Junco *J. p. palliatus*, Santa Catalina Mountains, Arizona, USA, Sept 1992. On this dorsal view notice the chestnut color of the mantle extends onto the scapulars. The tertials are broadly edged with chestnut and narrowly tipped with white. Note the broad, rounded tail feathers (Rick and Nora Bowers).

50.4 Juvenile/First-winter Yellow-eyed Junco *Junco p. palliatus*, Mount Lemon, Arizona, USA, Sept 1992. Similar to adult, but with a duller iris and some retained juvenile streaking on mantle and head. This individual has yet to replace the juvenile wing-coverts which form spotted wing-bars (David D. Beadle).

50.5 Juvenile Yellow-eyed Junco *J. p. palliatus*, Chiricahua Mountains, Arizona, USA, July 2000. Differs from adult in having iris brown. The head, malar area and breast are extensively streaked like other juvenile juncos but note largely rufous tertials and wing-coverts (Larry Sansone).

51 McCown's Longspur

(Calcarius mccownii)

Measurements
Length: 13.0–15.0 cm; 5.1–5.9 in.
(males slightly larger).
Wing: 80–94 mm; 3.1–3.7 in.
(males larger).
Mass: males av. = 26.7 g; females av. =
24.7 g.

The facial pattern of breeding male
McCown's Longspurs is distinctive: they
have a **black cap, malar stripe, and
breast band, and whitish side of face
and throat**, and a large pinkish bill.
Their median-coverts are rusty, giving
them a rusty shoulder, and when they fly
they flash a lot of **white in the tail**.
Females are similarly patterned, but have
little or no black markings, and are grayish rather than white on the face and throat.
In winter, their feathers are tipped with buff (although there is a limited Prealternate
molt, they essentially wear into their breeding plumage). McCown's Longspur's tail
pattern is distinctive: the outermost rectrix is nearly pure, the middle two brown, and
the others tipped with brown, making an **inverted 'T' pattern** in flight.

Habitat
McCown's Longspurs are birds of the sparse, dry high plains, typically in places where
heavily grazed shortgrass is interspersed with cactus and scattered shrubs, and where
there is little litter. Unlike Chestnut-collared Longspurs, they often forage in fallow
fields. In winter, they are found in shortgrass pastures or bare dirt fields.

Behavior
The aerial display flight of the male is striking. With slow, stiff wing-beats, the male
rises to 20 m high, singing and gliding back to the ground. During courtship, individuals of either sex will raise one wing or both while on the ground. Territorial males
chase intruders from their territory and occasionally chase females. In winter,
McCown's Longspurs tend to be found in flocks, often with other longspurs (especially Chestnut-collared) and Horned Larks. When on the ground, they may crouch
down into a depression where they are difficult to see, and the flock flushes explo-
sively when approached. In spite of their preferred open, shortgrass habitat, they can
be difficult to see.

Voice
Territorial males sing a distinctive warbling, musical song, *see see see mee see me hear
me hear me see*. The song is frequently sung during an elaborate, stiff-winged aerial

display flight, but may be sung from a fence, rock, or the ground; females have been reported to sing. During flight, they give a dry rattle, ***chip-pur-r-r-r***. Call notes are a two-noted ***prit-tup*** or ***chit-it***, or a single ***whit***.

Geographic variation None described.

Similar species

Although in breeding plumage, the longspurs are relatively easy to separate, identification can be more difficult in winter (see Appendix 2). Juvenile McCown's Longspurs have a slightly streaked breast, but in winter they are the only longspur with an unstreaked breast. Although ventral streaking is faint on some other wintering longspurs, **Lapland Longspurs** always show some streaking on their flanks. McCown's Longspurs usually show some chestnut on the lesser and median-coverts, and appear to be pale, relative to the other longspurs. The mantle streaking is not so distinct as that on other longspurs. When flushed, McCown's Longspurs show a lot of white in the tail, separating them from either **Smith's** or **Lapland longspurs**; if well seen, the tail pattern can also be used to separate them from **Chestnut-collared Longspurs**, but this usually is not a useful mark. McCown's Longspur has a pinkish bill with a dark tip, but other longspurs may be similarly colored. Relative to other longspurs, especially **Chestnut-collared Longspurs**, McCown's Longspurs are large-billed and chunky, long-winged, and short-tailed. In contrast, the **Chestnut-collared Longspur** is small and delicate looking, and seems to have relatively short wings, as well as faint streaking on the breast; males usually show chestnut in their collar and black on the breast and belly (male **Lapland Longspurs** may also show chestnut in their collar and black on their breast). **Smith's Longspurs** are a warm rusty buff overall, especially on their underparts; other longspurs are usually white-bellied. **Vesper Sparrows** also show white in their tail and have rusty lesser-coverts, but are streaked below, have a white eye-ring, and do not act like longspurs.

Distribution

Breeds from s Alberta, sw and s-central Saskatchewan, south through w North Dakota, w and n-central South Dakota, Montana, and extreme se Idaho, to w Nebraska and n-central Colorado.

Winters from California (rare), central and especially se Arizona, s and e New Mexico, and w Kansas (sporadic), south through central Oklahoma, s-central Texas to ne Sonora, Chihuahua, w Coahuila, and n Durango. Commonest in winter in sw Kansas and w Texas.

Migrates mostly through western Great Plains. Spring migration starts in Feb, with a peak in Mar; fall migration occurs mostly in Oct.

Conservation status

McCown's Longspur has declined not only in abundance but in range since 1900. At the turn of the Century, they bred south to w Oklahoma, and east to ne North Dakota and sw Minnesota. The reasons for this are not clear, but the habitat of the Great Plains was greatly changed by the near extirpation of the bison, the fencing of pastures, and the cultivation of grain crops. It is possible that the suppression of prairie fires has contributed to their decline. Today, McCown's Longspurs are most common in dry, grazed, even heavily grazed pastures, which are unsuitable for cultivation, so there is no reason to suppose that they will significantly decline from present numbers.

Molt

The Prebasic I plumage is acquired by a partial Prebasic I molt in July to Sept that involves most of the body feathers, but not the wing feathers. There is a limited Prealternate I molt from Feb to Apr that involves most of the body feathers but no flight feathers. The Definitive Basic plumage is acquired by a complete Definitive Prebasic molt from late July to late Sept; the Definitive Prealternate molt is like the Prealternate I molt in extent and timing.

Description

Fairly large in size; sexually and seasonably variable. **Adult males in summer** (May–Aug)—**Head:** forehead and anterior part of crown black (depending on wear, feathers may be buff-tipped); supercilium, supraocular spot, and lores white; ear-coverts white under and behind eye, gray toward neck; malar stripe black; throat white; **back:** nape gray, with brownish streaks; mantle, scapulars, and tertials brown, with pale edges; **rump:** and uppertail-coverts grayish, with darker centers; uppertail-coverts long, extending half way down tail; **tail:** middle two rectrices brown; outer-most rectrix white; others brown-tipped, with brown variably extending up the outer web somewhat more on the innermost white rectrices; **wing:** coverts chestnut; greater-coverts and secondaries broadly, but not distinctly edged with white; inner webs of wing feathers whitish, making underside of the wing appear white; **under-parts:** chin and throat white; breast with a crescent-shaped broad black band; belly and flanks grayish-white; undertail-coverts white; **bill:** black; **legs** and **feet:** grayish-brown; **iris:** brown or black.

Adult males in winter (Sept–Apr)—Like summer male, but black areas on head concealed by brown tips to feathers, and breast by buffy tips.

Adult females (May–Aug)—**Head:** crown grayish-brown, with indistinct brown streaks; supercilium whitish buff; ear-coverts whitish buff becoming brown toward the neck; malar and eyeline stripes grayish-brown; **back:** brown with dark brown centers to mantle feathers giving the back a streaked appearance; **rump:** and uppertail-coverts brown; **tail:** pattern same as adult male; **underparts:** throat buffy pale gray; breast band grayish-white; belly pale; **wing:** brown with varying amounts of cinnamon in the lesser and median-coverts (apparently varies with age), inner webs of wing feathers whitish; **bill:** pinkish or light brown, with dark tip; **legs** and **feet:** brownish; **iris:** black.

Females in winter (Sept–Apr)—Like summer female, but feathers edged with buffy, and streaks on back less distinct.

First-winter (after Aug)—Resemble adults, but are less brightly colored and buffier; females in their first year have little chestnut in the wing.

Juveniles (May–Aug)—Resemble females in winter, but are distinctly streaked on the breast and flanks.

Hybrids

There is a hybrid McCown's X Chestnut-collared Longspur.

References

Dechant *et al.* (1999d), Dunn and Beadle (1998), Pyle (1997), Rising (1996), With (1994).

51.1 Male McCown's Longspur, w. Montana, USA, June 1997. This breeding male in slightly worn plumage should present few identification hazards. Apart from the chunky, block-headed shape and deep-based bill the overall plumage pattern is unique. Note especially the gray face and underparts with contrasting white throat and supercilium and black crown, malar stripe and gorget on breast. The median-coverts are mostly rich chestnut and contrast greatly with the rest of the wing. Even with the tail closed a substantial amount of white is evident, especially at the feather bases, but note that this is not always easy to observe (Brian E. Small).

51.2 Male McCown's Longspur, w Montana, USA, June 1997. Another view of a breeding male. The solid black gorget is well displayed here. The remaining underparts are gray, mottled darker, blending to white on undertail-coverts. The thick bill is completely black (Brian E. Small).

51.3 Female McCown's Longspur w Montana, USA, June 1997. This breeding female in slightly worn plumage is quite different from the male. The head pattern is rather plain and mostly brown and buff with a whitish supercilium and black-streaked crown. The bill is bright pink with a small black tip. The median-coverts show a reduced amount of rufous-chestnut with buffy fringes and black centers. Note here the shortish primary extension with three evenly spaced tips showing (Brian E. Small).

51.4 Male McCown's Longspur San Rafael Valley, Arizona, USA, Jan 1999. The almost solid black gorget on the breast and largely chestnut median-coverts immediately identify this bird as a male. Otherwise it resembles a female though perhaps with a slightly stronger malar stripe. The bill on this winter bird is dull pinkish with a darker culmen (Jim Burns/Natural Impacts).

51.5 Male McCown's Longspur, Lancaster, Los Angeles Co., California, USA, Dec 1991. This bird is similar to that depicted in Fig. 51.4, but shows less abrasion on the underparts and therefore a less prominent blackish gorget. The median-coverts are largely chestnut with sharply defined buff fringes (Larry Sansone).

51.6 McCown's Longspur, Lancaster, Los Angeles Co., California, USA, Dec 1991. A back view of a winter bird, quite probably a male judging by the largely chestnut median-coverts. The general chunky aspect of the species is well demonstrated here as is the habit of wing-drooping with slightly raised tail (Larry Sansone).

51.7 Female McCown's Longspur, Lancaster, Los Angeles Co., California, USA, Nov 1991. The somewhat bland head pattern without an obvious dark border to the ear-coverts and lack of obvious rufous or chestnut in the median-coverts easily identify this bird as a female. The underparts are whitish with a buffy wash across the breast and some blurry brown streaking on breast sides and along upper flanks (Larry Sansone).

51.8 Female McCown's Longspur, s California, USA, Dec 1991. Another view of a winter female. Again, the often-quoted House Sparrow-like head pattern is evident, as is the lack of chestnut in the median-coverts. The bill is largely pinkish (Herbert Clarke).

52 Lapland Longspur

(Calcarius lapponicus)

Measurements
Length: 13.5–17.3 cm; 5.3–6.8 in.
Wing: 88–101 mm; 3.5–4.0 in.
   (males larger).
Mass: 23.5–32.5 g (Alaska).

Lapland Longspurs are large sparrows. Breeding males have a **black face, outlined with a buffy white or white supercilium and post-auricular stripe** that runs to the upper breast, a **bright rusty back or crown and nape**, and a **bright yellow bill with a black tip**. Females have a **pale buffy supercilium and earcoverts, which are outlined by blackish eyeline and moustachial stripes**; the pale side of neck is highlighted by a narrow **rusty collar**. There is a crescent-shaped black bib surrounding the white throat.

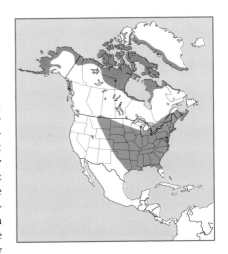

Habitat
Lapland Longspurs breed in the high arctic where they can be found in a variety of tundra habitats. They are most common in fairly wet tundra. In migration and winter they can be found in shortgrass prairie, fallow fields, or near beaches.

Behavior
Males arrive on the breeding grounds shortly before females and, weather permitting, start to defend and advertise territories. They commonly give a flight-song, and chase intruders from their territory, but also will sing from a rock, the top of a sedge tussock, or even a telephone wire. During courtship, the pair engages in reciprocal chasing. When flushed from the nest, the female may give a distraction display, alarm notes, or both, but usually does not fly far from the nest. In migration and winter, Lapland Longspurs characteristically form large flocks, sometimes of over a million individuals. Especially in the east, where these longspurs are not particularly common, they are often found with pipits or Horned Larks, and Snow Buntings. When flushed, flocks will fly around a field and drop back into the short vegetation that is characteristic of their habitat, and can be very difficult to see, once on the ground. If one approaches slowly it is possible to walk into the midst of a flock on the ground – and still not see the longspurs!

Voice
The song of the Lapland Longspur is a variable, almost squeaky, melodious *churtle churtle seerilee-seerilee-serrilee seetle-we-we-you*, first rising slightly, then descend-

ing slightly. The song is often given during a flight display in which the male will rise 3–15 m and glide back to earth with his wings held above his back. The sharp rattle, *pit-tic* or *pit-tic-tic* is frequently given in flight; this call is similar to the rattle of Smith's Longspur (which, however, is sharper and louder) and that of McCown's Longspur. Laplands often intersperse rattles with musical *teu* notes, which resemble those of Snow Buntings.

Similar species

Lapland Longspurs are the commonest and most widespread of the longspurs. Breeding longspurs are easily identified, but wintering ones can be difficult, in part because they are commonly difficult to see well. There is considerable white in the outer two rectrices of both **Smith's** and Lapland longspurs which can often be seen when they are in flight; **McCown's and Chestnut-collared longspurs** have considerably more white in their tails. The ear-coverts of Lapland Longspurs are framed with dark brown, and the edges of the secondaries, tertials, and coverts are edged with rufous. Lapland (and Smith's) Longspurs are long-winged with long primary tip projection (the tips of the longest primaries extend well beyond the tips of the tertials). Lapland Longspurs often occur in mixed flocks (with other longspurs, Horned Larks, Snow Buntings). When flushed, longspurs often fly as a group and drop back into the field where they often seem to disappear. The call notes are distinctive. See Appendix 2.

Geographic variation

Three subspecies from North America are generally recognized, *C. l. lapponicus* of the eastern arctic and Eurasia, *C. l. alascensis* of the western Canadian arctic and Alaska, and *C. l. coloratus* of northwestern Siberia and occasionally on the western Aleutian Is., Alaska. *C. l. alascensis* is paler than *C. l. lapponicus* on average, but variation is clinal. *C. l. coloratus* is darker than the others with a dark back and wing-coverts, and wing edges bright chestnut. Some put longspurs from the eastern arctic in the subspecies *C. l. subcalcaratus*.

Distribution

Breeds from w and n Alaska, n Yukon, Banks, Prince Patrick, Melville, Bathurst and central Ellesmere islands south to central Alaska, n Mackenzie, s Keewatin, n Manitoba, n Ontario, n Quebec and Labrador.

Winters from coastal Alaska, s British Columbia, se Alberta, s Quebec, New Brunswick, Prince Edward I., and Nova Scotia south through central Montana, central Wyoming and e Colorado, to e and central Texas, Louisiana, Alabama, and n Florida. Commonest in central Plains (Kansas, Oklahoma).

Migrates through Canada and the United States, primarily east of the Rocky Mountains. Fall migration occurs from mid-Aug through Dec, with a peak in mid-Oct to early Nov; spring migration from mid-Feb through early May, with a peak in Mar; in Ontario, the spring migration is mainly in late Apr to early May.

Conservation status

This is an abundant species; they breed in habitats that are of little economic value and have been little disturbed by people. In migration and winter their numbers in any given area may show considerable variation, but this probably reflects variation in food availability and weather.

Molt

The Prebasic I molt is partial and involves some to all median-coverts and sometimes some of the greater-coverts, but no tertials or rectrices; it takes place on the breeding ground from July to Sept. Prealternate molts are limited to body feathers, especially those around the head and breast, and occurs Mar to May. The Definitive Basic molt is complete, and takes place July to Sept.

Description

Large and long-winged. **Adult males** (May–Aug)—**Head:** crown black, flecked with varying amounts of buff or pale buff; side of face and throat black; supraloral spot may have some flecks of buff; eye-stripe wide and bright pale buffy or white, connecting with a bright buffy post-auricular stripe that runs to the upper breast; **back:** nape and side of neck rusty or rufous, variously flecked with buff (affected by wear); mantle brown with blackish centers, and variously edged with pale buff, giving the back a streaked appearance; **rump:** and uppertail-coverts blackish-brown to brown with broad pale buffy edges; **tail:** outer two rectrices blackish, with white on the outer webs and at the tips of the inner webs; **wing:** brown, with indistinct pale edges to feathers; coverts and scapulars with buffy brown edges; **underparts:** chin, throat, and breast black, with varying amounts of white on the sides of the breast; flanks white, with black streaking; lower breast and belly white; undertail-coverts white; **bill:** bright yellow, with black tip; **legs** and **feet:** black; **iris:** black.

    Adult males in winter (Sept–Apr)—The black on the head is confined to the crown, the posterior and lower borders of the ear-coverts, and a patch on the chest, and is obscured by the pale brownish tips to the feathers; although there is a limited prealternate molt, the birds mostly wear into summer plumage, so become progressively more brightly colored toward the end of the winter. The throat is whitish; the rusty collar is somewhat obscured by buffy feather tips, and the bill dull orange.

    Adult females (May–Aug)—Resemble adult male, but have brownish ear-coverts, bordered with black, a white throat, and less rust on the collar.

    Females in winter (Sept–Apr)—Resemble male in winter, but may be somewhat duller, and there is often no trace of rust on the neck.

    Juveniles (June–July)—Crown, back, and rump dark brown, with broad pale or rusty edges to the feathers; throat and breast streaked with brown; belly pale buff; greater-coverts and tertials broadly edged with rufous buff; tail pattern as in adults.

Hybrids None reported.

References Dunn and Beadle (1998), Dunning (1993a), Pyle (1997), Rising (1996).

52.1 Male Lapland Longspur *C. l. alascensis*, Nome, Alaska, USA, June 1998. This breeding male is unmistakable. The combination of chestnut nape and striking pied head pattern is unique. Note also the bold black streaking on the flanks. The moderately stout bill is yellow with a dusky tip (Brian E. Small).

52.2 Male Lapland Longspur *C. l. alascensis*, Cambridge Bay, NWT, Canada, July 1996. Another view of a breeding male. The mantle is brown boldly streaked black with obvious whitish braces (similar to Smith's Longspur). Notice the very long primary projection and the shape of the black centers to the tertials. The chestnut fringe to the greater-coverts and tertials is sun-bleached and abraded on this slightly worn individual (James M. Richards).

52.3 Female Lapland Longspur *C. l. alascensis*, Cambridge Bay, NWT, Canada, July 1990. This breeding female is in slightly worn plumage typical by mid-summer. The head pattern is distinctive. Note especially the bold and complete black border to the ear-coverts and the wide whitish supercilium blending into the pale lores and central ear-coverts. This bird shows little brownish chestnut on the finely streaked nape (James M. Richards).

52.4 Female Lapland Longspur *C. l. alascensis*, Cambridge Bay, NWT, Canada, July 1996. Another breeding female, but notice how extensive the pale chestnut nape patch is. This is quite variable on adult females. The amount of black on the otherwise white underparts is also variable with this bird showing quite extensive black centers on the breast, forming a gorget. The bill is ochre-yellow with a dusky tip and culmen (James M. Richards).

52.5 Lapland Longspur, Ontario, Canada, Sept 1995. This fall bird (probably a female due to the lack of any rufous on the nape) is similar in appearance to a breeding female, although it is distinctly more buffy overall, especially on the head, with deeper chestnut edges to the greater-coverts and tertials. The complete black border to the ear-coverts and long primary extension (six tips showing here) are characteristic. The bill is dark pink with a dusky tip and culmen (Mike McEvoy).

52.6 Male Lapland Longspur, Lancaster, Los Angeles Co., California, USA, Nov 1991. This winter male shows a limited amount of chestnut on the nape and is possibly in its first winter. The long primary extension is nicely illustrated here with six tips projecting beyond the tertials. Primaries 9, 8, and 7 are closely bunched at the tip with long gaps between primaries 7, 6, 5 and 4. The tips of primary 3 and primary 2 are just visible underneath the longest tertial. Note the shape of the black centers to the tertials, which closely resemble many of the Old World emberizid buntings (Larry Sansone).

52.7 Male Lapland Longspur, Serilveda Dam, Los Angeles Co., California, USA, Dec 1990. This winter bird shows much chestnut on the nape and extensive black mottling on the breast and flanks and might possibly be an adult. Note the distinctive head pattern. The boldly streaked lateral crown-stripes contrast with the wide creamy supercilium and central crown-stripe. Notice also how the wide chestnut edges to the greater-coverts form a distinct panel on the wing (Larry Sansone).

52.8 Juvenile Lapland Longspur *C. l. alascensis*, Prudhoe Bay, Alaska, USA, July 1995. The bold blackish streaking on the buffy breast, flanks, and head easily identify this bird as a juvenile. Notice the loose appearance of the body feathers. The median-coverts show an obvious black stripe along the shaft, causing the white median bar to appear spotted. The deep chestnut panel on the greater-coverts is very noticeable (Kevin T. Karlson).

53 Smith's Longspur

(Calcarius pictus)

Measurements
Length: 14–17 cm; 5.5–6.7 in.
Wing: 86–96 mm; 3.4–3.8 in. (males slightly larger).
Mass: 22.0–31.8 g.

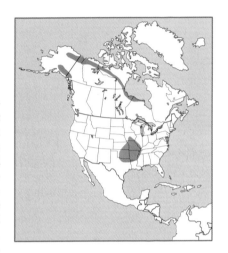

Smith's Longspur is a fairly large, long-winged sparrow of open country and wet tundra. In summer, they have a rich **buffy tan nape, chin, breast, and belly;** males have a **black crown, and a broad white supercilium, and white ear-coverts, boldly outlined in black.** Females are similarly patterned, but are brown where the males are black, and have thin brown streaks on their breasts. Their outer two **rectrices are white.** Wintering birds resemble breeding females.

Habitat
Smith's Longspurs breed in subarctic moist tundra at the edge of the tree line, where they are found in sedges and grasses interspersed with clumps of heath and small trees. In migration they can be found in fallow fields, but are more common in short-grass prairie (often where there is three-awn grass), golf courses, and airports.

Behavior
Smith's Longspurs arrive on their breeding grounds later than Laplands. Males start to sing almost immediately upon arrival. When the females are laying, males frequently chase each other, often giving the rattle call. No territories or pair bonds in the usual sense are formed, as one female will copulate with 1–3 males and each male will copulate with 1–3 females. In migration and winter they form fairly tight flocks. Such flocks are often rather large, consisting of around 200 individuals, and usually contain only Smith's Longspurs, although occasionally other longspurs or Snow Buntings. Smith's Longspurs run rather than hop, and often will run a short distance before taking flight.

Voice
The male's song is somewhat like that of a Chestnut-sided or Yellow warbler, **ta ta tee twe twe twee-werr-tee we chew**. The first notes are weak, and the song increases in strength to the emphatic **we chew** at the end. The call is a staccato rattle, **tic-tic-tic-tic**, which may be given on the ground, but is commonly given in flight (in any season). They also give a sneezy **syn** call.

Similar species

At all times of the year, Smith's Longspur can be distinguished from the other longspurs by the nearly uniform buffy tan plumage. The dark frame around the ear-coverts is not distinct (as it is in **Lapland Longspurs**). Unlike Lapland Longspurs, their lateral crown-stripes are not distinct. Like Lapland Longspurs, the primary projection of Smith's Longspur is long; they have less white in the tail than either **McCown's** or **Chestnut-collared longspur**. Their lower bill is flesh-colored. The rattle call is sharper and louder than that of Lapland Longspur. Smith's Longspurs are less often found in mixed flocks than are the other longspurs. See Appendix 2.

Geographic variation

None described.

Distribution

Breeds from n and e-central Alaska and adjacent Yukon and British Columbia east across n Yukon, s Keewatin, ne Manitoba, and n Ontario.

Winters in s-central Kansas south through Oklahoma, Arkansas (especially in nw), Mississippi, and w Tennessee south to n Alabama (rare) and n Texas, and locally south to s-central Texas (Waco, Austin). They are commonest in s-central Kansas to central Oklahoma, and very rare in California (most records from Oct).

Migrates through the Great Plains east to Ohio; commoner in Ohio, Indiana, and Illinois in the spring than the fall. Spring migration begins in early Mar, with a peak in mid-Mar, and lasts into late May in the northern prairies and Yukon Territory. They leave their breeding grounds at the end of Aug, and migration continues into early Dec, with a peak in Oct.

Conservation status

The breeding habitat of Smith's Longspurs has been little disturbed, and the species has probably been little affected by human activities.

Molt

The Prebasic I molt is partial and begins in July to Sept on the breeding grounds; it involves body feathers but remiges and rectrices are not replaced. The Prealternate I molt is probably like the Definitive Prealternate molt, and involves extensive molt of head and body feathers and some of the smaller wing-coverts; it begins in Mar and is complete by late Apr. The Definitive Basic molt is complete and occurs July to Sept on the breeding grounds.

Description

Fairly large sized, with long wings; sexually dimorphic. **Adult males in summer—** *Head:* forehead and crown dark brown or black, often flecked with white toward the back of the crown; supercilium, lores, and supraloral spot white; ear-coverts white, boldly outlined by wide, black post-ocular and moustachial stripes, and boldly edged with black toward the neck; malar stripe white; *back:* nape bright buffy; *rump:* and back black with feathers edged in bright buff, making it appear streaked; *wing:* brown; anterior lesser-coverts black; posterior lesser-coverts white; median and greater-coverts narrowly edged with whitish, forming one or two indistinct wing-bars; *underparts:* uniformly warm ochraceous buff; *bill:* dusky, with darker tip and brownish-yellow base; *legs* and *feet:* pale to dark brown; *iris:* brown.

Adult males in winter (Sept–Apr)—The black on the head is replaced by streaked brown, and the throat and breast are thinly streaked; otherwise like summer males, but the median and greater-coverts are more distinctly tipped white. The summer plumage is obtained through wear and a rather extensive pre-alternate molt, more extensive than in other longspurs.

Summer females (May–Aug)—*Head:* patterned as summer male, but crown dark brown, flecked with buff; supercilium, lores, and ear-coverts light buffy brown, boldly edged with dark brown; *back* and *rump:* dark brown, with broad buffy edges to the feathers; *tail:* dark brown, with lateral two rectrices mostly white; *wing:* brown with posterior lesser-coverts white, and edges of median and greater-coverts tipped in pale buff; *underparts:* uniformly ochraceous buff, with breast thinly streaked with brown; *bill:* dusky, with darker tip and brownish-yellow base; *legs* and *feet:* brown; *iris:* brown.

Females in winter (Sept–Apr)—Like winter male, but paler, and without black and pure white on lesser-coverts.

Juveniles (July–Sept)—Similar to adults in winter, but perhaps somewhat more heavily streaked on the throat and breast; young apparently complete their postjuvenal molt south of the breeding grounds.

Hybrids
None reported.

References
Briskie (1993), Dunn and Beadle (1998), Rising (1996).

53.1 Male Smith's Longspur, Churchill, Manitoba, Canada, June 1996. This adult male in full breeding plumage is unmistakable. The rich buffy orange underparts and collar and pied head pattern are distinctive. Note also the extensive amount of white on the lesser-coverts (Kevin T. Karlson).

53.2 Female Smith's Longspur, Churchill, Manitoba, Canada, July 1989. This breeding female (with quite extensive wear on wings and tail) is essentially a muted version of the male. The underparts and collar are paler and buffier with more extensive brown streaking and the head pattern less distinct, though note the obvious whitish central crown-stripe. The pale braces on the largely black mantle show nicely here (James M. Richards).

53.3 Female Smith's Longspur, Polar Bear Prov. Park, Ontario, Canada, July 1970. The pale buff ground color to the face and underparts are nicely depicted on this breeding female. Note the fine blackish streaking on the brown lateral crown-stripes contrasting with the whitish central stripe (Dr. George K. Peck).

53.4 Smith's Longspur, Kern Co., California, USA, Sept 1996. This bird shows a distinct blackish border surrounding the whitish ear-coverts and is probably a male. The greater-coverts and tertials show blended rusty edges and two distinct wing-bars are formed by neat white tips to the median and greater-coverts. The longish primary projection is well illustrated here with four tips visible. Primary 7 forms the tip while the tip of primary 4 is just visible from underneath the folded tertials (Brian E. Small).

53.5 Smith's Longspur, Kern Co., California, USA, Sept 1996. Same bird as Fig. 53.4. The warm buffy cinnamon underparts contrast with the paler throat. Fine brown streaking is evident across the breast and along the flanks. Note the white submoustachial stripe extends back behind the blackish border to the ear-coverts. A substantial amount of white is visible on the lesser-coverts, another feature to support this bird being a male. Note the dark-flesh colored legs (blackish on other Longspurs) (Brian E. Small).

53.6 Smith's Longspur, Island Beach, New Jersey, USA, Oct 1995. Concentrating on the head note the shape of the bill compared with Lapland Longspur. It is relatively fine with a straight culmen. The dark border to the rear edge of the ear-coverts is broken beneath the dark eye-line. Also, Smith's tends to have quite a pronounced whitish eye-ring which is rather noticeable here (Kevin T. Karlson).

53.7 Female Smith's Longspur, Death Valley National Park, California, USA, Oct 1997. The subdued brown surrounding to the buffy brown ear-coverts and the limited amount of white in the lesser-coverts indicate that this bird is a female. Well shown here is the extent of white in the outer two tail feathers (Larry Sansone).

53.8 Female Smith's Longspur, Death Valley National Park, California, USA, Oct 1997. Another view of the bird in Fig. 53.7. Note the relatively blended appearance of the head markings with fine blackish streaking on crown also invading the narrow buffy supercilium. The submoustachial stripe is washed with buff and the whole appearance shows less contrast than the suspected male in Figs. 53.4 & 53.5. Also note the extent and spacing of the primary extension. Three tips are obvious (with primary 8 and primary 4 just visible), but note especially the big step between primary 6 and primary 5 (Larry Sansone).

53.9 Female Smith's Longspur, Death Valley National Park, California, USA, Oct 1997. Same bird as in Figs. 53.7 & 53.8. The rather fine bill shape is well shown here. The underparts are a rich buffy color blending into a paler throat. Note the blurry brown streaking across breast and the relatively subdued brown and buff head pattern (Larry Sansone).

54 Chestnut-collared Longspur

(Calcarius ornatus)

Measurements

Length: 12–15 cm; 4.7–5.9 in.
Wing: 78–90 mm; 3.1–3.5 in.
  (males somewhat larger).
Mass: 17–23 g.

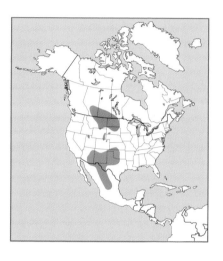

Chestnut-collared Longspur is the smallest of the longspurs. Males in breeding plumage are unmistakable: the **black chest and belly** are distinctive, and at a distance displaying males initially look like small blackbirds. They also have a **bright ochre face, black crown and strip behind the eye, white supercilium**, a black spot or line on the side of the face, and a conspicuous chestnut collar, and show a lot of **white in the tail**. Females are plain brown, with no black or white on the head, but a pale buff supercilium; the chestnut collar is obscure, and the dark of the breast and belly is reduced or absent. Their tail pattern is like that of males.

Habitat

Chestnut-collared Longspurs are locally abundant in native shortgrass prairie, particularly areas that have rather recently been burned or heavily grazed. Grasslands with dense litter accumulations are avoided. In drier shortgrass prairie, Chestnut-collared Longspurs prefer moister and more densely vegetated areas than McCown's Longspurs. In winter, they are found in short or tall grass, fallow fields, or mowed alfalfa.

Behavior

Territorial males are frequently involved in chases, and do a lot of flight-singing, although less than McCown's Longspurs. Displaying males will rise from the ground with rapidly beating wings, circle and sing, then drop back to the ground. Breeding males characteristically sit on top of a tall bunch of grass, a weed or small bush, where they are distinctive; they often sing from these perches. Females are more difficult to see. They usually walk away from the nest before flying, and may give a distraction display that involves showing the white in the tail. In winter, Chestnut-collared Longspurs are usually found in small flocks. Often these flocks are comprised only of Chestnut-collared Longspurs, but often they also contain other longspurs (especially McCown's) or Horned Larks.

Voice

The song of the Chestnut-collared Longspur is musical, and has the qualities of the song of the Western Meadowlark. It generally lasts 2–3 s, and contains 7–8 phrases, each made up of several notes. The song becomes buzzy toward the end. The flight call is a distinctive *til-lip* or *cheed-lup*, the first syllable accented. The call note is a whistled *wheer*, or, when alarmed, a rattling *tri-ri-rip*, or *tzip*.

Similar species

The Chestnut-collared Longspur is clearly the smallest of the longspurs; it also has a small bill, especially compared with **McCown's Longspur**, and appears to be round-winged and short-tailed. Like McCown's Longspur, the primary projection is short, relative to that of either **Smith's** or **Lapland longspurs**. There is a pale spot on the back edge of the ear-coverts; Smith's and Lapland longspurs may have this, but it is generally not so distinct. The calls are distinctive. There is a lot more white in the tail of Chestnut-collared Longspurs than in other sparrows, other than McCown's Longspurs; tail pattern is usually not helpful in separating these two. Note, however, the rather large conical bill, and the lack of a spot on the back of the ear-coverts on McCown's Longspur. See Appendix 2.

Geographic variation

None described.

Distribution

Breeds from se Alberta and s Saskatchewan east to s Manitoba, North Dakota, and w Minnesota, south through central and e Montana, e Wyoming and South Dakota, to ne Colorado, and occasionally w Nebraska.

Winters from s California, e Arizona, and s-central Kansas south into w Texas, se Sonora, Zacatecas and Aguascalientes, rarely east to the Panhandle of Florida. They are commonest in w Kansas south to w Texas and s New Mexico.

Migrates through the western Great Plains east of the Rocky Mountains, and uncommonly through California. Fall migration starts in mid-Sept, and continues through mid-Oct. Spring migration begins by mid-Feb, and they arrive on their breeding grounds by late Apr. Wanders to east coast (vary rare).

Conservation status

The conversion of native prairie to agricultural land has had a significant negative impact on the numbers of Chestnut-collared Longspurs, which have disappeared from much of their historical breeding range. In Saskatchewan, numbers decline in the first year following burning, but they increase in the second year. Heavily grazed areas are preferred to mowed ones, and they may avoid periodically hayed or cultivated fields. They formerly bred south to western Kansas, and commonly east to western Minnesota (where they now are only local breeders).

Molt

The Basic I plumage is acquired by a partial Prebasic I molt that includes the body feathers, lesser and median-coverts, and probably the greater-coverts and tertials, but not the remiges or rectrices; this occurs in July to Sept. There is a limited Prealternate molt in Feb to Apr that is restricted to the head region, throat, and breast. The Definitive Basic molt is complete and takes place July to Sept.

Description

Medium-sized sparrow; sexually dimorphic. **Males in summer** (Apr–Aug)—*Head:* crown black, with a white spot in the middle at the back; eye-stripe (behind eye), and spot on the lower part of ear-coverts black; supercilium white; lores, side of face, and throat pale yellow ochre; ***back:*** nape chestnut; back and rump brown, with feathers broadly to narrowly edged with pale buff; ***tail:*** outer two rectrices (5th and 6th) mostly white; rectrices 2, 3, and 4 white with dark tips; middle pair of rectrices brown and pointed; ***underparts:*** chin and throat pale ochre-buff; breast, flanks, and belly black, often flecked with varying amounts of dark chestnut; lower belly and undertail-coverts white; ***wing:*** brown, with greater-coverts and tertials broadly edged with buff; anterior lesser-coverts black; posterior lesser-coverts white; ***bill:*** tip dark brown or black; remainder grayish or dull yellow; ***legs*** and ***feet:*** dull pink to brown; ***iris:*** brown.

Adult males in winter (Aug–Apr)—Like summer males, but black of head and breast and chestnut of neck obscured by brownish or dull buffy tips to feathers (they wear into summer plumage); bill brownish.

Adult females (Apr–Aug)—*Head:* crown beige, thinly streaked with dark brown; supercilium and lores pale buff; side of face brown, thinly streaked with darker brown; ***back*** and ***rump:*** brown (nape may be tinged with chestnut), thinly streaked with darker brown; ***tail:*** pattern as in male, but lighter brown; ***wing:*** brown, with greater-coverts and tertials broadly edged with buff; anterior lesser-coverts black; posterior lesser-coverts white; ***underparts:*** throat buffy; breast, flanks, and belly buffy gray, thinly streaked with brown, usually with varying amounts of dark brown to blackish feathers; undertail-coverts buffy; ***bill:*** dull brown; base of upper bill and tomium paler, sometimes dull pink; ***legs*** and ***feet:*** dull to pale brown, feet darker; ***iris:*** brown.

Females in winter (Sept–Mar)—Like summer female, but feathers tipped with buff.

Juveniles (July–Aug)—Crown and back dark brown, with feathers edged with pale buff; throat pale buffy gray, lightly speckled with brown; chest and flanks buffy, streaked with brown; belly paler, and lightly streaked; tail pattern as in adults; bill gray-brown; legs and feet flesh-colored.

Hybrids

There is a specimen of a Chestnut-collared X McCown's longspur from Saskatchewan.

References

Dechant *et al.* (1998d), Dunn and Beadle (1998), Hill and Gould (1997), Rising (1996), Sibley and Pettingill (1955).

54.1 Male Chestnut-collared Longspur, Benton Lake NWR, Montana, USA, July 1997. This breeding male presents few identification problems. The combination of pale ochre face, chestnut nape and black breast and belly is unique. Note also the white supercilium and gorget contrasting with the black crown, eye-stripe and rear edge to ear-coverts (Brian E. Small).

54.2 Male Chestnut-collared Longspur, Benton Lake NWR, Montana, USA, July 1997. Another view of a breeding male. The upperparts are brown with blackish streaking and relatively diffused pale braces. The wings show obscure pale buffy tips to the median and greater-coverts. Rather strikingly, when one can see them, the lesser-coverts are black with a white bar on the innermost row. Note also the extensive amount of white on the outer tail feathers, especially at the base (Brian E. Small).

54.3 Female Chestnut-collared Longspur, Moose Jaw, Saskatchewan, Canada, June 1968. This breeding female is essentially brown, streaked darker above and pale below. Note the head pattern with quite a broad creamy supercilium contrasting with blackish post-ocular stripe and border to rear edge of ear-coverts. There is a very faint wash of chestnut on the sides of the nape as well as black centers to some feathers on the breast (just visible). The moderate-sized bill is gray. Note especially the short primary projection (Dr. George K. Peck).

54.4 Female Chestnut-collared Longspur *Calcarius ornatus*, Sonoita, Arizona, USA, Mar 1989. On this bird notice contrast between the whitish throat and the remaining buffy-gray underparts. The breast is finely and evenly streaked darker. Note also the sharp thin blackish malar stripe (Rick and Nora Bowers).

54.5 Chestnut-collared Longspur, Van Nuys, Los Angeles Co., California, USA, Nov 1991. Notice the overall shape of the bird and the moderate size of the bill, obviously smaller than Lapland and McCown's, but deeper based than Smith's. This bird seems to show quite a lot of shaded black on the belly (the result of broad pale fringes to all feathers, reduced by wear) and is probably a first-winter male. Note also the relatively plain wings with the greater-coverts and tertials edged buff and tipped whitish (Larry Sansone).

54.6 Chestnut-collared Longspur, Van Nuys, Los Angeles Co., California, USA, Nov 1991. Possibly the same bird as Fig. 54.5. On this view notice the very short primary extension with only three tips showing. Primary 7 forms the tip with only a small gap between it and primary 6. Apart from the tip of primary 5 all the other primaries are mostly hidden by the tertials. Note the fairly uniform appearance of the streaked upperparts lacking obvious pale braces often prominent on Smith's and Lapland (Larry Sansone).

55 Pine Bunting

(Emberiza leucocephalos)

Measurements
Length: 16.5 cm; 6.5 in.
Wing: 84–100 mm; 3.3–3.9 in. (males larger).
Mass: 24–36 g.

Adult male Pine Buntings have a distinctive head pattern, with a **white cheek and crown, black lateral crown-stripes, a broad chestnut stripe through the eye**, and a chestnut chin and throat. Adult females have a less distinct facial pattern, with a pale supercilium, grayish ear-coverts with a pale spot near the posterior edge, and brownish or rusty brown streaks on the breast and flanks. Males in the first winter are like adults, but are less brightly colored, and have a streaked crown, and rusty streaks on their underparts.

Habitat
In the breeding season, Pine Buntings nest in the edge of sparse forests and clearings, with overgrown bushes.

Behavior
During the breeding season, males sing vigorously from the tops of small trees, and chase one another in the air. In winter, they are often in flocks, but only single birds have been reported in North America.

Voice
The song is long and repetitious, and resembles that of the Yellowhammer; it is described as *sri-sri-sri-sri-sri-zyyh*. There is considerable variation, and an individual may sing several different song types. A *tsik*, *tic*, or *twik* note is given both when perched and in flight.

Similar species
Female Reed Buntings are similar to female Pine Buntings, but have brownish ear-coverts, without the light spot, and have a paler supercilium and submoustachial stripe, and a darker malar stripe. Female Rustic Buntings are similar, but are more brightly patterned, with rustier markings on the breast and flanks. Female and winter Smith's Longspurs are buffier in hue, and not so heavily streaked below. None of the North American sparrows (with the exception of the juncos, Vesper and Lark sparrows, and longspurs) have conspicuous white in the tail.

Geographic variation
None in our area; *E. l. leucocephalos* is the subspecies that has been found in North America.

Distribution
Breeds in the Palearctic, from Finland east to nw Siberia.

Winters in s China. Fall migration is Aug to Nov; spring migration is Mar to June. Reported twice from Attu, Aleutian Is., Alaska: 19 Nov 1985 (male); 6 Oct 1993 (first-year male).

Molt

The Prebasic molt is partial, and involves head and body feathers and coverts; it takes place prior to the fall migration. The Definitive Basic molt is complete, and occurs mid-Aug to mid-Sept.

Description

Large; sexually dimorphic. **Adult males** (Feb–Aug)—*Head:* forehead, lateral crown-stripes, and back of neck black; remainder of crown and nape white; eyeline stripe and lores broad, and brick red, contrasting with white ear-coverts, which are narrowly edged with black on both upper and lower margins; side of neck with a narrow pale or white streak; *back:* mantle light rufous-cinnamon, streaked with dark brown; *rump:* and uppertail-coverts deep rufous-cinnamon, slightly mottled with pale buff; *tail:* brownish-black; outer rectrices edged with white on inner webs toward tip; outermost rectrix edged with white, with black toward base and tip; *wing:* grayish-black, edged with cinnamon-rufous; coverts edged with cinnamon-rufous; *underparts:* chin and throat brick red, contrasting with the white ear-coverts and a white band across the upper breast; breast and flanks rusty; belly whitish; *bill:* upper mandible slate-gray to brownish-black; lower mandible pale horn-color; *legs:* pale flesh-brown; *iris:* dark brown.

Males in winter (Sept–Jan)—Similar to males in summer, but the feathers are tipped with brown, obscuring the cinnamon and white markings on the head; they have a thin eye-ring. First-winter males are duller in coloration than adult males. There is a partial facial molt in Feb–Mar, but otherwise males wear into summer plumage.

Adult females (May–Sept)—*Head:* forehead brown with cinnamon mottling; crown streaked with pale buff and dark brown; supercilium and lores pale; eye-stripe dark brown, ear-coverts grayish brown, edged with dark brown, and with a pale spot on the back margin; submoustachial stripe whitish, malar dark; throat whitish; *back, wings,* and *tail* similar to adult male; *underparts:* chin and throat pale, breast and flanks streaked with chestnut; belly white; soft parts colored as in males.

Females in winter (Sept–Apr)—Like adult males, but duller in coloration.

Juvenile—Like females but duller in coloration, with a dull cinnamon rump and streaked back.

Hybrids

Hybridizes freely with the Yellowhammer (*E. citrinella*) where their ranges overlap in western Siberia.

References

Cramp and Perrins (1994), Kessel and Gibson (unpublished).

55.1 Male Pine Bunting, China, July. This handsome breeding-plumaged male displays the characteristic, largely chestnut and white head pattern. Note especially the conspicuous white patches on the crown and ear-coverts (Goran Ekstrom).

55.2 Female Pine Bunting. A washed-out version of male but head mostly pale gray, whiter on crown. Ear-coverts and throat with blackish lines and some rufous speckling within the supercilium and malar area. Note the quite extensive rufous mottling and streaking on breast and flanks (Urban Olsson).

55.3 Male Pine Bunting, Dagenham Chase, Gr. London, UK, Feb 1992. In non-breeding plumage (as here) the chestnut head markings are scaled with white and the whitish crown patch less obvious. The back is pale grayish-buff, tinged with rufous on the scapulars and streaked with black. This contrasts with the rufous rump and uppertail-coverts which are broadly fringed with grayish-buff (David M. Cottridge/Windrush Photos).

55.4 Female Pine Bunting, Big Waters, Tyne & Wear, UK, Mar 1990. Similar to breeding female (Fig. 55.2) but with much subdued head pattern, lacking extensive chestnut. The supercilium, central ear-covert patch, submoustachial and throat are whitish contrasting with brownish lateral crown stripe and surround the ear-coverts. The crown shows some whitish streaking in the central stripe. The underparts, including the throat, are whitish with dusky malar stripe and streaking on breast-sides and flanks (George Reszeter).

56 Little Bunting

(Emberiza pusilla)

Measurements
Length: 13–14 cm; 5.1–5.5 in.
Wing: 67–76 mm; 2.6–3.0 in. (males slightly larger).
Mass: 11.0–14.0 g.

The Little Bunting is a small bunting with a **flat forehead**, a small, **sharply pointed bill**, short neck, short legs, and a short tail. In profile, the upper mandible is flat or slightly concave. The dull chestnut cheeks and median crown-stripe of adults, and the thin eye-ring are distinctive.

Habitat
Little Buntings breed in moist shrubby tundra, in willows along rivers through the boreal forest, or in open forests. In western Siberia they are often in dwarf birch or spruce, and in northern Russia in alders and willows in river valleys. In winter, they are found in short grass on hillsides and in plains.

Behavior
The flight of the Little Bunting is light and fast, like a small finch, but not undulating. On the ground, it creeps, and nervously flicks its wings. In migration it often forms flocks, but North American records are of single birds. Territorial males sing from the tops of small trees.

Voice
The song is quiet and sweet, and consists of buzzy phrases and clicks, such as *srri zee srri see sip sip sip zrree dz-oo dz-oo*. Migrants give paired hard, sharp **tik tik, tzik tzik,** or *pick pick* notes.

Similar species
The combination of the small size, bill shape, and eye-ring separate Little Bunting from female **Reed Buntings**, which can be similar to female Pine Buntings. Reed Buntings have a thicker bill, which appears to be relatively shorter than that of the Little Bunting, and the upper mandible is slightly convex in profile. Little Bunting has a rather small head, with a flat forehead; Reed Buntings have a larger, more rounded head. Little Buntings have short legs and short, rectangular tails; Reed Buntings have longer tails (this may not be obvious), and they frequently spread their tails. **Rustic Buntings** are similar in shape, but larger, have a more rounded head, and often show a ragged crest (Little Buntings can show this). Little Buntings have a broad chestnut or buffy central crown-stripe, whereas Rustic Buntings have a thin pale buffy stripe. The facial markings of the Rustic Bunting are sharper than those of the Little Bunting, and the Little Bunting has buffy cinnamon ear-coverts and lores. The pale spot at the back of the ear-coverts is bright in Rustic Buntings, and obscure in Little Buntings.

Geographic variation
None described.

Distribution

Breeds in the Palearctic, from n Finland east to n Siberia, south to Lake Biakal and the Sea of Okhostsk.

Winters in e Asia, south to n Burma, and east to n India, and rarely continental Europe, the British Isles, North Africa, and the Philippines. Fall migration is Aug to Nov; spring migration is Mar–May. There are three records for North America, an immature found aboard ship in the Chukchi Sea, 280 km northwest of Icy Cape, Alaska, on 6 Sept 1970, and an immature male collected at Shemya I., Aleutian Is., Alaska, on 8 Sept 1977. One was seen at Point Loma, San Diego County, California (Oct).

Molt

The Prebasic I molt is partial, and involves the head and body feathers, and lesser and median upper wing-coverts, and sometimes some of the greater-coverts and tertials; it occurs from July to early Sept. There is a partial Prealternate molt and involves feathers on the side of the head, chin, and throat; it occurs on the wintering range, Feb to Apr. The Definitive Basic molt is complete, and occurs from July to early Sept.

Description

Adults—Small; sexes similar. *Head:* median crown-stripe, ear-coverts, and lores cinnamon-buff, the latter narrowly outlined with dark brown eyeline and moustachial stripes; posterior border of ear-coverts dark brown, often with a pale spot at the back; lateral crown-stripes dark brown; supercilium pale cinnamon-buff, paler than ear-coverts; *back*, *rump*, and uppertail coverts brownish, and dark brown streaks; *tail:* brownish-black; outer rectrices mostly white, with some dark brown on inside and tip; variable, but little white in the second outermost rectrix; *wing* brownish, edged with buff; median and greater-coverts edged with pale buff, forming two wing-bars; *underparts:* chin and upper throat buffy; lower throat whitish; breast and flanks brown streaked; belly whitish; *bill:* upper mandible grayish-black, with cutting edges paler; lower mandible pale flesh-pink (fall) to dull gray with a pink tinge (spring); *legs:* pale reddish-flesh; *iris:* red-brown or dark brown (gray-brown in first fall).

Fall and winter (Sept–Apr)—Similar to adults, but warmer in hues, with streaking less sharply defined.

Juveniles—Like females but more yellowish-buff in coloration, stripes on the head indistinct, and ventral streaking more extensive.

Hybrids None reported.

References Cramp and Perrins (1994), Kessel and Gibson (1978).

56.1 Adult Little Bunting, Beidaihe, China, May. The pale chestnut ear-coverts, lores and crown, black lateral crown-stripe and bold whitish eye-ring are distinctive. Like Rustic Bunting shows a pale spot in the ear-coverts. Note that the thin black moustachial stripe fades before reaching the base of the bill. The submoustachial stripe and underparts are white contrasting with thin black malar and streaking across breast (David Tipling/ Windrush Photos).

56.2 Little Bunting, Lashford Lane Fen. Oxon, UK, Mar 1988. On this early spring bird the head pattern is pale with buffy wash on the supercilium and submoustachial stripe. Upperparts finely streaked black with some chestnut in scapulars. Buff tips to median and greater-coverts form two obscure wing-bars. Note the typical *Emberiza* tertial pattern. The fine bill with straight culmen is well shown here (George Reszeter).

57 Rustic Bunting

(Emberiza rustica)

Measurements
Length: 14.5–15.5 cm; 5.7–6.1 in.
Wing: 73–83 mm; 2.9–3.3 in. (males slightly larger).
Mass: 17.7–24.3 g.

Rustic Buntings are medium-sized sparrows with white underparts and **bold rusty spots or streaks on their breast.** Adult males have a **black head**, with a grayish-white median crown-stripe, a white spot on the nape, a white supercilium, and a white spot on the back of the black ear-coverts. Females and first-winter birds are similarly patterned, but with brown on the crown and grayish-brown ear-coverts. Juveniles may be less rusty on the breast.

Habitat
Breeds in low bushes in wet tundra, and in open coniferous forests, streamside thickets. In winter, they are found in bushy areas, grasslands, open woods, and cultivated fields.

Behavior
On the breeding grounds, male Rustic Buntings sing from an exposed perch, with their crown raised; singing begins in spring migration. When agitated, they raise their crown and flick their tail. When flushed from the ground, they fly up into trees. Their flight is quick, and slightly undulating. In migration and winter, Rustic Buntings are gregarious, and flocks of up to five birds have been recorded in Alaska, although many records are of single birds.

Voice
The song is a short, clear, and melodious *dudeleu-deluu-delee*. It has the melancholy quality of that of the Lapland Longspur. The flight-call is a double *tic tic*, like that of the Little Bunting, or *tic tic tic*; a faint *tsip* is given in flight.

Similar species
Female **Reed Buntings** are similar to female Rustic Buntings, but not rusty, and lack the light spots on the nape and ear-coverts. The bill of Reed Buntings appears to be relatively blunt, not sharp like that of Rustic and Little buntings. **Little Buntings**, are small, short-legged, and have a flat forehead; Rustic Buntings have a peaked crown; the rump of Little Bunting is brownish, whereas that of Rustic Bunting is rusty brown. **Red Fox Sparrows** are red, but are much larger, lack black on the head, and like most of the North American sparrows (with the exception of the juncos, Vesper Sparrow, Lark Sparrow, and longspurs) lack conspicuous white in the tail.

Geographic variation
None in our area. The Siberian subspecies, *E. r. latifascia* is doubtless the one that strays to North America. The geographic variation in this species is slight, but Siberian birds are said to have black, rather than brownish-black caps and ear-coverts, and more rufous in the tail.

Distribution

Breeds in the Palearctic, from n Scandinavia east to n Siberia.

Winters in China, Japan, and Commander (Komandorskiye) Is. (rare). Fall migration is Aug to Nov; spring migration is Mar to June. Rare in spring migration in w and central Aleutian Is. (mid-May through June), and very rare in fall migration (mid-Sept through Oct); casual on St. Lawrence I. (June), and in winter in interior Alaska (Fairbanks). Casual south to British Columbia (Queen Charlotte Is.: Queen Charlotte City (Oct), Masset (Aug); Vancouver I.: Jordan River, Nov [wintered]; Tofino [wintered]), Washington (Kent Ponds, King Co. [two records; wintered]), Oregon (Multnomah Co., Nov; Lane County, Apr), and to California (Humboldt Co., Jan; Kern Co., Nov; San Mateo Co., Nov).

Molt

The Prebasic I molt is partial and does not involve remiges or rectrices; it takes place mid-June to late Sept. There is a partial Prealternate molt that involves head and throat feathers; this occurs in Mar to May. The Definitive Basic molt is complete and takes place late June to late Sept.

Description

Medium-sized; sexually dimorphic. **Adult males** (Feb–Aug)—*Head:* black mottled with brown in unworn birds; median crown-stripe usually grayish-white; white spot on nape; supercilium white; supraloral spot and ear-coverts black, with a white spot on the back of the coverts; submoustachial stripe bold and white; malar stripe rusty, extending to bill; throat white; *back:* nape rusty, with a white spot at the back of the head; mantle rusty, streaked with dark brown; *rump:* and uppertail-coverts deep rufous-cinnamon; *tail:* blackish; outer rectrices edged with white on inner webs toward tip; outermost rectrix (6th) mostly white, with black toward base and tip; 5th rectrix with white on the inner web toward the tip; *wings:* dark brown, with secondaries and tertials edged with cinnamon-rufous; middle and greater-coverts white tipped, forming two wing-bars; *underparts:* chin and throat white, contrasting with bright rusty streaks, often forming a band across the upper breast; flanks rusty streaked; belly white; *bill:* pinkish-gray at base, dark gray at tip; *legs:* pale flesh-brown; *iris:* dark brown.

Males in winter (Sept–Jan)—Similar to males in summer, but the feathers are tipped with brown, obscuring the black markings on the head. First-winter males probably are duller in coloration than adult males. There is a partial head molt in March, but otherwise males wear into summer plumage.

Adult females (May–Sept)—Similar to males, but duller, with the nape spot inconspicuous, and black markings brown to dark brown.

Females in winter (Sept–Apr)—Like adult females, but duller in coloration; the supercilium and submoustachial stripes are buffy.

Juveniles—Like females but duller and buffier in coloration.

Hybrids None reported.

References Cramp and Perrins (1994), Kessel and Gibson (1978).

57.1 Adult male Rustic Bunting, Arthog Bog, Gwynedd, UK, Apr 1991. This strikingly plumaged spring male is unlikely to be mistaken for any other bunting. The bold pied head pattern and largely chestnut nape, scapulars, breast-band and flank streaking is unique. Note the slightly raised crown feathers forming a short crest (George Reszeter).

57.2 Rustic Bunting, Tresco, Isles of Scilly, UK, Oct 1994. This probable first-winter bird is similar to adult female but with buff suffusion to supercilium and submoustachial stripe. Note the dark bordered brown ear-coverts with a prominent pale spot along rear edge. The upperparts are buffy brown streaked darker with some chestnut on nape and scapulars. Heavy reddish-brown streaking on breast and flanks. Note the shape of the black centers to the tertials (similar to Lapland Longspur) (George Reszeter).

57.3 Male Rustic Bunting, China. Non-breeding males appear very similar to females but tend to be slightly brighter overall with whiter post-ocular stripe and bolder black border to the ear-coverts (Urban Olsson).

57.4 Rustic Bunting, Japan, Jan 1999. Ageing and sexing of winter birds in the field is problematic and often not possible. This individual shows typical pattern of rufous on scapulars, across breast and along flanks (Mike Danzenbaker).

58 Yellow-throated Bunting

(Emberiza elegans)

Measurements
Length: 15.0–15.5 cm; 5.9–6.1 in.
Wing: 62–81 mm; 2.4–3.2 in. (males somewhat larger).
Mass: no information.

Male Yellow-throated Buntings have a distinctive **black and yellow head with a short crest, and a black breast.** Females and juveniles are duller in color, and the black markings are replaced by brown.

Habitat
Yellow-throated Buntings are found on grassy slopes, fairly dry, thinly wooded areas where they prefer young trees, conifers, and thickets.

Behavior No information.

Voice
The song is a soft twitter, **tswit-tsu-ri-tu witt tsuri weee-dee tswit-tsuri-tu.** The call is a sharp **tzik.**

Similar species
The facial pattern of birds of both sexes is unmistakable; the crest is distinctive.

Geographic variation
Three subspecies have been recognized, but they are not well established and need further study. *E. e. elegans* of Manchuria and Siberia is the one most likely to appear in North America. They are duller in coloration than *E. e. elegantula* of central China.

Distribution
Breeds from s Siberia, Manchuria, and n Korea south to s China.

Winters from e China, s Korea, and Japan south to s China and Burma. One record for North America: Attu, Aleutian Is., 25 May 1998.

Molt
There is a partial Prebasic I molt in June to Sept that involves head and body feathers, upperwing-coverts, and tertials. The Definitive Basic molt in June to Sept is complete. There may be a partial Prealternate molt involving head feathers.

Description
Medium-sized; sexually dimorphic. **Adult breeding males—Head:** crown and side of face black; supercilium whitish around eye and yellow behind eye; throat yellow; ***back:*** nape and sides of neck gray; mantle rusty with beige streaks; ***rump:*** and upper-tail-coverts gray-brown; ***wing:*** brown, with pale tips to the coverts; ***tail:*** brown; ***underparts:*** pale buff with streaking on the side of breast and flanks; ***bill:*** blackish; ***legs*** and ***feet:*** pale pinkish-brown; ***iris:*** dark brown.

Adult males in winter—Like breeding male, but black feathers are somewhat obscured by brown edges.

Males in first winter—Like adult male, but the dark on the head is less well developed.

Adult females—Are patterned like adult males, but brown where the males are black, and yellow areas are duller.

Juveniles—Crown and ear-coverts pale brown, with thin streaking on breast; lack crest.

Hybrids None reported.

References Byers *et al.* (1995), Flint *et al.* (1984), Meyer de Schauensee (1984).

58.1 Male Yellow-throated Bunting, China, May. Easily recognized by the black mask and crown with contrasting yellow throat and hindcrown. The crown feathers form a distinct erect crest. Note also the boldly streaked back and whitish wing-bars (Goran Ekstrom).

58.2 Female Yellow-throated Bunting, China, Apr. Like a dull version of the male with brownish crown and ear-coverts, paler, buffy-yellow hindcrown and throat and no obvious dark gorget (although this is variable) on breast (Urban Olsson).

58.3 Male Yellow-throated Bunting, Japan, Oct 1997. The underparts of this non-breeding bird are whitish with a distinct blackish gorget across breast. The flanks are tinged with buff and finely streaked with chestnut and black (Mike Danzenbaker).

59 Yellow-breasted Bunting

(Emberiza aureola)

Measurements
Length: 14.0–15.0 cm; 5.5–5.9 in.
Wing: 72–81 mm; 2.8–3.2 in. (males somewhat larger).
Mass: 20.5–22.5 g.

Yellow-breasted Buntings are brightly colored, medium-sized sparrows. Males are **unmistakable**. Females have dark **rusty brown lateral crown-stripes**, and a paler buffy median crown-stripe, and a prominent whitish supercilium and yellow supraloral spot; they have a streaked breast and flanks, and most have a yellowish wash to their underparts; the ear-coverts are buffy, outlined with brown, and with a pale spot toward the upper back.

Habitat
Yellow-breasted Buntings nest in wet streamside thickets of willow and birch, interspersed with grass, or in damp sedge meadows with sparse shrubs. In winter, they are found in grassland, hedgerows, and gardens.

Behavior
All North American records are of single birds. Breeding males start to sing shortly after arriving on the breeding grounds; they sing from the tops of trees or bushes. Yellow-breasted Buntings are gregarious outside of the breeding season, and flocks can be quite large.

Voice
The song is short and melodious, written as *tyy-tyy-tsyy-tsitsi-tuu* or *tsiu-tsiu-tsiu vue-vue tsia-tsia trip-trip*. A hard *tsik* or *thip* note may be given in rapid succession when the bird is perched or in flight. There is also a soft *tsee* note.

Similar species
Males in all plumages are bright yellow below, with a dark chestnut band across their breast, white lesser and median-coverts, forming a white patch on the wing; they are unmistakable. Females resemble some of the other female *Emberiza*, but are distinctly yellowish in hue, have a conspicuous pale supercilium, and the back is streaked with brown and buff. Females in winter superficially resemble winter Bobolinks, which are substantially larger. Yellow-breasted Buntings appear to be rather chunky and short-tailed.

Geographic variation
None in our area. The specimen was identified as *E. a. ornata*, which breeds in eastern Siberia and Japan. *E. a. ornata* tend to be darker on the back, have deeper yellow underparts, and a blacker (often black) bar on the chest than birds from the western Palearctic.

Distribution

Breeds in the Palearctic, from central Finland east to ne Siberia (Kamchatka, Commander [Komandorskiye] Is.), and Japan.

Winters from ne India east to se Asia, and occasionally to Great Britain, w Europe, and the Philippines. Fall migration is July–Sep.; spring migration is Apr–June. There are four records for Alaska: a first spring male was seen on St. Lawrence, Alaska, 26–27 June 1978; an adult male was collected at Attu I., Aleutian Is., 26 May 1988; a female was seen at Buldir I., Aleutians, 20–25 June 1988; and an adult male was seen at Buldir on 13 June 1990.

Molt

There is a partial Prebasic I molt that takes place Aug to early Oct that involves body feathers, wing-coverts and tertials. There is a partial Prealternate molt of head, throat, and some breast feathers; this takes place in Mar to May. The Definitive Prebasic molt is complete and occurs Aug to early Oct; this molt may occur at stopping-over places during migration.

Description

Medium-sized; sexually dimorphic. **Adult males in summer** (Feb–Aug)—*Head:* face black, with a dark chestnut nape extending variably onto the crown; *back* and *rump:* dark chestnut with variable black streaks (the back tends to be darker in eastern birds); *tail:* brown-black edged with rust; white on outer two rectrices; *wing:* dark brown; secondaries and tertials edged in chestnut; lesser and median-coverts white, greater-coverts tipped in white, forming a wing-bar; *underparts:* chin and upper throat black; lower throat bright yellow, with a dark chestnut (sometimes black) breast-band; breast and belly otherwise bright yellow, becoming paler toward tail, with chestnut streaking on the flanks; undertail-coverts buffy white; *bill:* upper mandible dark horn-colored, with a paler cutting edge; lower mandible is pale pink; *legs:* pink or straw-colored; *iris:* dark. First-year males resemble winter males, but have some black on their throat.

Males in winter (Sept–Apr)—Similar to males in summer, but the feathers are tipped with buff, somewhat obscuring the bright colors; the throat is yellow. There is a partial facial molt in Mar–May, but otherwise males wear into summer plumage. First-winter males resemble females.

Adult females (May–Sept)—*Head:* lateral crown-stripes dark brown, separated by a narrow pale median crown-stripe; supercilium is broad, and nearly white above the eye; supraloral spot yellow; ear-coverts buffy, outlined with a dark eye and moustachial stripes, with a pale spot on the brown back margin of the coverts; *back:* nape grayish-brown, mantle streaked with brown and buff; *wing:* brown, with tips of median and greater-coverts tipped in buff, forming two wing-bars; tertials are edged and tipped with buff or chestnut; *underparts:* washed with yellow, paler on throat and toward tail, thinly streaked with brown on breast and flanks; *tail:* brown, with white in outer two rectrices; soft part colors like males.

Females in winter (Sept–April)—Like adult females, but duller in coloration.

Juveniles—Like females but duller in coloration.

Hybrids None reported.

References Cramp and Perrins (1994).

59.1 Adult male Yellow-breasted Bunting, China, May. This handsome bunting is easily recognized by the combination of dark chestnut upperparts, black face and throat and bright yellow underparts. Note also the chestnut streaking along flanks and the striking white patch on the wing. The bill is rather pale pink with a grayish culmen (Goran Ekstrom).

59.2 Adult male Yellow-breasted Bunting. Another view of a male; this individual is in transitional plumage. Note the black face and throat and the bright yellow underparts crossed by a narrow chestnut band on breast (Urban Olsson).

59.3 Adult female Yellow-breasted Bunting, ne China, May. The complete dark border (narrower on the upper rear edge) to the ear-coverts, broad pale supercilium and lack of obvious malar stripe are clearly shown here. The underparts are pale with quite a strong yellow suffusion on the breast and flanks and streaking confined to the sides of the breast and flanks (David Tipling/Windrush Photos).

59.4 Female Yellow-breasted Bunting, China, May. Another spring individual, somewhat paler than Fig. 59.3. The upperparts are crisply streaked with black and the rump lacks any strong rufous tones (Goran Ekstrom).

59.5 Juvenile Yellow-breasted Bunting, Portland, Dorset, UK, Sept 1993. Similar to adult female. Note the distinctive blackish border to the ear-coverts, streaked lateral crown-stripes contrasting with whitish central stripe and the weak malar stripe. The upperparts are brown streaked blackish with striking whitish braces. Note also the very fine streaking on the breast and flanks (George Reszeter).

60 **Gray Bunting**

(Emberiza variabilis)

Measurements
Length: 14–17 cm; 5.5–6.7 in.
Wing: 76–91 mm; 3.0–3.6 in. (males slightly larger).
Mass: 26.6 g.

Gray Bunting males are nearly **uniformly gray**, with a large, sharp, pale yellowish or pinkish bill. Females are brown, with a pale supercilium, extensive ventral streaking, and a bright rusty tail. Neither sex has white in the tail.

Habitat
The Gray Bunting breeds in coniferous and mixed forests and thickets of dwarf bamboo, principally in hilly country. In winter, they are found in hill forests with dense understory.

Behavior
In migration and winter, Gray Buntings are typically found in pairs of small flocks, but in North America records are of single birds. In their breeding habitat they are apparently difficult to see.

Voice
The song is described as a series of loud fluty notes, a short *youee-tseeye-tseeye.* The call note is soft *tsik.*

Similar species
Males are unmistakable; they may resemble 'Slate-colored' Juncos, but juncos have a white belly and conspicuous white in the tail. Females resemble other female *Emberiza*, but lack the white in the tail, and have a rusty tail.

Geographic variation
None described.

Distribution
Breeds in the Palearctic, on se Kamchatka Peninsula, Kuril I., s Sakhalin I., and locally in central Honshu and Hokkaido. Winters in Japan and Ryukyu Is. There are two North American records, both from the Aleutian Is.: an adult male collected at Shemya I. 18 May 1977, and an immature male at Attu I., 29 May 1980.

Molt
The Prebasic I molt is partial and includes body feathers, wing-coverts, and tertials; it takes place in July to Sept. The Definitive Basic molt is complete and takes place at the same time.

Description
Large; sexually dimorphic. **Adult males**—Uniformly gray, with indistinct black streaking on the back and belly; *bill:* upper mandible pale horn-colored; lower

mandible yellowish or pinkish, darker toward tip; *legs:* dull pink; *iris:* dark.

First-winter males—Grayish on the face and belly, which is lightly streaked with rusty and perhaps black; back rusty and streaked with brown; crown pale rusty gray.

Adult females—*Head:* forehead and crown dark chestnut with a pale median crown-stripe; supercilium and lores pale; eye stripe brown, ear-coverts pale brown, thinly edged with darker brown; submoustachial stripe whitish; malar thin and dark; throat whitish; *back:* buffy brown, streaked with brown; *rump* and *tail:* bright rusty, with no white in tail; *wings:* brown, with edges of secondaries rusty; median and greater-coverts dark and white tipped, forming two wing-bars; *underparts:* chin and throat pale, breast and flanks streaked with pale chestnut-brown; belly white, faintly washed with yellowish-buff; soft parts colored as in males.

Females in winter—Like adult males, but probably duller in coloration.

Juveniles—Resemble females, but are more heavily streaked below.

Hybrids None recorded.

References Byers *et al.* (1995), Kessel and Gibson (1978).

60.1 Male Gray Bunting, Apr. Mostly slate-gray with olive wash on head, back and flight-feathers. Note the black streaking on the mantle and the black centers to the median and greater-coverts (Urban Olsson).

60.2 Male Gray Bunting, Japan, Oct 1997. A chunky slaty-gray bunting lacking white in tail. The stout bill is pinkish-flesh with a darker culmen (Mike Danzenbaker).

60.3 Male Gray Bunting, Japan, Oct 1997. The upperparts of this non-breeding adult/first-winter bird are mostly buff, tinged with gray and boldly streaked black. The tertials are broadly edged with pale chestnut and the median and greater-coverts are narrowly tipped buff, forming indistinct bars. Note the olive-buff suffusion on the head typical of winter birds (Mike Danzenbaker).

61 Pallas's Bunting

(Emberiza pallasi)

Measurements
Length: 13–15 cm; 5.1–5.9 in.
Wing: 68–77 mm; 2.7–3.0 in. (males slightly larger).
Mass: 13.6–16.4 g.

Breeding male Pallas's Buntings have a **black head**, with a **broad contrasting white submoustachial stripe and nape**, and a **blackish tail**, contrasting with a **whitish rump**; they are unmistakable; males in winter are similar, but the black feathers of the head are tipped with brown. Females are pale in hue, with a pale supercilium, faint breast streaking, and a pink lower mandible.

Habitat
Breeds in cool, dry areas in overgrown thickets and dry tundra, including mountain tundra.

Behavior
Pallas's Buntings are found singly or in flocks, in bushes or on the ground. North American records have been of single birds.

Voice
The song is a soft trill, *chi chi chi chi chi*, or a cricket-like *tsisi tsisi tsisi tsisi*. The call is a quiet *tsiup* or *tsee-see*.

Similar species
Males are similar in pattern to male **Reed Buntings**, but are much paler overall, with a whitish rather than a gray rump. The coverts and secondaries of Reed Buntings are edged in rust; those of Pallas's Bunting are pale. Female Reed Buntings are similar to female Pallas's Buntings, but darker in hue, with a more pronounced brown malar streak, and more ventral streaking. As in males, the coverts and secondaries of Reed Buntings are edged with rusty; those of Pallas's Buntings are pale buff. The ear-coverts of Reed Buntings are darker and less uniformly colored than those of Pallas's. The back streaking is more striking on Pallas's Bunting than on Reed Bunting. In winter, female Pallas's Buntings have no or faint streaking on their crown, whereas Reed Buntings usually show distinct lateral crown-stripes. The upper mandible of Pallas's Bunting is nearly straight, and there is a distinct contrast between the dark upper mandible and the pale pinkish lower mandible (the bill is usually all black in breeding males); the upper mandible of Reed Bunting is slightly convex, and the bluish-gray lower mandible contrasts little with the upper.

Geographic variation
None in our area; *E. pallasi polaris* of Siberia is probably the race that occurs in Alaska. Eastern birds are paler than western ones.

Distribution

Breeds in the e Palearctic, from Siberia south to w and ne China, Tibet, and Manchuria.

Winters in China and Korea. Fall migration is in Aug–Oct; spring migration early Mar through mid-May. Three records (all spring) from Alaska: Barrow, 11 June 1968 (adult male); St. Lawrence I., 28 May 1973 (adult male); Buldir I., Aleutian Is., June 1992 (female).

Molt

The Prebasic I molt is partial and involves head and body feathers, lesser and median upperwing-coverts, and a variable number of greater coverts; the molt occurs in Aug to mid-Sept. The Definitive Basic molt is complete and starts in late July and is generally finished in Aug.

Description

Medium-sized; sexually dimorphic. **Adult males** (May–Aug)—*Head:* black, with bold white submoustachial stripes and a white collar; *back:* nape white; mantle pale buff to whitish, boldly striped with black; *rump:* white and unpatterned; uppertail-coverts pale and faintly streaked; *wing:* dark brown, with pale edges to secondaries; tertials with black centers; lesser-coverts bluish-gray; median and greater-coverts are tipped with white or buff, forming two wing-bars; *tail:* black; outermost rectrix (6th) mostly white; 5th with white at the tip of the inner web; wing grayish-black, edged with cinnamon-rufous; coverts edged with cinnamon-rufous; *underparts:* chin and throat black; breast, belly, and undertail-coverts buffy white to white; *bill:* upper mandible grayish-black; lower mandible pinkish-gray; bill of breeding males black; *legs:* flesh-brown or light brown; *iris:* brown or dark brown.

Males in winter (Sept–May)—Similar to males in summer, but the feathers are tipped with brown, obscuring the black and white markings on the head. First-winter males are duller in coloration than adult males. Although there may be a limited face molt, males wear into summer plumage.

Adult females (May–Sept)—*Head:* crown pale brown, with faint streaks; supercilium and lores pale buff; ear-coverts buff, faintly outlined with pale brown; submoustachial stripe pale buff; malar stripe thin, brown; *back:* brown, with sharp brown streaks; *wings:* brown, with edges of median and greater-coverts whitish buff, forming two wing-bars; *tail:* brown; patterned like male's; *underparts:* chin, throat, breast, flanks, and belly pale with faint or no streaking on the flanks; soft parts colored as in males. Winter females are slightly buffier.

Juveniles—Like females but duller in coloration, with a dull cinnamon rump and streaked back.

Hybrids None reported.

References Cramp and Perrins (1994), Kessel and Gibson (1978, unpublished).

61.1 Male Pallas's Bunting, China, May. Overall pattern similar to Reed Bunting but more pallid-looking with cleaner, unstreaked underparts. The bill shows a straight culmen (distinctly curved on *pyrrhulina* Reed Bunting). The diagnostic blue-gray lesser-coverts are just visible here and are an important distinction from the rufescent coverts of Reed Bunting (Goran Ekstrom).

61.2 Male Pallas's Bunting, Beidaihe, China, Apr 1986. Another view of a male in transitional plumage. Note the striking head pattern, clean whitish underparts and blue-gray lesser-coverts. Also, the wing-bars are distinctly pale buff compared with the rufous wing-bars on Reed Bunting (Urban Olsson).

61.3 Female Pallas's Bunting, China, May. Lacks the head pattern of male. Note the grayish supercilium, white submoustachial stripe and contrasting blackish malar stripe and frame around brownish ear-coverts. The straight culmen is a good distinction from female *pyrrhulina* Reed Bunting (Goran Ekstrom).

61.4 Female Pallas's Bunting, Beidaihe, China, Apr. The lesser-coverts are mostly hidden but appear quite dull and grayish without rufescent tones. Note also the buffy wing-bars and general paleness of the upperparts. The underparts are clean white with little brown streaking on flanks (Urban Olsson).

61.5 Pallas's Bunting, China, 14 Oct 1992. Overall paler and finer-billed (straight culmen) than *pyrrhulina* form of Reed Bunting. Sandy-brown head and upperparts with paler supercilium and mantle braces. Underparts uniform creamy-white. Median and greater-coverts and tertials broadly edged buff. Ill-defined darker border to ear-coverts and malar stripe (Goran Ekstrom/Windrush Photos).

62 Reed Bunting

(Emberiza schoeniculus)

Measurements
Length: 15–16.5 cm; 5.9–6.5 in.
Wing: 76–86 mm; 3.0–3.4 in. (males slightly larger).
Mass: 17.3–26.5 g.

Breeding male Reed Buntings have a **black head**, with a **broad contrasting white submoustachial stripe and nape**, a dark back, streaked with black, a gray rump, and a blackish tail, **white in the outer two rectrices**; they are unmistakable; males in winter are similar, but black of head is less distinct. Females are brown, with broad, pale or whitish supercilium and submoustachial streaks, the latter outlined by a thin brown moustachial stripe and a broad brown malar stripe, streaked breast and flanks, and white outer tail feathers.

Habitat
Breeds in reeds and thickets along streams and around lakes. In winter, Reed Buntings are found in marshes and pastures.

Behavior
Reed Buntings typically are found in pairs or in flocks, in bushes or on the ground. North American records have been of single birds. Breeding males typically sing from a high point in their territories; they are easily approached and easy to see.

Voice
The song is a short, rather disjointed staccato repeated loud trill, ***shree-shree-teeree-teeree***, or ***tsee tsee tsea tsisirr***, that is described as squeaky or tinkling. The call note is a distinct ***tzween***, rising at the end, a soft ***tseek-tseek***, or a short ***bzree***.

Similar species
Males are similar in pattern to male **Pallas's Buntings**, but are darker overall, with a gray rather than whitish rump that does not contrast strongly with the back and tail colors. The coverts and secondaries of Reed Buntings are edged in rust; those of Pallas's Bunting are pale. Female Reed Buntings are similar to female Pallas's Buntings, but darker, with a pronounced brown malar streak, and more ventral streaking. As in males, the coverts and secondaries of Reed Buntings are edged with rusty; those of Pallas's Buntings are pale buff. The ear-coverts of Reed Buntings are darker and less uniformly colored than those of Pallas's. The back streaking is more striking on Pallas's than on Reed Bunting. There is, however, considerable geographic variation in Reed Buntings, and eastern Siberian birds are paler (more like Pallas's Buntings) than western ones, and the females have a rustier crown, and less ventral streaking. In winter, female Pallas's Buntings have no or faint streaking on their crown, whereas Reed Buntings usually show distinct lateral crown-stripes. The upper mandible of Pallas's Bunting is nearly straight, and there is a distinct contrast between the dark upper mandible and the pale pinkish lower mandible (the bill is usually all black in breeding males); the upper mandible of Reed Bunting is slightly convex, and bluish-gray lower

mandible contrasts little with the upper. Winter Rustic Buntings are rusty, especially on the breast and flanks, and have a distinctive white spot behind their ears.

Geographic variation

None in our area; marked, but clinal in the Palearctic. *E. s. pyrrhulina* of southeastern Siberia west to Kamchatka, and south to Manchuria and Japan is the race that has been collected in Alaska. *E. s. pyrrhulina* is paler in coloration and larger billed than birds from western Europe, with the crown of the female somewhat rufous, and with reduced breast streaking.

Distribution

Breeds from the British Isles, Scandinavia, n Russia and n Siberia south to the Mediterranean region, Iran, s Siberia, Kamchatka and n Japan.

Winters from the southern part of the breeding range south to nw India, ne China, and s Japan.

Migrates casually in spring migration in the w Aleutian Is., Alaska (6 records, from 22 May–4 June).

Molt

The Prebasic I molt is partial, involving head and body feathers, most of the coverts, many or all tertials, and sometimes rectrices; it occurs in Aug to Sept. The Prealternate molt is partial, and involves head, breast, and sometimes mantle feathers, and a few tail feathers; it occurs in Feb to Mar. The Definitive Basic molt is complete, and takes place (in western Europe) in late summer.

Description

Medium-sized; sexually dimorphic. **Adult males** (May–Aug)—*Head:* black, with bold white submoustachial stripes and a white collar; *back:* nape white; mantle brown to rusty brown, boldly striped with black; *rump* and uppertail-coverts with a few dark streaks; *wing:* dark brown, with rusty edges to secondaries; tertials with black centers; lesser-coverts rusty; median and greater-coverts are dark brown to black edged with rusty and tipped with buff, forming indistinct wing-bars; *tail:* black; outermost rectrix (6th) mostly white; 5th with considerable white in the inner web; *underparts:* chin and throat black; breast, belly, and undertail-coverts white; *bill:* upper mandible grayish-black; lower mandible pinkish-gray or pinkish-brown; *legs:* pinkish-brown or brown; *iris* brown or dark brown.

Males in winter (Sept–May)—Similar to males in summer, but the feathers are tipped with brown, slightly obscuring the black and white markings on the head. First-winter males are duller in coloration than adult males. Although there may be a limited face molt, males wear into summer plumage.

Adult females (May–Sept)—*Head:* lateral crown-stripes light rusty brown; median crown-stripe buff brown, with faint streaks; supercilium and lores pale buff; ear-coverts brownish-buff, outlined with pale brown; submoustachial stripe pale buff; malar stripe broad and dark brown; *back* brown, with sharp brown streaks; *rump:* pale brown, with darker centers to feathers; *wings:* brown; lesser-coverts rusty; edges of median and greater-coverts and tertials rusty; *tail:* brown; patterned like male's; *underparts:* chin, throat, breast, flanks, and belly pale with faint or no streaking on the flanks; soft parts colored as in males. Winter females are slightly buffier.

Juveniles—Like females but duller in coloration, with a dull cinnamon rump and streaked back.

Hybrids None described.

References
Cramp and Perrins (1994), Flint *et al.* (1984), Kessel and Gibson (1978, unpublished).

62.1 Male Reed Bunting *E. s. pyrrhulina*, Beidaihe, China, Apr 1986. Similar to male Pallas's Bunting in transitional plumage but note the larger bill with obviously curved culmen. The underparts are sullied whitish with quite heavy streaking on breast and flanks (Urban Olsson).

62.2 Adult female Reed Bunting *E. s. pyrrhulina*, Fuku, Japan, Oct 1984. Similar to female Pallas's Bunting but note bill shape and obviously rufous lesser-coverts and wing-bars. Note also more extensive fine streaking on breast and flanks and darker lateral crown-stripes (Urban Olsson).

62.3 First-winter male Reed Bunting *E. s. pyrrhulina*, Fuku, Japan, Oct 1984. Very similar to non-breeding female (Fig. 62.2) but with some blackish mottling within brown ear-coverts and lateral crown stripes and some white patches (feather bases) visible on the neck-sides (Urban Olsson).

63 **Snow Bunting**

(Plectrophenax nivalis)

Measurements
Length: 15–18 cm; 5.9–7.1 in.
   (males slightly larger).
Wing: 95–116 mm; 3.7–4.6 in.;
   113–119.5 mm western Aleutian Is.
Mass: 34.0-56.0 g.

The Snow Bunting is a large, chunky bunting, with a **white or dusky head and belly, black-tipped white wings, a black back**, and white edges to its tail.

Habitat
Snow Buntings breed in the high Arctic in sparse, dry, rocky areas, such as shores, mountain slopes, and outcrops. In migration and winter they are characteristically found in fields, pastures, and along the shore.

Behavior
In winter, Snow Buntings are usually found in flocks, often fairly large ones. As they move through a field, they appear to 'roll' along, like blowing snow, as the birds toward the back of the flock leap-frog over those in front. Although they usually stay on the ground, they not infrequently fly into a tree or land on fences or telephone wires. Particularly where they are uncommon, they may associate with other species, such as Horned Larks or Lapland Longspsurs, but where they are common, they are more often in pure flocks. On the ground, they run rather than hop, and their flight is undulating. Flocks of males arrive on the breeding grounds well before females. As the weather gets warmer, they establish territories. Chases, fights, and flight-singing is common (see **Voice**). During the molt in late summer, they become quieter and more secretive; some can barely fly at this time.

Voice
The song of the Snow Bunting is a short, musical *turee turee tureee turiwee*, or *sir plee si-chee whee-cher*. This is often given during an elaborate flight-display during which the male rises to 15 m and then glides into the wind with his wings held in a 'V' above his body. The call notes have been written as *chee*, or a high-pitched *tweet*.

Similar species
In all plumages, Snow Buntings are unmistakable. **McKay's Bunting** is much whiter: male McKay's Buntings have a white back and rump, little black in their tail, and usually no black in the bend of their wings. Females have a whitish rather than a brownish back, with little black in the tail.

Geographic variation
Two subspecies from North America are generally recognized, *P. n. townsendi* which breeds and is probably resident in the Pribilof and the western Aleutian islands, Alaska, and *P. n. nivalis* which is found throughout the rest of the American range. *P. n. townsendi* is relatively large and large-billed, with little or no buffy tinge on the body plumage. Two other subspecies are found in the Old World. The subspecies are poorly defined because of clinal variation and high within group variability.

Distribution
Circumpolar; in North America *Breeds:* n Alaska the Canadian arctic archipelago, greenland and from w and sw Alaska south in the mountains to s Alaska, nw British Columbia, nw and central-e Mackenzie, central and se Keewatin, Ninavut n Quebec and n Labrador.

Resident in the Pribilof and Aleutian Is.

Winters from w Alaska, nw British Columbia across s Canada north to central Alberta, central Saskatchewan, s Manitoba, s Ontario, and s Labrador, south through British Columbia along the coast to nw California and e Washington, Oregon, Idaho, n Utah, n Colorado, n Kansas, central Illinois, n Indiana, central Ohio, Pennsylvania, and south along the coast to North Carolina, and rarely south to n Texas.

Migrates through southern Canada and the northern United States. During fall migration the peak departure occurs in mid- to late Sept and continues through Dec; spring migration Mar through April, and May in the northern part of its range.

Conservation status
Although at times large numbers may perish in bad weather, neither their breeding nor wintering habitats have been significantly affected by human activities, and there is no reason to suppose that their abundance has changed in recent times.

Molt
The Prebasic I molt is partial, involving head and body feathers, lesser, median and sometimes inner greater wing-coverts, and tertials; this begins three weeks after fledging. There is no Prealternate molt. The Definitive Basic molt is complete; it begins in mid-July and is completed by early Sept.

Description
Large and chunky; sexually dimorphic. **Summer males** (Apr–Aug)—*Head:* white, sometimes with some black in the crown; *back:* black, sometimes mottled with brown; *rump:* black, mottled with white; uppertail-coverts white; *tail:* outer three rectrices white, thinly tipped with black on the outer web; other rectrices with little white; *wing:* greater-coverts, innermost secondaries, alula, and scapulars black; primaries black with white bases; median and lesser-coverts white; *underparts:* white; *bill:* black; *legs* and *feet:* brown, dark gray, or black; *iris:* dark brown or black.

Adult males in winter (Sept–Apr)—Like summer males, but the white areas are washed with pale rusty brown, particularly on the nape, crown, ear-coverts, and breast; black feathers on back and tail are edged with frosty brown; bill yellowish. Although there is a limited pre-alternate molt of the face feathers, adults wear into breeding plumage.

First-winter males—Like adult males, but the juvenal wing, greater-coverts, and tail feathers are retained, and they may have darker wings, and more buffy on the crown, back, and underparts than adults.

Adult females (Apr–Aug)—Like adult males, but the crown is more likely to be dusky, and the black areas duller, often brownish.

Females in winter (Sept–Apr)—Like winter males.

First-winter females—Like adults, but with darker secondaries, buffier head and browner underparts.

Juveniles (July–Aug)—Crown, back, and breast mottled grayish-brown; back black, edged with buff; rump rusty brown; flanks pinkish; belly white; white on wings and tail as in adults; bill yellowish.

Hybrids There is limited hybridization with McKay's Bunting.

References Lyon and Montgomerie (1995), Pyle (1997), Rising (1996).

63.1 Male Snow Bunting, Cambridge Bay, Nunavut, Canada, July 1990. The pied appearance of this breeding male is unmistakable. The white head and underparts contrast with black mantle and central tail. The wings are white with mostly black primaries, primary coverts, alula and tertials. The bill is wholly black (Dr. George K. Peck).

63.2 Female Snow Bunting, Cambridge Bay, Nunavut, Canada, July 1990. This breeding female is like a drab version of the male with white in the wing restricted to a panel formed by white edges and tips to the greater-coverts and secondaries. The head is sullied with gray and buff with quite distinct though fine black streaking on the crown. The black mantle feathers are edged with buff (mostly abraded on this worn mid-summer individual). The bill shows some horn color at the base (Dr. George K. Peck).

63.3 Female Snow Bunting, Nome, Alaska, USA, June 1998. Another breeding female, this time in fresher plumage. Note the streaked crown and nape, sullied face and crisp pale fringes to the black mantle feathers (Brian E. Small).

63.4 Juvenile Snow Bunting, Cornwallis I., Nunavut, Canada, July 1989. The gray head and black and buff streaked mantle easily identify this bird as a juvenile. The whitish broken eye-ring is also quite noticeable. The greater-coverts and tertials are broadly edged with pale chestnut and only the secondaries are edged white. Note the loose quality of the body feathers typical of juvenile birds (Mark K. Peck).

63.5 Male Snow Bunting, Island Beach, New Jersey, USA, Oct 1986. Winter birds are variable, but the extent of white on the wing of this individual suggests a male in its first winter. The secondaries show extensive black centers and the primary coverts are black edged buff. Note the rounded black centers to the scapulars, a pattern typical of males (Kevin T. Karlson).

63.6 Male Snow Bunting, near Sacramento, California, USA, Nov 1977. Another view of a winter male showing the broad buff edges to the black mantle feathers (lost with abrasion) and extensive buff and brown suffusions on the head. The scapulars show rounded black centers. Note the very long primary extension, black legs and deep yellow bill (Herbert Clarke).

63.7 Female Snow Bunting, Jones Beach State Park, New York, USA, Jan 2000. Similar to winter male but note the dark bases to the greater-coverts and the pointed dark centers to the scapulars. Ageing can be problematic but what little we can see of the primary-coverts (mostly blackish) suggest a first-winter bird (Michael D. Stubblefield).

63.8 Snow Buntings in flight, Jones Beach State Park, New York, USA, Jan 2000. A nice study showing variation of wing pattern between males and females (Michael D. Stubblefield).

64 McKay's Bunting

(Plectrophenax hyperboreus)

Measurements
Length: 15–19 cm; 5.9–7.5 in.
Wing: 104–119 mm; 4.1–4.7 in.
(males slightly larger).
Mass: ca. 43 g.

McKay's Bunting is a large, chunky sparrow that is **white except for the wing-
tips, and the tip of the center of the
tail.** Females have some dark mottling
on the back.

Habitat
McKay's Buntings nest in upland, rocky
tundra. In winter, they occur principally
along the coast.

Behavior
The behavior of McKay's Bunting is
doubtless much like that of the Snow Bunting, but little has been written about it.
Flight-singing occurs.

Voice
Vocalizations are like those of Snow Buntings.

Similar species
See **Snow Bunting.**

Geographic variation
None described.

Distribution
Breeds on islands in the Bering Sea (Hall and St. Matthew islands, and occasionally
others).

Winters along the coast of the Bering Sea in w Alaska from Nome south and west
to Cold Bay.

Conservation status
At present they are not threatened.

Molt
Presumably like those of the Snow Bunting.

Description
Large and chunky; sexually dimorphic. **Summer males (Apr–Aug)—*Head:* white;
back: white, rarely with a few narrow black streaks, and the posterior scapulars with

black blotches; *rump:* white; uppertail-coverts white; *tail:* outer four rectrices white; middle two to four rectrices black-tipped; *wing:* white, with tips of outer five primaries black; tertials black; alula white, sometimes with some black; *underparts:* white; *bill:* black; *legs* and *feet:* brown to black; *iris:* black.

Winter males (Sept–Apr)—Variable, like summer males, but the crown, ear-coverts and breast are lightly washed with pale rusty brown; black feathers on back and tail are lightly edged with frosty brown; bill yellowish or pinkish. Adults appear to wear into breeding plumage.

Adult females (Apr–Aug)—Like adult males, but the crown may be dusky, and the back narrowly streaked with black; the alula is black. The middle two rectrices are dusky to the base; the others may be dusky on the inner webs.

Adult females in winter (Sept–Apr)—Like winter males, but average darker; variable.

First-winter females—Like adults, but with darker secondaries, a buffier head and browner underparts.

Juveniles (July–Aug)—Crown, back, and breast mottled grayish-brown; back black, edged with buff; rump rusty brown; flanks pinkish; belly white; white on wings and tail as in adults; bill yellowish. They are paler on average than juvenile Snow Buntings.

Hybrids

There is limited hybridization with Snow Buntings (e.g. St. Lawrence I., and perhaps the Pribilof Is.). There is a lot of variability in the amount of black on the wings, suggesting that hybridization may be more frequent, but the range of variability in Snow Buntings is poorly known.

References Lyon and Montgomerie (1995), Rising (1996).

64.1 Male McKay's Bunting, Gambell, Alaska, June 1989. Similar in overall structure to Snow Bunting but almost wholly white in this plumage. The outer primaries are tipped black and the bill and legs are blackish (Paul Lehman).

64.2 Male McKay's Bunting, Gambell, Alaska, June 1989. This rear view nicely captures the reduced amount of black on this otherwise strikingly white bird. Note the thin line formed by the narrow black inner webs to the tertials and the tiny black tips to the central pair of tail feathers (Paul Lehman).

Appendix I

Fall Chipping, Clay-coloured, and Brewer's sparrows at a glance (Rising, 1996)

Characteristic	Chipping	Clay-colored	Brewer's
Crown	Medium brown, sometimes with some red; thin black streaks; median stripe indistinct or missing	Buff brown; with thin brown streaks; median stripe paler buff; usually visible	Buff brown; thin brown streaks; median stripe usually missing
Supercilium	Distinct; pale whitish buff	Distinct; buffy	Indistinct; grayish buff
Lores	Dark	Pale	Pale
Post-ocular Stripe	Dark & broad	Dark & broad	Thin & indistinct
Ear-coverts	Brown; moustachial stripe indistinct	Light brown; darkly outlined moustachial distinct	Plae grayish brown; moustachial indistinct
Malar	Pale grayish buff; indistinct	Buff; distinct	Whitish; indistinct
Nape	Brown; dark streaks	Often grayish; paler streaks	Light brown; thin streaks
Side of neck	Gray; contrasts with ear-coverts	Gray; contrast with ear-coverts	Grayish buff or gray; contrasts with ear-coverts
Tertials	Edged with rusty brown	Edged with pale rusty brown	Edged with pale rusty brown
Breast	Pale grayish brown	Pale buff	Pale grayish buff
Rump	Grayish; often washed brown	Buffy-brown	Buffy-brown

Appendix 2

Winter Longspurs at a glance (Rising, 1996)

Characteristic	McCown's	Lapland	Smith's	Chestnut-collared
Bill	Stout; pink with dark tip	Dark or pinkish with dusky tip	Horn with dusky tip	Pinkish with dusty tip
Facial pattern	Indistinct,with pale supercilium	Ear-coverts distinctly outlined; malar stripe dark	Ear-coverts distinctly outlined, showing pale interior spot	Indistinct: malar may be brownish
Nape	Pale brown or grayish; indistinctly streaked	Dark brown; may show rust	Buffy tan; thin streaks	Pale brown; may show rust
Breast, flanks, and belly	Pale; unstreaked; may show black; white belly	Whitish; streaked; white belly	Buffy; lightly streaked; buffy belly	Pale buff; lightly streaked or blackish flecked; pale buff belly
Primary projection beyond tertials	Long (short tailed)	Long	Long	Short
Coverts	Medians rusty in males; light buff in females	Brown greaters edged with rusty	Lessers and medians white edged or white	Brown; may show white lessers
Tail	White extensive	White limited to outer 2 feathers	White limited to outer 2 feathers	White extensive

Glossary

Alternate plumage. The plumage that replaces the basic plumage. In many sparrows this is incomplete, that is to say, not all of the basic plumage is replaced. Some sparrows lack an alternate plumage.

Alula. A number of small feathers attached to the first digit, at the bend of the wing.

Basic plumage. The plumage that replaces either the Juvenal plumage or the alternate plumage. The first basic plumage (or Basic I plumage) replaces the Juvenal plumage. In most sparrows later basic plumages are like the first basic plumage, or only little different; these are called the Definitive Basic plumage.

Braces. Pale parallel streaks on the back.

Culmen. The upper mandible or bill.

Family. A taxonomic category containing one to several genera. The New World sparrows are often put in the Family Emberizidae. In zoological nomenclature, all families end in the suffix -idae.

Genus. A subdivision of the Family containing one to several species. A genus containing only one species is called a monotypic genus. The plural is genera.

Hallux. The first toe, directed backwards in sparrows and other songbirds.

Juvenal plumage. The plumage that replaces the natal down.

Juvenile. In sparrows, a juvenile is a bird in Juvenal plumage. More generally, juvenile can be used to refer to any sub-adult bird, that is a bird that can not yet breed. All north temperate sparrows, however, reach reproductive maturity in the spring following their birth.

Mandible. Strictly, the mandible is the bone (several fused bones) of the lower jaw and its horny covering, and in this sense is contrasted with maxilla. More generally, however, the term refers to the bill, with upper mandible and lower mandible being commonly used.

Nominant form (subspecies). The subspecies that has the same subspecific and specific name, e.g. *Melospiza melodia melodia*.

Presupplemental molt. In some species of sparrows there is an extra molt of some of the body feathers, and occasionally of some of the coverts that occurs before the First Prebasic molt. This has been called a Presupplemental molt.

Species. Variously defined, but commonly as 'Groups of interbreeding populations that are reproductively isolated from other such groups.' Generally, individuals from different species do not interbreed and produce viable, fertile offspring. If this occurs only occasionally, or is geographically restricted, the two groups are considered to be effectively reproductively isolated, and may be treated as two different species. For example, Nelson's Sharp-tailed Sparrows and Saltmarsh Sharp-tailed Sparrows interbreed occasionally and locally in southern Maine, but are now considered to be two different species because they differ behaviorally, morphologically, and biochemically in a number of ways.

Spishing or (pishing). A whispery or squeaky noise made to attract songbirds.

Subspecies. A geographically and morphologically defined population (or group of populations) of one species.

Tomium (tomial). The cutting edge of the mandible.

Xeric. Dry habitat.

References

[Note: For additional references, see the references listed in Rising, 1996.]

Adams, M. T. and K. B. Bryan. 1999. Botteri's Sparrow in Trans-Pecos, Texas. *Texas Birds* 1:6–13.

Aldrich, J. W. 1984. *Ecogeographical variation in size and proportions of Song Sparrows* (Melospiza melodia). Ornitho. Monogr. No. 35, American Ornithologists' Union, Washington, DC.

American Ornithologists' Union. 1957. *Check-list of North American Birds.* 5th edition. American Ornithologists' Union, Baltimore, MD.

American Ornithologists' Union. 1998. *Check-list of North American Birds.* 7th edition. American Ornithologists' Union, Washington, D.C.

Ammon, E. M. 1995. Lincoln's Sparrow (*Melospiza lincolnii*). In *The Birds of North America* (A. Poole and F. Gill, eds.). The Birds of North America, Inc., Philadelphia, PA.

Austin, Jr., O. L. (Ed.) 1968. *Life Histories of North American Cardinals, Buntings, Towhees, Finches, Sparrows, and Allies.* Bull. 237 U. S. Nat. Mus. Parts 2 and 3. Bull. 237 U. S. Nat. Mus. Parts 2 and 3, Smithsonian Institution, Washington, D.C.

Banks, R. C. 1964. Geographic variation in the White-crowned Sparrow, *Zonotrichia leucophrys. Univ. Caligornia Publs. Zool.* 70: 1–123.

Banks, R. C. 1970. Re-evaluation of two supposed hybrid birds. *Wilson Bulletin* 82:331–332.

Behrstock, R. A., C. W. Sexon, G. W. Lasley, T. L. Eubanks, and J. P. Gee. 1998. First nesting records of Worthen's Sparrow *Spizella wortheni* for Nuevo León, Mexico, with a habitat characterisation of the nest site and notes on ecology, voice, additional recent sightings and leg coloration. *Cotinga* 8:27–33.

Bond, G. M. and R. E. Stewart. 1951. A new Swamp Sparrow from the Maryland coastal plain. *Wilson Bull.* 63: 38–40.

Briskie, J. V. 1993. Smith's Longspur (*Calcarius pictus*). In *The Birds of North America,* No. 34 (A. Poole and F. Gill, eds.). The Birds of North America, Inc., Philadelphia, PA.

Browning, M. R. 1980. Taxa of North American birds described from 1957 to 1987. *Proc. Biol. Soc. Washington* 105: 414–419.

Brush, T. 1998. Olive Sparrow (*Arremonops rufivirgatus*). In *The Birds of North America,* No. 325 (A. Poole and F. Gill, eds.). The Birds of North America, Inc., Philadelphia, PA.

Buckelew, Jr., A.R. and G. A. Hall. 1994. *The West Virginia Breeding Bird Atlas.* Univ. Pittsburgh Press, Pittsburgh, PA.

Busby, W. H. and J. L. Zimmerman. 2001. *Kansas Breeding Bird Atlas.* University Press of Kansas, Lawrence, KS (in press).

Byers, C., U. Olsson, and J. Curson. 1995. *Buntings and Sparrows / A Guide to the Buntings and North American Sparrows*. Pica Press, Sussex.

Carey, M., D. E. Burhans, and D. A. Nelson. 1994. Field Sparrow (*Spizella pusilla*). In *The Birds of North America*, No. 103 (A. Poole and F. Gill, eds.). The Birds of North America, Inc., Philadelphia, PA.

Cartwright, B. W., T. M. Shortt, and R. D. Harris. 1937. Baird's Sparrow. *Trans Royal Canadian Institute* 21:153–197.

Chilton, G., M. C. Baker, C. D. Barrentine, and M. A. Cunningham. 1995. White-crowned Sparrow (*Zonotrichia leucophrys*). In *The Birds of North America*, No. 183 (A. Poole and F. Gill, eds.). The Birds of North America, Inc., Philadelphia, PA.

Collins, P. W. 1999. Rufous-crowned Sparrow (*Aimophila ruficeps*). In *The Birds of North America*, No. 472 (A. Poole and F. Gill, eds.). The Birds of North America, Inc., Philadelphia, PA.

Cramp, S. and C. M. Perrins (eds.). 1994. *Handbook of the Birds of Europe the Middle East and North Africa*. Oxford Univ. Press, Oxford, UK.

Cully, Jr., J. F. and H. L. Michaels. 2000. Henslow's Sparrow habitat associations on Kansas tallgrass prairie. *Wilson Bulletin.* 112:115–123.

Dechant, J. A., M. L. Sondreal, D. H. Johnson, L. D. Igl, C. M. Goldade, M. P. Nenneman, and B. R. Euliss. 1998a. *Effects of management practices on grassland birds: Clay-colored Sparrow.* Northern Prairie Wildlife Research Center, Jamestown, ND.

Dechant, J. A., M. L. Sondreal, D. H. Johnson, L. D. Igl, C. M. Goldade, M. P. Nenneman, and B. R. Euliss. 1998b. *Effects of management practices on grassland birds: Baird's Sparrow.* Northern Prairie Wildlife Research Center, Jamestown, ND.

Dechant, J. A., M. L. Sondreal, D. H. Johnson, L. D. Igl, C. M. Goldade, M. P. Nenneman, and B. R. Euliss. 1998c. *Effects of management practices on grassland birds: Grasshopper Sparrow.* Northern Prairie Wildlife Research Center, Jamestown, ND.

Dechant, J. A., M. L. Sondreal, D. H. Johnson, L. D. Igl, C. M. Goldade, M. P. Nenneman, and B. R. Euliss. 1998d. *Effects of management practices on grassland birds: Chestnut-collared Longspur.* Northern Prairie Wildlife Research Center, Jamestown, ND.

Dechant, J. A., M. L. Sondreal, D. H. Johnson, L. D. Igl, C. M. Goldade, A. L. Zimmerman, and B. R. Euliss. 1998e. *Effects of management practices on grassland birds: Le Conte's Sparrow.* Northern Prairie Wildlife Research Center, Jamestown, ND.

Dechant, J. A., M. L. Sondreal, D. H. Johnson, L. D. Igl, C. M. Goldade, B. D. Parkin, and B. R. Euliss. 1999a. *Effects of management practices on grassland birds: Field Sparrow.* Northern Prairie Wildlife Research Center, Jamestown, ND.

Dechant, J. A., M. L. Sondreal, D. H. Johnson, L. D. Igl, C. M. Goldade, B. D. Parkin, and B. R. Euliss. 1999b. *Effects of management practices on grassland birds: Lark Sparrow.* Northern Prairie Wildlife Research Center, Jamestown, ND.

Dechant, J. A., M. L. Sondreal, D. H. Johnson, L. D. Igl, C. M. Goldade, M. P. Nenneman, and B. R. Euliss. 1999c. *Effects of management practices on grassland birds: Nelson's Sharp-tailed Sparrow*. Northern Prairie Wildlife Research Center, Jamestown, ND.

Dechant, J. A., M. L. Sondreal, D. H. Johnson, L. D. Igl, C. M. Goldade, P. A. Rabie, and B. R. Euliss. 1999d. *Effects of management practices on grassland birds: McCown's Longspur*. Northern Prairie Wildlife Research Center, Jamestown, ND.

Dechant, J. A., M. L. Sondreal, D. H. Johnson, L. D. Igl, C. M. Goldade, A. L. Zimmerman, and B. R. Euliss. 1999e. *Effects of management practices on grassland birds: Lark Bunting*. Northern Prairie Wildlife Research Center, Jamestown, ND.

Dechant, J. A., M. F. Dinkins, D. H. Johnson, L. D. Igl, C. M. Goldade, and B. R. Euliss. 2000. *Effects of management practices on grassland birds: Vesper Sparrow*. Northern Prairie Wildlife Research Center, Jamestown, ND.

Dickerman, R. W. 1961. Hybrids among the fringillid genera *Junco-Zonotrichia* and *Melospiza*. *Auk* 78:627–634.

Dickerman, R. W. 1968. A hybrid Grasshopper X Savannah Sparrow. *Auk* 85:312–315.

Dobbs, R. C., P. R. Martin, and T. E. Martin. 1998. Green-tailed Towhee (*Pipilo chlorurus*). In *The Birds of North America*, No. 368 (A. Poole and F. Gill, eds.). The Birds of North America, Inc., Philadelphia, PA.

Doyle, T. J. 1997. The Timberline Sparrow, *Spizella* (*breweri*) *taverneri*, in Alaska, with notes on breeding habitat and vocalizations. *Western Birds* 28:1–12.

Dudley, S., T. Benton, P. Fraser, and J. Ryan. 1996. *Rare Birds Day by Day*. T. & A. D. Poyser, London, UK.

Dunn, J. L. and D. Beadle. 1998. Longspurs / Distribution and identification in basic plumage. *Birders Journal* 7:68–93.

Dunn, J. L., K. L. Garrett, and J. K. Alderfer. 1995. White-crowned Sparrow subspecies: Identification and distribution. *Birding* 27:183–200.

Dunning, Jr., J. B. 1993a. *CRC Handbook of Avian Body Masses*. CRC Press, Boca Raton, Florida.

Dunning, Jr., J. B. 1993b. Bachman's Sparrow (*Aimophila aestivalis*). In *The Birds of North America*, No. 38 (A. Poole and F. Gill, eds.). The Birds of North America, Inc., Philadelphia, PA.

Dunning, Jr., J. B., R. K. Bowers, Jr., S. J. Suter, and C. E. Bock. 1999. Cassin's Sparrow (*Aimophila cassinii*). In *The Birds of North America*, No. 471 (A. Poole and F. Gill, eds.). The Birds of North America, Inc., Philadelphia, PA.

Eitniear, J. C. 1997. White-collared Seedeater (*Sporophila torqueola*). In *The Birds of North America*, No. 278 (A. Poole and F. Gill, eds.). The Birds of North America, Inc., Philadelphia, PA.

Falls, J. B. and J. G. Kopachena. 1994. White-throated Sparrow (*Zonotrichia albicollis*). In *The Birds of North America*, No. 128 (A. Poole and F. Gill, eds.). The Birds of North America, Inc., Philadelphia, PA.

Flint, V. E., R. L. Boehme, Y. V. Kostin, and A. A. Kuznetsov. 1984. *A Field Guide to Birds of the USSR*. Princeton Univ. Press, Princeton, NJ.

Garrett, K. L., J. L. Dunn, and R. Righter. 2000. Call notes and winter distribution in the Fox Sparrow complex. *Birding* 32: 412–417.

Garrido, O. H. and A. Kirkconnell. 2000. *Field Guide to the Birds of Cuba*. Cornell Univ. Press, Ithaca, NY.

Gauthiar, J. and Y. Aubry (eds.). 1996. *The Breeding Birds of Quebec: Atlas of the Breeding Birds of Southern Quebec*. Prov. Quebec Soc. Protection of Birds, and Canadian Wildlife Service, Montreal, PQ.

Greenlaw, J. S. 1993. Behavioral and morphological diversification in Sharp-tailed Sparrows *(Ammodramus Caudacutus)* of the Atlantic Coast *Auk* 110:286–303.

Greenlaw, J. S. 1996a. Spotted Towhee *(Pipilo maculatus)*. In *The Birds of North America*, No. 263 (A. Poole and F. Gill, eds.). The Birds of North America, Inc., Philadelphia, PA.

Greenlaw, J. S. 1996b. Eastern Towhee *(Pipilo erythrophthalmus)*. In *The Birds of North America*, No. 262 (A. Poole and F. Gill, eds.). The Birds of North America, Inc., Philadelphia, PA.

Greenlaw, J. S. and J. D. Rising. 1994. Sharp-tailed Sparrow *(Ammodramus caudacutus)*. In *The Birds of North America*, No. 112 (A. Poole and F. Gills, eds). The Birds of North America, Inc., Philadelphia, PA.

Groschupf, K. 1992. Five-striped Sparrow *(Aimophila quinquestriata)*. In *The Birds of North America*, No. 21 (A. Poole and F. Gill, eds.). The Birds of North America, Inc., Philadelphia, PA.

Herkert, J. R. 1998. *Effects of management practices on grassland birds: Henslow's Sparrow*. Northern Prairie Wildlife Research Center, Jamestown, ND.

Hill, D. P. and L. K. Gould. 1997. Chestnut-collared Longspur *(Calcarius ornatus)*. In *The Birds of North America*, No. 288 (A. Poole and F. Gill, eds.). The Birds of North America, Inc., Philadelphia, PA.

Hoag, D. J. 1999. Hybridization between Clay-colored Sparrow and Field Sparrow in northern Vermont. *Wilson Bull.* 111:581–584.

Howell, S. N. G. and S. Webb. 1995. *A guide to the birds of Mexico and northern Central America*. Oxford Univ. Press, Oxford, UK.

Hubbard, J. P. 1972. The nomenclature of *Pipilo aberti* Baird (Aves: Fringillidae). *Proc. Biol. Soc. Washington* 85:131–138.

Hubbard, J. P. 1975. Geographic variation in non-California populations of the Rufous-crowned Sparrow. *Nemouria*, No. 15.

Hubbard, J. P. 1977. The status of Cassin's Sparrow in New Mexico and adjacent states. *American Birds* 31:935–941.

Humphrey, P. S. and K. C. Parkes. 1959. An approach to the study of molts and plumages. *Auk* **76**:1–31.

Hyde, A. S. 1939. *The life history of the Henslow's Sparrow,* Passerherbulus henslowi *(Audubon)*. Misc. Publ. No. 41, Univ. Michigan, Ann Arbor, MI.

Johnson, N.K. and J.A. Marten. 1992. Macrogeographic patterns of morphometric and genetic variation in the Sage Sparrow complex. *Condor* 94: 1–19.

Johnson, R. R. and L. T. Haight. 1996. Canyon Towhee *(Pipilo fuscus)*. In *The Birds of North America*, No. 264 (A. Poole and F. Gill, eds.). The Birds of North America, Inc., Philadelphia, PA.

Jones, A., W. G. Shriver, N. L. Bulgin, and P. D. Vickery. Identification of a probable Grasshopper X Song sparrow hybrid in Massachusetts. MS submitted.

Kaufman, K. 1990. *Advanced birding*. Houghton Mifflin Co., Boston, MA.

Kessel, B. and D. D. Gibson. 1978. *Status and Distribution of Alaska Birds*. Studies Avian Biol. No. 1, Cooper Ornith. Soc., Lawrence, KS.

Kingery, H. E. (Ed.). 1998. *Colorado Breeding Bird Atlas*. Colorado Wildlife Heritage Foundation, Denver, CO.

Klicka, J., R. M. Zink, J. C. Barlow, W. B. McGillivray, and T. J. Doyle. 1999. Evidence supporting the recent origin and species status of the Timberline Sparrow. *Condor* 101:577–588.

Knapton, R. W. 1994. Clay-colored Sparrow (*Spizella pallida*). In *The Birds of North America*, No. 120 (A. Poole and F. Gill, eds.). The Birds of North America, Inc., Philadelphia, PA.

Levine, E. (Ed.) 1998. *Bull's Birds of New York*. Comstock Publ. Assoc., Ithaca, NY.

Linsdale, J. M. and E. L. Sumner, Sr. 1934. Variability in the weight in the Golden-crowned Sparrow. II. Environmental control of reproductive and associated cycles. *Condor* 51:88–96.

Lowther, P. E., K. D. Groschupf, and S. M. Russell. 1999. Rufous-winged Sparrow (*Aimophila carpalis*). In *The Birds of North America*, No. 422 (A. Poole and F. Gill, eds.). The Birds of North America, Inc., Philadelphia, PA.

Lyon, B. and R. Montgomerie. 1995. Snow Bunting and McKay's Bunting (*Plectrophenax nivalis* and *Plectrophenax hyperboreus*). In *The Birds of North America*, No. 198–199 (A. Poole and F. Gill, eds.). The Birds of North America, Inc., Philadelphia, PA.

Marshall, J. T. Jr. 1948. Ecological races of Song Sparrows in the San Francisco Bay region Part II. Geographical variation. *Condor* 50: 233–256.

Martin, D. J. 1977. Songs of the Fox Sparrow. I. Structure of song and its comparison with song in other Emberizidae. *Condor* 79:209–221.

Martin, J. W. and B. A. Carlson. 1998. Sage Sparrow (*Amphispiza belli*) In *The Birds of North America*, No. 326 (A. Poole and F. Gill, eds.). The Birds of North America, Inc., Philadelphia, PA.

Martin, J. W. and J. R. Parrish. 2000. Lark Sparrow (*Chondestes grammacus*). In *The Birds of North America*, No. 488 (A. Poole and F. Gill, eds.). The Birds of North America, Inc., Philadelphia, PA.

McWilliams, G. M. and D. W. Brauning. 2000. *The Birds of Pennsylvania* Cornell Univ. Press, Ithaca, NY.

Meyer de Schauensee, R. 1984. *The Birds of China*. Smithsonian Inst. Press, Washington, D.C.

Middleton, A. L. A. 1998. Chipping Sparrow (*Spizella passerina*). In *The Birds of North America*, No. 334 (A. Poole and F. Gill, eds.). The Birds of North America, Inc., Philadelphia, PA.

Miller, A. H. 1941. Speciation in the avian genus *Junco*. *Univ. California Pubs. Zool.* 44: 173–434.

Mowbray, T. B. 1997. Swamp Sparrow (*Melospiza georgiana*). In *The Birds of North America*, No. 279 (A. Poole and F. Gill, eds.). The Birds of North America, Inc., Philadelphia, PA.

Murray, B. G. Jr. 1969. A comparative study of Le Conte's and Sharp-tailed sparrows. *Auk* 86:199–231.

Naugler, C. T. 1993. American Tree Sparrow (*Spizella arborea*). In *The Birds of North America*, No. 37 (A. Poole and F. Gill, eds.). The Birds of North America, Inc., Philadelphia, PA.

Norment, C. J. and S. A. Shackleton. 1993. Harris' Sparrow (*Zonotrichia querula*). In *The Birds of North America*, No. 64 (A. Poole and F. Gill, eds.). The Birds of North America, Inc., Philadelphia, PA.

Norment, C. J., P. Hendricks, and R. Santonocito. 1998. Golden-crowned Sparrow (*Zonotrichia atricapilla*). In *The Birds of North America*, No. 352 (A. Poole and F. Gill, eds.). The Birds of North America, Inc., Philadelphia, PA.

Oberholser, H. C. 1974. *The Bird Life of Texas*. Vol. 2. Univ. Texas Press, Austin, Texas.

Patten, M. A., S. F. Bailey, and R. Stallcup. 1998. First records of the White-winged Junco for California. *Western Birds* 29:41–48.

Payne, P. A. 1979. Two apparent hybrid *Zonotrichia* sparrows. *Auk*: 96:595–599.

Petersen, W. R. 1999. New England region. *North American Birds* 53:363–366.

Phillips, A., J. Marshall, and G. Monson. 1964. *The birds of Arizona*. Univ. Arizona Press, Tucson, AZ.

Pinel, H. W., W. W. Smith, and C. R. Wershler. 1993. *Alberta Birds, 1971–1980. Vol. 2. Passerines*. Nat. Hist. Occ. Paper No. 20, Prov. Mus. Alberta, Edmonton, AB.

Post, W. 1998. The status of Nelson's and Saltmarsh Sharp-tailed Sparrows on the Waccasassa Bay, Levy County, Florida. *Florida Field Naturalist* 26: 1–6.

Post, W. and J. S. Greenlaw. 1994. Seaside Sparrow (*Ammodramus maritimus*). In *The Birds of North America*, No. 127 (A. Poole and F. Gill, eds.). The Birds of North America, Inc., Philadelphia. PA.

Pruitt, L. 1996. *Henslow's Sparrow / Status Assessment*. U. S. Fish & Wildlife Service, Bloomington, IN.

Pyle, P. 1997. *Identification Guide to North American Birds. Part 1 Columbidae to Ploceidae*. Slate Creek Press, Bolinas, CA.

Pyle, P. and D. Sibley. 1992. Juvenal-plumaged Le Conte's Sparrows on migration. *Birding* 24: 70–76.

Quay, T. L., J. B. Funderburg, Jr., D. S. Lee, E. F. Potter, and C. S. Robbins. 1983. *The Seaside Sparrow, Its Biology and Management*. Occ. Papers North Carolina Biol. Survey, 1983–5.

Raffaele, H., J. Wiley, O. Garrido, A. Keith, and J. Raffaele. 1998. *A Guide to the Birds of the West Indies*. Princeton Univ. Press, Princeton, NJ.

Ridgway, R. 1901. *The Birds of North and Middle America, Part I*. Bull. U. S. Nat. Mus., No. 50, Smithsonian Inst., Washington, D.C.

Rimmer, C. C. 1986. Identification of juvenile Lincoln's and Swamp sparrows. *J. Field Ornithol.* 57:114–125.

Rising, J. D. 1996. *A Guide to the Identification and Natural History of the Sparrows of the United States and Canada.* Academic Press, London, UK.

Robbins, C. S. (Ed.). 1996. *Atlas of the Breeding Birds of Maryland and the District of Columbia.* Univ. Pittsburgh Press, Pittsburgh, PA.

Rotenbury, J. T., M. A. Patten, and K. L. Preston. 1999. Brewer's Sparrow (*Spizella breweri*). In *The Birds of North America*, No. 390 (A. Poole and F. Gill, eds.). The Birds of North America, Inc., Philadelphia, PA.

Russell, S. M. and G. Monson. 1998. *The Birds of Sonora.* Univ. Arizona Press, Tucson, AZ.

Schulenberg, J. H., G. I. Horak, M. D. Schwilling, and E. J. Finck. 1994. Nesting of Henslow's Sparrow in Osage County, Kansas. *Bull. Kansas Ornithol. Soc.* 44:25–28.

Shane, T. G. 1972. The nest site selection behavior of the Lark Bunting, *Calamospiza melanocorys.* M. Sci. Thesis, Kansas State University, Manhattan.

Shane, T. G. 1996. The Lark Bunting: in peril or making progress? *J. Colorado Field Ornithologists* 30:162–168.

Shane, T. G. 1998. The North American migration count: Lark Bunting status. *J. Colorado Field Ornithologists* 32:234–236.

Shane, T. G. 2000. Lark Bunting (*Calamospiza melanocorys*). In *The Birds of North America*, No. 542 (A. Poole and F. Gill, eds.). The Birds of North America, Inc., Philadelphia, PA.

Shane, T. G. and S. S. Seltman. 1995. The historical development of wintering Lark Bunting populations north of the thirty seventh parallel. *Bull. Kansas Ornithol. Soc.* 46:36–39.

Sibley, C. G. and O. S. Pettingill, Jr. 1955. A hybrid longspur from Saskatchewan. *Auk* 72:423–425.

Smith, M. R., P. W. Mattocks, Jr., and K. M. Cassidy. 1997. *Breeding Birds of Washington State.* Seattle Audubon Soc. Publs. Zool. No 1, Seattle, WA.

Sullivan, K. A. 1999. Yellow-eyed Junco (*Junco phaeonotus*). In *The Birds of North America*, No. 464 (A. Poole and F. Gill, eds.). The Birds of North America, Inc., Philadelphia, PA.

Sutton, G. M. 1935. The juvenal plumage and post juvenal molt in several species of Michigan sparrows. *Bull. 3, Cranbrook Institute Sci.,* Bloomfield Hills, MI.

Swanson, D. A. 1998. *Effects of management practices on grassland birds: Savannah Sparrow.* Northern Prairie Wildlife Res. Center, Jamestown, ND.

Tenney, C. R. 1997. Black-chinned Sparrow (*Spizella atrogularis*). In *The Birds of North America*, No. 270 (A. Poole and F. Gill, eds.). Birds of North America, Inc., Philadelphia, PA.

Tweit, R. C. and D. M. Finch. 1994. Abert's Towhee (*Pipilo aberti*). In *The Birds of North America*, No. 111 (A. Poole and F. Gill, eds.). The Birds of North America, Inc., Philadelphia, PA.

Vickery, P. D. 1996. Grasshopper Sparrow (*Ammodramus savannarum*). In *The Birds of North America*, No. 239 (A. Poole and F. Gill, eds.). The Birds of North America, Inc., Philadelphia, PA.

Walk, J. W., E. L. Kershner, and R. E. Warner. 2000. Nocturnal singing in grassland birds. *Wilson Bull.,* 112:289–292.

Walters, M. J. 1992. *A Shadow and a Song.* Chelsea Green Publ. Co., Post Mills, VT.

Webb, E. A. and C. E. Bock. 1996. Botteri's Sparrow (*Aimophila botterii*). In *The Birds of North America*, No. 216 (A. Poole and F. Gill, eds.). The Birds of North America, Inc., Philadelphia, PA.

Wege, D. C., S. N. G. Howell, and A. M. Sada. 1993. The distribution and status of Worthen's Sparrow *Spizella wortheni*: a review. *Bird Conservation International* 3:211-220.

Wheelwright, N. T. and J. D. Rising. 1993. Savannah Sparrow (*Passereulus sandwichensis*). In *The Birds of North America*, No. 45 (A. Poole and F. Gill, eds.). The Birds of North America, Inc., Philadelphia, PA.

Willoughby, E. J. 1986. An unusual sequence of molts and plumages in Cassin's and Bachman's sparrows. *Condor* 88:461–472.

Willoughby, E. J. 1991. Molts of the Genus *Spizella* (Passeriformes, Emberizidae) in relation to ecological factors affecting plumage wear. *Proc. Foundation of Vert. Zool.* 4:247–286.

With, K. A. 1994. McCown's Longspur (*Calcarius mccownii*). In *The Birds of North America*, Inc., No. 96 (A. Poole and F. Gill, eds.). The Birds of North America, Inc., Philadelphia, PA.

Wolf, L. L. 1977. Species relationships in the avian genus *Aimophila*. *Ornith. Monogr.* No. 23, American Ornithologists' Union, Lawrence, Kansas.

Woolfenden, G. E. 1956. Comparative breeding behaviour of *Ammospiza caudacuta* and *A. maritima*. *Univ. Kansas Publ., Mus. Nat. Hist.* 10:45–75.

Zimmerman, J. L. 1988. Breeding season habitat selection by the Henslow's Sparrow (*Ammodramus henslowii*) in Kansas. *Wilson Bull.* 100:632–649.

Zink, R. M. 1986. Patterns and evolutionary significance of geographic variation in the Schistacea group of fox sparrows (*Passerella iliaca*). *Ornithol. Monogr.* No. 40, American Ornithol. Union, Washington, D.C.

Zink, R. M. 1993. Gene flow, refugia, and evolution of geographic variation in the Song Sparrow (*Melospiza melodia*). *Evolution* 47:717–729.

Zink, R. M. 1994. The geography of mitochondrial DNA variation, population structure, hybridization, and species limits in the fox sparrow (*Passerella iliaca*). *Evolution* 48:96–111.

Zink, R. M. and D. L. Dittmann. 1993. Gene flow, refugia, and evolution of geographic variation in the Song Sparrow (*Melospiza melodia*). *Evolution* 47: 717–729.

Zink, R. M. and A. E. Kessen. 1999. Species limits in the Fox Sparrow. *Birding* 31:508–517.

Index